EVALUATION OF EVIDENCE

Evaluation of Evidence addresses the question: should the law restrict the freedom of judges in assessing the probative value of evidence in the criminal process? Tracing the treatment of evidence from premodern to modern times, Mirjan Damaška argues that there has always been some appreciation of rules regarding the use and value of evidence, and these rules should not be viewed askance as a departure from ideal arrangements. In a time when science and technology have the ability to contribute to factual inquiry, there needs to be acceptance of rules that corroborate evidence produced by our native sensory apparatus.

Mirjan Damaška is Sterling Professor Emeritus of Law and Professorial Lecturer in Law at Yale Law School. He is a fellow of the American Academy of Arts and Sciences, and a member of the Croatian Academy of Sciences and Arts and the International Academy of Comparative Law. He is the author of over 100 articles and six books, including *The Faces of Justice and State Authority* (1986) and *Evidence Law Adrift* (1997).

ASCL STUDIES IN COMPARATIVE LAW

ASCL Studies in Comparative Law is designed to broaden theoretical and practical knowledge of the world's many legal systems. With more than sixty years' experience, the American Society of Comparative Law have been leaders in the study and analysis of comparative law. By promoting the investigation of legal problems in a comparative light, whether theoretical or empirical, as essential to the advancement of legal science, they provide an essential service to legal practitioners and those seeking reform of the law. This book series will extend these aims to the publication of monographs and comparative studies of specific legal problems.

The series has two general editors. Mortimer Sellers is Regents Professor of the University System of Maryland and Director of the Baltimore Center for International and Comparative Law. He is an Associate Member of the International Academy of Comparative Law. Vivian Curran is Distinguished Professor of Law at the University of Pittsburgh School of Law.

Series Editors

Vivian Curran *University of Pittsburgh*
David Gerber *Chicago-Kent College of Law*
Mortimer Sellers *University of Baltimore*

Editorial Board

Richard Albert *University of Texas*
David Clark *Willamette University*
Helge Dedek *McGill University*
James Feinerman *Georgetown University*
Richard Kay *University of Connecticut*
Maximo Langer *University of California Los Angeles*
Ralf Michaels *Duke University*
Fernanda Nicola *American University*
Jacqueline Ross *University of Illinois*
Kim Lane Scheppele *Princeton University*
Franz Werro *Georgetown University*

External Advisory Board

Josef Drexl *University of Munich*
Diego Fernandez Arroyo *Institut d'etudes politiques de Paris*
Hongjun Gao *Tsinghua University*
Michele Grazidei *University of Turin*
Ko Hasegawa *University of Hokkaido*
Hisashi Harata *University of Tokyo*
Andreas Heinemann *University of Zurich*
Christophe Jamin *Institut d'etudes politiques de Paris*
Yong-Sun Kang *Yonsei University*
Claudia Lima *Marques Federal University of Rio Grande do Sul*
Bertil Emrah *Oder Koc University*
Amr Shalakany *American University of Cairo*

Evaluation of Evidence

PREMODERN AND MODERN APPROACHES

MIRJAN DAMAŠKA
Yale University, Connecticut

CAMBRIDGE
UNIVERSITY PRESS

University Printing House, Cambridge CB2 8BS, United Kingdom

One Liberty Plaza, 20th Floor, New York, NY 10006, USA

477 Williamstown Road, Port Melbourne, VIC 3207, Australia

314–321, 3rd Floor, Plot 3, Splendor Forum, Jasola District Centre,
New Delhi – 110025, India

79 Anson Road, #06–04/06, Singapore 079906

Cambridge University Press is part of the University of Cambridge.

It furthers the University's mission by disseminating knowledge in the pursuit of
education, learning, and research at the highest international levels of excellence.

www.cambridge.org
Information on this title: www.cambridge.org/9781108497282
DOI: 10.1017/9781108667326

© Mirjan Damaška 2019

This publication is in copyright. Subject to statutory exception
and to the provisions of relevant collective licensing agreements,
no reproduction of any part may take place without the written
permission of Cambridge University Press.

First published 2019

Printed and bound in Great Britain by Clays Ltd, Elcograf S.p.A.

A catalogue record for this publication is available from the British Library.

Library of Congress Cataloging-in-Publication Data
NAMES: Damaška, Mirjan R., 1931– author.
TITLE: Evaluation of evidence : pre-modern and modern approaches / Mirjan Damaška,
Yale University, Connecticut.
DESCRIPTION: Cambridge, United Kingdom ; New York, NY, USA : Cambridge
University Press, 2018. | Series: ASCL studies in comparative law | Includes
bibliographical references and index.
IDENTIFIERS: LCCN 2018042763 | ISBN 9781108497282 (hardback)
SUBJECTS: LCSH: Evidence (Law) | BISAC: LAW / Evidence.
CLASSIFICATION: LCC K2261 .D349 2018 | DDC 347/.06–dc23
LC record available at https://lccn.loc.gov/2018042763

ISBN 978-1-108-49728-2 Hardback

Cambridge University Press has no responsibility for the persistence or accuracy of
URLs for external or third-party internet websites referred to in this publication
and does not guarantee that any content on such websites is, or will remain,
accurate or appropriate.

To the memory of Marija, meorum finis amorum

Nous voulons vous donner de vastes et d'étranges domaines,
Où le mystère en fleurs s'offre à qui veut le cueillir.

–Apollinaire

Contents

Acknowledgments		*page* viii
	Prologue	1
1	The Origin of Roman-Canon Legal Proof in Criminal Cases	10
2	Epistemic Foundations	27
3	Orientation in the Labyrinth	47
4	The Two-Eyewitnesses Rule	59
5	The Probative Impact of Confessions	69
6	The Negative Effect of Legal Proof	81
7	The Rejection of Persuasive Evidence	92
8	Evading the Roman-Canon Full Proof Standard	105
9	Recapitulation	113
10	Continental Successors to Roman-Canon Legal Proof	118
11	Roman-Canon Legal Proof and Common Law Evidence	128
	Epilogue	138
Index		149

Acknowledgments

This book derives from an interest in the history of criminal justice, an interest I have cultivated as a hobby for almost all of my professional life. Although most of my publications have been in other areas, I started taking notes on my readings in the history of criminal justice long before settling in America. Scribbled mostly in my native Croatian, these notes now overflow the drawers of my office cabinets. Five years ago, I decided to recast some of them into a book on a topic with possible contemporary relevance. The evaluation of evidence emerged as the most promising candidate. Executing the project turned out to be a solitary enterprise, however, because my notes were barely legible to others. I also found it difficult to find an assistant with sufficient knowledge of legal Latin. It was only in the academic year 2014–15 that I was fortunate to find an outstanding assistant, Mr. John Wei, then a student at Yale Law School. He helped me in locating many sources to which my notes only alluded, and on several occasions he was also able to establish the proper context of opinions expressed by late medieval legal authorities. For his skillful assistance I owe him a debt of gratitude. Heartfelt thanks go also to Mr. Mike Widener, curator of the rare books collection at Yale's Lillian Goldman Law Library. He saw to it that I promptly acquired whatever literature I needed. I wish that the dedication of the book could express how five years of work on it helped alleviate the years of grief caused by the passing of Marija, my life companion.

Prologue

Should the law restrain the freedom of the trier of facts to determine the value of evidence in criminal cases? This question intensely preoccupied nineteenth-century lawyers. On the continent of Europe, the triggering event for mulling it over was the challenge which the French revolutionary idea of free evaluation of evidence presented to traditional legal proof rules of Roman-canon origin. In England, responsible for stirring the debate was Jeremy Bentham's scathing critique of the subjection of fact-finding activity to legal regulation. Although his primary target was rules on the admissibility of evidence, he also lambasted rules of weight. In the battle over the fate of the *ancien régime*'s justice system, which relied on legal proof rules, the debate became politicized and acrimonious. As the conceptual scaffolding for this debate, continental legal theorists posited a stark contrast between two fact-finding schemes – one rejecting and the other adopting legal constraints on the fact-finders' assessment of the value of evidence. English jurors were placed in the former and continental professional judges in the latter scheme. In this Manichaean opposition, English jurors appeared completely free from legal constraints, while continental judges seemed like robotic implementers of Roman-canon rules on the quantity and quality of evidence, required to arrive at factual findings irrespective of their personal assessment of evidence. This opposition was accepted as true in common law countries and became the dominant account of how factual findings were made on the continent during the *ancien régime*. The account stuck like a burdock, and still represents the conventional view in both continental and Anglo-American lands. It is usually accompanied by an evolutionary theory, holding that the assessment of evidence untethered from legal rules is the cornerstone of enlightened justice, and represents the irreversible stage in the evolution of forensic fact-finding. The evolution started with irrational appeals to God, was followed by blind reliance on Roman-canon legal proof, and culminated in the assessment of

2 *Prologue*

evidence free from legal chains. In this progressivist vision of the path leading to free evaluation of evidence, any regression appears like a return to the dark Middle Ages.

This study will challenge not only the conventional account of the opposition between Roman-canon and modern approaches to rules on the assessment of evidence, but also the view that the absence of these rules represents the apogee of the historical development of forensic fact-finding. Yet because of the byzantine complexities of the Roman-canon fact-finding scheme, the major part of the study will necessarily be devoted to reconstructing the scheme and examining how it functioned in the dominant form of the *ancien régime*'s criminal process.

THE ROAD MAP OF INQUIRY

The study will include eleven short chapters and an Epilogue. The opening chapter will explore the genesis of the Roman-canon fact-finding scheme in criminal cases. It is hazardous, of course, to speculate about what induced Roman-canon jurists to adopt the scheme. The dry bones of texts they left behind, and on which we must rely, can too easily be covered with contemporary flesh and blood, and nonexistent motives attributed to those who wrote them. In a triumph of temerity over scruple, the study will nevertheless venture an answer to the multifaceted and contested issue of the scheme's origin. Two families of theories dealing with the subject will be examined and found wanting. The attraction of the scheme's progenitors to rules on the value of evidence will be attributed not only to the allure of Roman law and certain biblical texts, but also to the needs of the court organization pioneered by the Church of Rome for the supervision of decisions made on the lower echelons of authority. In regard to crimes which entailed sanguinary punishments, the attraction to rules of this nature, the study will propose, was reinforced by Christian moral theology. The unsettling undertow beneath these rules will then be ascribed to the demands of harsh criminal policy that sprang up in late medieval times. The realization of this policy required that a large dose of discretion be granted to judges in the implementation of rules on the value of evidence. If applied mechanically, Roman-canon authorities recognized, these rules would often produce inaccurate verdicts.

Chapter 2 will seek to reconstruct the epistemic assumptions of Roman-canon evidence which are of interest to this study. On this issue conventional wisdom finds a stark difference between modern and premodern fact-finding schemes. The study will first address the question whether late medieval architects of Roman-canon evidence really believed that fidelity to proof-sufficiency rules guaranteed accurate outcomes. If such a belief existed, it would support the conventional opinion that these rules were automatically applied. Is it true, the study will ask, that the progenitors of the Roman-canon system disregarded sensory experience and defended claims to factual knowledge by blind invocation of authoritative rules?

Prologue

This theme will be examined through the writings of the greatest late-medieval jurists on the nature of factual inquiry. Stitched into the tapestry of the law, their preference of direct over circumstantial evidence will then be canvassed. The chapter's end will be devoted to the sensitive and emotionally charged question, rife with clamorous dissents, whether the use of coerced confessions in the inquisitorial process was rational.

After these preliminaries, Chapter 3 will prepare the reader for the review of those parts of the Roman-canon fact-finding scheme that are capable of revealing the extent to which Roman-canon judges were bound by law in assessing the value of evidence. This approach will necessitate a somewhat unconventional tour of Roman-canon evidence. Separately considered will be situations in which observance of legal proof could require the judge to convict defendants whom he considered innocent, and situations in which these rules could require him to abstain from convicting defendants whom he considered guilty. The former situation will be referred to as the *positive* effect of legal proof and the latter as its *negative* effect. These two possible effects will be analyzed against the background of the highest Roman-canon standard of full proof (*probatio plena*) required for the imposition of sanguinary punishments (*poenae sanguinis, poenae ordinariae*). This standard required either the testimony of two unimpeachable eyewitnesses to the crime or the defendant's confession.

Chapters 4 and 5 will then explore whether the highest Roman-canon standard of proof ever produced the positive effect – that is, required the judge to convict a defendant even if he considered him innocent. Chapter 4 will explore the impact of the rule requiring two unimpeachable eyewitnesses, and Chapter 5 the impact of the rule requiring the defendant's in-court confession. Contrary to standard accounts, these rules never compelled the judge to impose blood punishment if he found the testimony of the two eyewitnesses or the defendant's confession unreliable. The conventional view, the study will claim, results from paying insufficient attention to activities the judge was expected to perform in establishing whether the required eyewitnesses were unimpeachable and the confession truthful.

Chapter 6 will address the negative effect of Roman-canon full proof. What was the judge supposed to do when full proof was missing, but other evidence in the case convinced him of the defendant's guilt? The study will show that the Roman-canon scheme was more rigid in this regard, and could require the judge to disregard his personal evaluation of the evidence. Only in its negative impact, then, did Roman-canon evidence generate a gap between legally mandated outcomes and outcomes favored by the inquisitorial process's hunt for the truth. The resulting tension produced a split in Roman-canon legal doctrine. A minority held that blood punishment could be imposed even in the absence of full proof if the probative force of legally insufficient evidence was overwhelming. Court practice, we will see, varied across continental jurisdictions.

4 *Prologue*

However, the extent to which the judge's fact-finding freedom was legally bound cannot properly be established by focusing solely on rules of proof sufficiency. Admissibility rules must also be considered. On first inspection this seems to be wrong, since the purpose of these rules is to exclude evidence from consideration by the judge, rather than to direct him how to assess their value. Yet as Chapter 7 will demonstrate, the institutional milieu of the inquisitorial process could obliterate the distinction between admissibility rules and rules of weight, since the judge was often exposed to reliable testimony of legally incompetent witnesses. When this occurred, the law required that he attribute no probative value to information he found convincing. Whether rules on this subject were firm or vacillated will be exposed to scrutiny.

Chapter 8 will look at instruments designed to reduce the damage which the negative effect of Roman-canon full proof caused to crime control interests. The need for these instruments was keenly felt by judges when their inability to find two eyewitnesses or to obtain a confession prevented them from imposing blood punishment on a defendant of whose guilt they were convinced on legally inadequate evidence. Their urge to punish, their *furor puniendi*, needed some release. As we will see, most important for providing this release was the possibility of imposing criminal sanctions milder than death or serious bodily punishment (*poena extraordinaria*). After we have examined the rules dealing with the evidence needed for imposing these punishments, it will became clear why a measure of fact-finding freedom burst into court practice as inevitably as trees leaf out in spring. Also useful in compensating for the judges' inability to impose blood punishment were intermediate judgments between conviction and outright acquittal. They enabled the imposition of onerous restrictions on the freedom of defendants who were in limbo, neither convicted nor fully acquitted. And as the finality of these judgments was suspended, the door was left open for the resumption of prosecution if full Roman-canon proof became available at a later date.

Chapter 9 will summarize findings about the degree to which Roman-canon fact-finding arrangements influenced the freedom of judges in assessing the value of evidence. The chapter will survey the pronouncements of Roman-canon jurists on the wiggle room judges enjoyed in implementing proof sufficiency rules. It will become obvious that this wiggle room accommodated the tension between legal proof and the need for effective law enforcement that characterized the Roman-canon fact-finding arrangements. The judges' limited discretion (*arbitrium regulatum*) will emerge as the key for unlocking the mystery of how evidence law was implemented in the inquisitorial process.

Chapters 10 and 11 will move from the historical to the comparative plane and interrogate what constraints on the judges' freedom to evaluate evidence persist in contemporary criminal procedure, and how they relate to constraints in the Roman-canon fact-finding scheme. Chapter 11 will examine this question in regard to procedures in the continental legal tradition, where the principle of free evaluation of evidence is now professed to be the lodestar. The evolution of this principle will be traced from its original French form of inscrutable personal conviction (*conviction intime*) to its now prevailing intersubjectively articulated variant (*conviction raisonnée*). It will turn out that this more recent variant tolerates significant limitations on judges' fact-finding freedom. Although legal doctrine denies legal character to most of these limitations, we will see that the denial is not realistic. In contrast to the Roman-canon system, however, the modern variant of these limitations eschews rules requiring a specified quantity and quality of evidence for conviction. It espouses instead a general proof-sufficiency formula requiring that evidence supportive of conviction must leave no doubt in the adjudicators' minds. But we will see that it also includes rules on steps judges must take in arriving at factual findings, and rules mandating disregard of some species of evidence, no matter how persuasive they may appear to judges. The constraining effects of these rules will exhibit open and subtle parallels to the negative effects of Roman-canon legal proof rules.

Chapter 11 will seek to establish whether functional counterparts of Roman-canon legal proof rules can be found in common law jurisdictions. Here the comparison of the two systems will be bedeviled by differences between the Roman-canon unitary and the common law bicameral trial court. The division of the latter in two parts will require separate consideration of the law's *aspirations* as reflected in the judge's instructions to the jury, and their *realization* in the jury's verdict. In regard to aspirations, unsuspected affinities will come into view with the Roman-canon fact-finding system. It is only when the realization of these aspirations becomes the subject of comparison that major contrasts with the Roman-canon system become evident in regard to the adjudicators' fact-finding freedom.

The Epilogue will pull together the threads of the study's narrative. Two contrary dispositions toward the adjudicators' freedom to evaluate evidence will be identified in both premodern and modern criminal procedure, neither disposition strong enough to defeat or put the other to flight. Quite understandably, then, it will transpire that the Roman-canon fact-finding scheme and its contemporary counterparts were not radically opposed, the former adopting, the latter rejecting legal constraints on the evaluation of evidence. It will emerge instead that they both adopted intermediate positions between these two extremes. More unexpectedly, the study will reveal the remarkable endurance of legal proof in its negative form. The argument will be made that this form does not deserve disparagement as the relic of an inferior stage in the evolution of forensic evidence. On the contrary, the study will attempt to show that well-chosen negative proof rules could be useful in contemporary procedural systems. And as scientific and technological advances produce knowledge capable of extending law into areas presently left to the adjudicators' innate cognitive processes, the importance of these rules is likely to grow and find burgeoning acceptance. The final pages of the study will then propose that the evaluation of evidence free from legal intrusion does not deserve to be hailed as an irreversible historical achievement and an ideal fact-finding arrangement.

6   *Prologue*

THE ELUSIVE UNITY OF ROMAN-CANON EVIDENCE

As most of the terrain to be traversed in this study will be in the domain of Roman-canon evidence law, it is worth stressing at the outset a difficulty that any cicerone must face in guiding the reader through this hugely varied legal landscape. The difficulty stems from the fact that Roman-canon evidence law changed greatly depending on the type of proceedings to which it applied. Civil and criminal evidence differed considerably, especially in respect of the judge's freedom to depart from the rules of evidence when they seemed to him over- or under-inclusive. But even criminal evidence – with which this study is solely concerned – constituted a single system only in its main outline. If one ventures beyond, differences surface between evidence in the two types of criminal proceedings developed by the Church of Rome and adopted later by secular jurisdictions. The older "accusatorial" type of proceeding (*processus per accusationem*) was patterned on the criminal process of the later Roman Empire. It was organized as a private prosecution, instituted on the initiative of a private prosecutor. He and the accused were required to submit evidence which was then developed by the judge. But as of the thirteenth century, this type of proceeding was gradually overshadowed – and in some places totally eclipsed – by the "inquisitorial" type (*processus per inquisitionem*), conceived as a judicially instituted and conducted investigation.[1] Here the active role of the judge in collecting evidence had a significant effect on its evaluation. Only the fact-finding scheme in this dominant form of the *ancien régime*'s criminal justice will be canvassed in this study.

Common features of Roman-canon evidentiary arrangements are difficult to pinpoint, however, even within this greatly narrowed focus. A principal reason for this difficulty is the polyphonic character of late medieval legal sources regulating these arrangements. Consider that Roman-canon evidence did not spring from a single legislative source, nor was it built like a coral reef, case by case. Rather it emerged from the work of late medieval university scholars and Church lawyers engaged in organizing the fragmentary evidence rules found in ancient Roman law and in scattered legal sources of the Church.[2] Where no consensus crystallized on an issue, judges would follow the opinions of jurists they considered

---

[1] For the description of the accusatorial process in Italian secular courts, see Hermann Kantorowicz, *Albertus Gandinus und das Strafrecht der Scholastik*, vol. 1, 87–120 (1907). On the rise of the inquisitorial process, see Winfried Trusen, "Von den Anfängen des Inquisitionsprozesses zum Verfahren bei der Inquisitio Haereticae Pravitatis," in Peter Segl (ed.), *Die Anfänge der Inquisition in Mittelalter*, 39–76 (1993). For a brief outline of criminal proceedings developed by the Church of Rome, see Mirjan Damaška, "The quest for due process in the age of inquisition," 60 *Am. J. Comp. L*, 919, 921–926 (2012).

[2] Secular scholars (*viri scolastici*) focused on the Digest, Code and Novels in Justinian's codification of Roman law, while lawyers of the Church focused on Gratian's Decretum. But although secular (civil) and ecclesiastical law were formally separated, their interpenetration was so intense that it is appropriate to term the final product "Roman-canon" evidence. It should be noted, however, that the final product of this fusion is often designated as *ius commune* evidence, or learned evidence law.

Prologue

most respected.[3] But even respected jurists sometimes equivocated on the question of how flexible the rules on the value of evidence ought to be. Often they also failed to indicate the type of criminal process to which their opinions on a point of evidence law related: many of their pronouncements seem to have been directed to the more sophisticated and theoretically challenging accusatorial form of criminal proceedings, rather than to the prevailing inquisitorial form of interest to this study. This decentralized mode of lawmaking produced uncertainties in the law, similar to those that arise in common law jurisdictions when several lines of precedents compete for recognition. In a word, legal waters were muddied at their source. Princely ordinances of the early modern period introduced more order in this scholarly law and reduced its dissonances. But they gave rise to changes in attitudes toward the rigidity of evidence rules, particularly in jurisdictions where codification of the law was coupled with institutional innovations, such as the separation of investigative functions from decision-making.[4] The decline in the importance of blood punishments in the early modern period was yet another source of changes, especially in regard to the scope of applicability of the Roman-canon full proof standard.

As a result of all these transformations doubts arise whether the Roman-canon fact-finding scheme can be perceived as a unity with common characteristics. Responsible for these doubts is the scheme's long life. Its roots were planted in the twelfth century, and its vocabulary and doctrinal framework completed a century later, at the time when the inquisitorial process was officially recognized by the Church of Rome. Once established, the scheme's *dur désir de durer* was long-lasting. Even in the nineteenth century, after the French revolutionary principle of free evaluation of evidence began its victorious march on the continent, the scheme did not completely disappear. Like light after sunset, much of its doctrinal framework survived in some continental countries.[5] To be sure, variety thrived within this stubbornly persisting framework – a variety due to stupendous and multifaceted changes that took place in Europe between the thirteenth and nineteenth centuries.[6] Nor was the variety limited to diachronic differences. Synchronic spatial

---

[3] On the details of this scholarly law in late medieval northern Italy, see Woldemar Engelmann, *Wiedergeburt der Rechtskultur in Italien*, 212–228 (1938). It is true that local customs, urban statutes and sporadic royal ordinances could supersede this law, but it still remained influential as an instrument for interpreting customs, statutes, and ordinances, or as a tool for filling gaps in legal sources.

[4] These two functions, as we will see, were usually fused in the medieval forms of the inquisitorial process.

[5] On the margins of continental legal culture, the final flickers of Roman-canon evidence lingered until the twentieth century. For the Kingdom of Serbia, see Tihomir Vasiljević, *Sistem Krivičnog Procesnog Prava*, SFRJ, 311 (1965).

[6] Contrary to what is often thought, however, early modern lawyers remained remarkably aloof from developments in science and philosophy relevant to truth-discovery. We will see that some intellectual historians valiantly but unsuccessfully struggled to prove that Roman-canon evidence law was affected by science and philosophy as of the seventeenth century.

8 *Prologue*

differences existed as well: even identical changes in the enveloping political, social, and intellectual environment did not always produce identical responses in criminal justice. But despite all this variety the unity preserving doctrinal framework persisted. The vocabulary and the conceptual apparatus crafted in late medieval times remained largely intact until the scheme was *in extremis*. So did the proof sufficiency rules and the downgrading of circumstantial evidence. The tension between legal proof rules and effective crime control likewise proved unvarying. Antithetical energies released by this tension generated an enduring fervor in both legal doctrine and court practice, responsible for producing the characteristic mélange of constraint and freedom in the evaluation of evidence.

The continuity of Roman-canon legal proof can easily be documented. Consider that seventeenth-century lawyers still read late medieval jurists and invoked their views as authoritative. A century later, a famous French lawyer, Muyart de Vouglans, castigated Cesare Beccaria for attacking Roman-canon evidence without familiarity with two sixteenth-century Italian jurists, who in turn sought support for their opinions in the writings of fourteenth-century scholarly jurists.[7] And in the nineteenth century, the learned German lawyer Carl Mittermaier could still not separate himself from a version of legal proof, despite his surprising familiarity with common law evidence. If you think about it, the longevity of the Roman-canon fact-finding scheme is nothing short of remarkable. It is as if categories of scholastic philosophy continued to be recognized by Marx and Engels, or as if the Byzantine pictorial style continued to inform Western painting from the time of Cimabue to the rococo frivolities of Boucher or Fragonard.

Features of the Roman-canon scheme relevant to the judge's freedom to evaluate evidence will be examined against the background of the scheme's most sophisticated strand, developed in northern Italy after the intellectual rebirth of the twelfth century. The strand will be used as a trunk for the scheme's branching variations. It was very influential in continental courts, and gained a quasicanonical status not only in the courts at the continent's center, but also in those on its margins. Among several late medieval expositors of the strand, special attention will be paid to a treatise of Albertus Gandinus and to the writings of two of the greatest fourteenth-century jurists, Bartolus de Saxoferrato and Baldus de Ubaldis. They made important contributions to Roman-canon evidence law, and their opinions carried great weight outside Italy for several centuries. Among several of their sixteenth-century successors, the study will most frequently refer to the opus of Prospero Farinacci, the "prince of criminal lawyers," whose books on procedure and evidence circulated widely across the European land mass. Among seventeenth-century authorities, most often cited will be the Dutch jurist Damhouder, and especially the somewhat younger German jurist and judge Benedict Carpzov. The latter's treatise on

---

[7] See Muyart de Vouglans, *Réfutation des Principes Hasardés dans le Traité des Délits et Peines*, 66–67 (Lausanne 1767).

criminal procedure, although devoted to the law of his native Saxony, was treated in several continental jurisdictions as if it possessed legislative force.[8] Sporadic glances at the French variant of legal proof will be based mainly on two eighteenth-century legal authorities, Daniel Jousse and Muyart de Vouglans.

The discussion of the Roman-canon fact-finding scheme will not be limited to its depiction in scholarly commentaries and treatises, however. Although the law as described by learned jurists did not float irrelevantly over actual goings-on in court-rooms, significant gaps are known to have existed – as they do in our time – between the arias of procedural doctrine and the recitative of court practice. But since archival studies of this practice are fragmentary and often inconclusive, the study will rely on legal opinions (*consilia*) delivered by Roman-canon legal experts in criminal cases, and on practitioners' manuals devoted to the collection of evidence in the inquisitorial criminal process. Leafing through these primary sources takes one, as through a magnifying glass, into many otherwise invisible facets of the Roman-canon fact-finding scheme.

Having marked the route to be travelled in this study, and alerted the reader to difficulties we will encounter along the way, let us now consider how the Roman-canon evidentiary arrangements for criminal cases came into being.

[8] See Roderick von Stintzing, *Geschichte der deutschen Rechtswissenschaft*, vol. 1, 1, 67 (München-Leipzig, 1884).

1

The Origin of Roman-Canon Legal Proof in Criminal Cases

The standard narrative depicts the Roman-canon fact-finding system as characterized by the mechanical application of rules on the quantity and quality of evidence. Two groups of theories attempt to explain the origin of this feature: one group envisions it as an outgrowth of magical beliefs, while the other sees it as a product of their rejection. This study does not propose to set out in tedious detail the many variant theories which fall into these two families of inquiry, but will only tease out those of their entailments that relate to the emergence of legal constraints on the fact-finder's freedom to consider the value of evidence. Theories explaining the origin of the Roman-canon fact-finding scheme as an outgrowth of magical beliefs will be rejected as untenable: chilly drafts blow through the holes in their historical tapestry. Theories attributing the origin of the scheme to the abandonment of magical belief will be found plausible but questionable. They deserve a fresh look because they rest on questionable assumptions about the role of reason at the time when the inquisitorial criminal process and its fact-finding arrangements were nascent. They also fail to account for the origin of strong countercurrents to the mechanical application of evidence rules. Having expressed misgivings about these theories, the study will offer an alternative view of the genesis of the Roman-canon fact-finding scheme.

ROMAN-CANON EVIDENCE AS THE OUTGROWTH OF ORDEALS

What all theories falling into this group have in common is the assumption that the Roman-canon fact-finding scheme was predicated on the belief that forensic oath possesses intrinsic probative value, so that unopposed sworn testimony of legally competent witnesses could automatically be credited.

The Old Numerical Variant

The oldest version of these theories used to be popular in Anglophone legal scholarship.[1] According to this version, the consequence of considering oaths

---

[1] An early believer in this version was Jeremy Bentham. See Jeremy Bentham, *Rationale of Judicial Evidence*, vol. 1, 94 (Littleton, ed.), (Colorado: Fred B. Rothman & Co, 1995). Its spread in Anglo-American legal literature is in large measure due to Wigmore's acceptance of the version. See John

inherently probative was the neglect of the content of sworn testimony. In other words, legally competent witnesses were confounded with credible ones. And since oaths were treated as equally probative, the larger number of witnesses prevailed over the smaller number when their sworn testimony supported conflicting factual propositions. As a result, we are told, the judge was reduced to the role of an accountant totaling proof fractions, and fact-finding assumed a "numerical" character. As will soon be documented, this understanding of the role of the oath cannot be squared with Roman-canon legal authorities of the time when the inquisitorial process came into its own. Although uncontested sworn testimony possessed great probative force, it was not automatically credited. It is true that Roman-canon jurists included the number of witnesses among the facts to be considered in resolving conflicts of sworn testimony, but they indicated that the number should not be the decisive consideration. The witnesses' social standing, they wrote, ought to be given greater weight than their numbers.[2] And while the emphasis on standing is alien to our present understanding, it demonstrates that the Roman-canon scheme is misrepresented if conceived as a numerical system. Most important, we will also see that great medieval jurists added the "verisimilitude" of sworn testimony as a factor to be considered in resolving testimonial conflict. Ultimately, they wrote, the matter should be left to the judge's discretion (*arbitrium*).[3]

The Oath As the Source of God's Truth

A relatively new theory situating the Roman-canon fact-finding scheme in the shadow of ordeals deserves to be considered in some detail, because of its ingenious attempt to account for the mix of supernatural and human in medieval society.[4] It was put forward in order to explain fact-finding arrangements that sprouted across Europe in response to the early thirteenth-century papal ban on the participation of clergy in most commonly used trials by ordeal. The ban created a crisis in the administration of justice, the theory claims, because late medieval people were still unprepared to face up to problems involved in fact-finding for the purpose of administering justice by reliance on their own resources. They continued to demand that the authority

---

Henry Wigmore, *Evidence in Trials at Common Law*, vol. 7, 325, 327, 329–330 (Chadbourn rev.) (Boston: Little Brown, 1978). We will see that a few Anglophone legal historians now reject this view.

[2] Medieval commentators of papal legislation claimed, for example, that it would be wrong to prefer the testimony of 100 sinners over that of a bishop.

[3] Traces of the numerical system, with its confusion of legal and credible witnesses, can be found in English procedural history. As late as the seventeenth century Sir Matthew Hale found it necessary to emphasize that jurors were not bound by sworn testimony. See Barbara J. Shapiro, *Beyond Reasonable Doubt*, 12, 261, n. 38 (Berkeley and Los Angeles: University of California Press, 1991). A century later, Geoffrey Gilbert still argued for reliance on the number of witnesses who gave evidence under oath. See Geoffrey Gilbert, *The Law of Evidence*, 5, 157 (First ed. Dublin, 1754).

[4] See George Fisher, The Jury's Rise as Lie Detector, 107 *Yale Law Journal*, 575, 590, 596–597 (1997).

behind court decisions be divine rather than human. The reluctance to accept the judgments of mere mortals was especially strong in the case of capital crimes, where the prevailing sentiment called for a purely divine source of guilt determination. Aware of this persisting sentiment, thirteenth-century lawgivers, including Roman-canon jurists, chose the oath as a convenient substitute for ordeals. The oath was convenient, the theory tells us, because of the wide-spread belief that God vouches for the truth of sworn testimonial statements. This belief made it possible for ordinary folks to imagine that the divinely sponsored oath, rather than human reasoning powers, was capable of screening out untrustworthy testimony and guaranteeing correct procedural outcomes. But in the administration of justice so understood, the conflict of sworn statements created a problem. Since it was difficult for people to imagine that God would send conflicting signals about the truth of testimony, or that humans could resolve the inconsistency of these signals, the legitimacy of the fact-finding scheme regarding oath as a channel to God's wisdom would have been imperiled. Faced with this predicament, legal authorities, including Roman-canon ones, erected three lines of defense against clashing sworn statements. The first line consisted of rules assisting the judge in reconciling discrepancies in testimonial assertions, enabling him to announce that no real conflict existed. If this strategy failed, the next line of defense was a series of testimonial disqualifications aimed at preventing most likely liars from testifying. And if even this measure failed, a "hierarchy" of oaths was set up in which weightier oaths eliminated lesser ones in a mechanical fashion. Structured in this way, the fact-finding scheme was capable of supporting the belief that procedural outcomes were oath-driven, and that judges were merely classifying and counting oaths, rather than settling testimonial conflict by the exercise of their own reasoning powers. Only in low-visibility ways was some elbow room left to the judges to enable them to assess the real probative value of testimony and dispense a rational form of justice. But the main purpose of Roman-canon, and indeed all premodern, fact-finding schemes was to assure the public that, at least in the case of capital crime, God had retained all decision-making power to himself.

What is one to make of this theory? The worldview of ordinary thirteenth-century people was in fact permeated with magical imaginings: the interpenetration of the sacred and the profane was part of medieval life, and human reflection only gradually outstripped the ritual invocation of the supernatural in the administration of justice. No wonder, then, that the papal ban on ordeals could not produce an immediate break with magical conceptions, and was destined to share the fate of repeatedly violated papal prohibitions of knightly tournaments. It is also quite unsurprising that some species of forensic oath exhibiting features associated with ordeals continued to be administered across the European land mass. Prominent among them was the so-called "purgatory oath" of the defendant, assisted by "oath-helpers" who swore to their belief in the rightness of the defendant's claim of innocence.[5] A variant of this purgatory oath – the *purgatio canonica* – was used by the medieval Church in proceedings against clerics about whom credible rumors of criminal activity circulated. But with the introduction of the inquisitorial process in the early thirteenth century the purgatory oath lost its importance in ecclesiastical, and gradually also in secular, proceedings.[6] Rather than relying on sworn opinions of innocence delivered by oath-helpers (*testes de credulitate*), the investigating judge preferred to rely on witnesses with actual knowledge of relevant facts (*testes de scientia*). They were examined and required to take the promissory oath to tell the truth. And instead of asking the defendant to swear to his innocence, the investigating judge preferred to subject him to interrogation about the facts of the case. In some jurisdictions, as we will see, the defendant was also required to take the promissory oath to truthfully answer questions asked of him. The theory under consideration is thus right in claiming that the oath continued to play an important role in the administration of justice after the decline of ordeals, smoothing the transition to modern ways of adjudicative fact-finding.

But was the oath of Roman-canon witnesses imagined as capable of inducing God to vouch for the truth of testimony and to miraculously intervene in ongoing proceedings to indicate testimonial falsity? As far as the Church of Rome is concerned, there is abundant evidence for a negative answer. Latin Christendom never conceived of oath as an instrument according a supernatural seal of approval to testimonial assertions.[7] Perjury was subjected to ecclesial penitential discipline as early as the ninth century, and gradually also to the jurisdiction of ecclesiastical courts.[8] For twelfth-century theologians like Peter Lombard it was a commonplace that oath did not exhibit a numinous character in the sense that false swearing would provoke immediate divine punishment. Distancing the human from discernible divine proximity was, after all, one of their main achievements. The oath did remain linked to the supernatural, but only in the sense that the fear of divine retribution – whether in this life or the next – constituted an inducement to truthful testimony. By provoking fear of God, the oath was meant to increase the likelihood of obtaining

---

5 On the margins of Western legal culture, oath-helpers continued to be used as late as the seventeenth century. See Joannes Kitonicz, *Processus Consuetudinarii Incliti Regni Hungariae*, Cap. 6, qu. 9 (Trnava: Fredericus Gall, 1724).

6 For an old but still valuable collection of primary sources on the purgatory oath, see Karl Hildebrand, *Die Purgatio Canonica et Vulgaris* (Munich, 1841).

7 "A man who takes an oath," wrote Augustine of Hippo in the fifth century, "may swear to both truth and falsity" (*falsum et verum jurare potest*). Relevant passages from his writings can be found collected in Paolo Prodi, *Das Sakrament der Herrschaft*, 47 (Berlin: Duncker & Humblot, 1997). For a distinction between ordeals and the oath in the theology of the late Middle Ages, see Gerard Courtois, Le serment: du désenchantement du monde à l'éclipse du sujet, in Raymond Verdier (ed.), *Le Serment* vol. 2, *Théories et devenir*, 7–8 (Paris: Editions du CNRS, 1991).

8 See, Stephan Kuttner, *Die juristische Natur der falschen Beweisaussage* (Berlin: Walter de Gruyter, 1931).

14   *The Origin of Roman-Canon Legal Proof in Criminal Cases*

truthful testimony, but it was not believed to be a sufficient condition for taking it as true. This more mundane understanding of both purgatory and testimonial oaths differed from our present understanding only in its psychologically coercive power, since the fear of hell as the consequence of perjury was, in the then-existing climate of Western consciousness, intense and omnipresent.

What about the laity? Did it believe that sworn statements were true by reason of divine epiphany? If it did, the theory could retain an explanatory force. For even if the ordeal-like understanding of the oath was alien to the Church, the understanding could still make the imposition of capital punishment palatable to simple, uneducated spirits. The idea that sworn assertions have a divine imprimatur could have been addressed to the *hoi polloi*, and the low-visibility license to disbelieve them to the judge. Yet, long before the thirteenth century's adoption of inquisitorial procedure, the realization that persons lie under oath, and that their lie is not miraculously revealed by divine intervention, was part of the lived experience of ordinary folks. Medieval preachers regularly inveighed against perjury, and complaints of false swearing in both judicial and extrajudicial settings were frequent from at least the eighth century.[9] This fact is hard to reconcile with the view that sworn testimony was considered presumptively true even in capital cases.

But more palpably damaging to the ordeal-like conception of the oath is the difficulty of reconciling it with the rules of the inquisitorial process. If uncontested testimony were really considered presumptively true, then rules concerning the interrogation of witnesses in this process would make no sense. As we will see, these rules required the judge to pay close attention to possible inconsistencies and signs of falsity in the assertions of witnesses.[10] Consider also the difficulties the theory faces in explaining how the understanding of the oath as a channel to God's wisdom can be reconciled with the resolution of testimonial conflicts. The three lines of defense the theory proposes do not fit the Roman-canon fact-finding scheme. Regarding the first defense line, it is true that Roman-canon judges were urged to resolve testimonial conflict by reconciling inconsistent statements. But rules to this

---

[9] In jurisdictions that came to rely on Roman-canon *testes de scientia*, false testimony was threatened with severe punishment, such as the cutting off of the perjurer's tongue or the hand used in swearing. We have even pictorial evidence of such punishments. See, e.g., Robert Fossier (ed.), *The Cambridge Illustrated History of the Middle Ages, Vol. 2: The Middle Ages, 950–1250*, 357 (Cambridge: Cambridge University Press, 1997).

[10] Since the theory is supposed to apply to European criminal justice generally, it is worth noting that it also encounters difficulties in explaining English felony trials from the period when only witnesses for the prosecution were permitted to testify under oath. According to contemporary accounts, the hallmarks of these trials were heated exchanges between the accused and prosecution witnesses, as well as a large number of acquittals. But if sworn testimony was meant to appear to the public as a source of God's truth, how can these features of the trial be explained? If human mediation of *conflicting* sources of divine truth was unacceptable, the disregard of *congruent* sworn testimony of prosecution witnesses would be even more so. And if sworn testimony disclosed God's truth only when the jury believed prosecution witnesses, but not when it disbelieved them, it would have been obvious to the public that the ultimate power was human rather than divine even in capital cases. Jury verdicts would not appear as arising independently from the choice of mere mortals.

effect did not stem from fears that the conflict might be interpreted by the public as amounting to inconsistent divine epiphanies of the truth. Rather, these rules were intended to facilitate the use of the highly exacting Roman-canon proof sufficiency standard requiring the concordant testimony of two eyewitnesses to the crime. The considerable difficulty of finding them was augmented by the requirement that inconsistencies in their testimony be removed or explained away in order to establish the congruity of what the witnesses asserted. Nor is it true that the consonance of witness assertions made their acceptance automatic. We will see that greatly similar testimonial accounts led to the suspicion of possible collusion, and that judges were warned to subject such accounts to careful scrutiny. If harmony of sworn statements was regarded as a divine sign of their reliability, judicial inquiry into sources of this harmony would be inappropriate and possibly even sacrilegious.

Regarding the second line of defense,[11] it is true that Roman-canon evidence law included a multitude of testimonial disqualification rules. But the reason for barring specified categories of persons from testifying was not to minimize testimonial clashes. Consider that the judge had to exclude a legally incompetent witness even if what he testified agreed with the testimony of a competent witness.[12] As will become clear when Roman-canon testimonial disqualifications are reviewed, their primary purpose was to block spurious sources of information from polluting the pool of evidence. Also instrumental were dangers to the souls of witnesses likely to perjure themselves. The third line of defense, the theory proposes, was constituted by a list of factors the judge was supposed to have in mind in deciding whose sworn testimony to credit. But contrary to what the theory would have us believe, these factors were not expressed in iron-clad, hierarchically structured rules excluding human judgment. When we subject them to scrutiny, it will transpire that they did not constitute what might now be termed a self-executing algorithm. They were in the nature of guidelines, advising the judge what factors to consider in deciding whom to believe. If he thought it appropriate, he could order witnesses whose accounts clashed to confront each other, and then decide whose testimony was more credible by observing their demeanour.

In sum, Roman-canon testimonial oath does not lend itself to the theory that the inquisitorial process treated oaths as channels of God's wisdom. Nor can this theory be reconciled with the rules of the inquisitorial criminal process. By ascribing a supernatural character of this kind to the oath, the theory casts a distorting light – an *ignis fatuus* – on the origin of Roman-canon evidence rules for criminal cases.

---

[11] It would have been more elegant for the theory to treat this line of defense as the first one, since testimonial inconsistencies presented problems in regard to assertions of legally competent witnesses.

[12] We will see that this possibility was not rare. Some reasons for incompetence could be established only in the course of examination, for example, and in the initial stage of the inquisitorial process the judge would examine all persons capable of furnishing information about the crime.

16 *The Origin of Roman-Canon Legal Proof in Criminal Cases*

ROMAN-CANON EVIDENCE AS A RADICAL BREAK WITH ORDEALS

The prevailing account of the origin of Roman-canon evidence stems from efforts to explain how the administration of justice on the continent of Europe and in England drifted apart from its medieval common roots. The narrative begins again with reference to tensions generated by the thirteenth-century papal prohibition of clerical participation in trials by ordeal. In contrast to the theory examined above, however, the account does not portray testimonial oaths as links to divine wisdom, or as another form of divine intervention in the administration of justice. On the heels of the papal decree, the account proposes, the administration of justice appeared severed from the divine and dependent on human agency. And in a further contrast to the aforementioned theory, the account does not maintain that in response to the papal ban a single premodern fact-finding system evolved throughout Europe. In England and most northern continental lands, the account tells us, the inscrutable judgment of God was replaced by the inscrutable judgment of the local community. *Vox populi* replaced *vox Dei*. Meanwhile, much of the rest of Europe gradually adopted the fact-finding model pioneered by the Church of Rome – a model in which mere mortals, judges, were tasked with administering justice. The transition from sacred to profane legitimacy of judgments was a radical departure from earlier medieval practice, generating unease about the dependence on human reasoning powers in adjudication. In particular, the *vox singuli* of a lone judge failed to inspire sufficient confidence. As a result, strict Roman-canon proof sufficiency rules appeared attractive and were widely adopted.[13]

This account of what transpired following the ban on ordeals may be helpful in explaining how the administration of justice in England and on the continent began to drift apart. When closely examined, however, it tells us little about the origin of the Roman-canon fact-finding scheme for criminal cases. To begin with, the exacting requirement for the testimony of two eyewitnesses was adopted by the Church of Rome long before the thirteenth-century papal ban on the use of ordeals. The adoption was part of the Church's late eleventh-century effort to introduce Roman law into its jurisprudence. The specific motive for requiring two eyewitnesses for conviction was to accord prelates a procedural instrument to defend themselves against malicious accusations.[14] The seeds of the ecclesiastical component of the Roman-canon full proof standard were thus planted long before the rise of the inquisitorial process. As far as the secular component of this standard is

---

[13] For a sampling of accounts of this nature, see R. C. Caenagem, The Law of Evidence in the Twelfth Century, in *Proceedings of the Second International Congress of Medieval Canon Law*, 297 (Rome: Biblioteca Apostolica Vaticana, 1965); Piero Fiorelli, *La Tortura Giudiziaria nel Diritto Comune*, vol. 1, 8 (Rome: Giuffrè, 1953); John Langbein, *Torture and the Law of Proof*, 6–7 (Chicago: University of Chicago Press, 1976).

[14] That the protection of prelates was the purpose of pre-inquisitorial ecclesiastical procedure was acknowledged by the "Qualiter et Quando" decree of Pope Innocent III, confirmed in 1215 by the Lateran General Council. See IV Lat., c. 8, lin. 22. For details, see Linda Fowler-Magerl, "'Ordines Iudiciarii' and 'Libelli de Ordine Iudiciorum'," 23 (Turnhout: Brepols, 1994).

Roman-Canon Evidence As a Radical Break with Ordeals

concerned, it is important to bear in mind that northern Italian city states – where the component evolved – did not use trials by ordeal at all.[15] This fact alone should give us pause in attributing the birth of the Roman-canon fact-finding scheme to the decline of this early medieval mode of dispensing justice.

But there is more. Generally speaking, thirteenth-century elites did not lack faith in human judgment.[16] It is true that the rebirth of reason is often attributed to the early modern period, when people began to perceive that revelation did not suffice to elucidate their relation to the world. Only as faith ceased efficiently to act on people's lives, we are told, did the knight errant of the human spirit sally forth to accept reason as the mediator between humankind and the world. Scientific discoveries of people like Kepler and Copernicus, and the writings of philosophers like Descartes and Locke, were the cockcrows of rationalism, ushering in the age of reason.[17] But this concept of reason – mathematical in its purest form – is too narrow in regard to many human activities. It hardly applies to ancient Greek philosophy, for example. In a more encompassing sense, reason implies thinking coherently and drawing logical inferences from facts known or assumed. And when *ratio* is understood in this way, reliance on reason appears to have increased so dramatically in the twelfth and thirteenth centuries that some scholars refer to the period as the age of the first enlightenment.[18] Note that the twelfth century was the age of great breakthroughs and innovations in various spheres of social life. The cessation of invasions from Asia was followed by rapid economic development, the rise of cities and markets, population growth and an exuberant revival of culture. This was especially true of northern Italy and southern France, the birthplaces of most of the founding fathers of Roman-canon evidence law.

Of special importance for the faith in human reasoning capacity were changes that took place in the Church of Rome. Up to the first millennium, the Church, perhaps haunted by the collapse of classical civilization, showed little interest in matters concerning terrestrial life: it directed its vision upward, toward heavenly rewards in the hereafter. This neglect of the "here and now" (*hic et nunc*) began to

---

[15] See Michele Taruffo, *La Semplice Verità*, 14 (Rome: Laterza, 2009).

[16] Even trials by ordeal did not entirely exclude reliance on human intelligence. In the medieval cultural milieu, the participation of clergy and the solemn preparation of ordeals produced distinctive demeanor evidence in the guilty and the innocent. This evidence was then used in calibrating the severity of tests comprising the ordeal, or the manner in which the results of tests were interpreted. See Rebecca V. Colman, Reason and Unreason in Early Medieval Law, 4, *Journal of Interdisciplinary History*, 571, 589 (1974). It should also not be overlooked that the objective of early medieval lawsuits was to resolve issues that exceeded the task of accurately establishing empirical facts. For the resolution of these issues, ordeals may have been rational instruments. See, Taruffo, *La Semplice Verità*, 4–13.

[17] See L. J. Cohen, Freedom of Proof, in William Twining (ed.), *Facts in Law*, 16 *Archives for Philosophy of Law and Social Philosophy*, 10–11 (Stuttgart: Franz Steiner, 1983).

[18] See the collection of essays in Kurt Flash and Udo Jeck, *Das Licht der Vernunft; Die Anfänge der Aufklärung im Mittelalter* (Munich: C.H. Beck, 1981). See also Benjamin Nelson, *On the Road to Modernity*, 192–193 (Lanham: Lexington Books, 1981).

18   *The Origin of Roman-Canon Legal Proof in Criminal Cases*

change in the later eleventh century, when the idea took wing that life on earth could be improved, and that a social order reflecting divine will could be created.[19] The resulting retreat of the Church from apocalyptic otherworldliness was manifested in many ways, but the weakening of theological mysticism is the most important for the purposes of this study. Observe that prior to the late eleventh century matters divine were treated as a subject unfit for exploration by the human intellect. But in the course of the twelfth century, prominent theologians – St. Anselm, for example – began to reflect about the sacred in terms of logic and dialectics, made accessible to them by newly available texts of classical antiquity. Voices could even be heard to the effect that all divine knowledge could be subject to rational scrutiny.[20] Crucial in this regard seems to have been the focus on Jesus, the second person of the Trinity. If God could assume human form, "rational" theologians argued, perhaps the mysteries of faith could be fitted into the constructs of human intellect.[21] And since theology was exalted in the Middle Ages as the queen of all intellectual disciplines, the use of *ratio* in matters divine encouraged its employment in other areas, including the administration of justice.

On all these grounds it is difficult to sustain the position that the distrust of human intellect induced Roman-canon jurists to develop mechanically applicable rules of proof sufficiency. Leave to one side that the articulation of these rules presupposed optimism about human intellectual capacity. More obvious in reflecting this optimism was the fact that the social milieu in which the Roman-canon fact-finding scheme was crafted displayed a tolerant attitude toward decision-making on the basis of discretion. This attitude is discernible in urban statutes of late medieval Italian city states which granted their rotating criminal judges full authority (*plenum et liberum arbitrium*) to subject to torture and punish defendants on evidence short of legally required proof.[22] Thirteenth-century jurists conceded that the demanding proof sufficiency rules of learned Roman-canon law (*ius commune*) could be trumped by municipal statutes, on condition that their provisions were not contrary to natural law.[23] Obviously, then, the confidence that legally unrestrained human discernment could be relied upon to find facts and determine criminal punishment was not absent from the birthplace of the Roman-canon fact-finding scheme.

---

[19] See Jaroslav Pelikan, *The Christian Tradition: The Growth of Medieval Theology*, vol. 3, 2–3 (Chicago: University of Chicago Press, 1971); Charles Taylor, *A Secular Society*, 68, 243, 258 (Cambridge MA: Harvard University Press, 2007).

[20] See Alain de Libera, Die Rolle der Logik im Rationalisierungsprozess des Mittelalters, in Kurt Flash and Udo Jeck, *Das Licht der Vernunft*.

[21] For conjectures in this regard, see Charles Taylor, *A Secular Society*, 94; Harold Berman, *Law and Revolution*, 158 (Cambridge, MA: Harvard University Press, 1983).

[22] See, e.g., Richard M. Fraher, Conviction According to Conscience: The Medieval Jurists' Debate Concerning Judicial Discretion and the Law of Proof, 7 *Law and History Review*, 23, 58, 87 n. 289 (1989).

[23] See Albertus Gandinus, Tractatus de Maleficiis, Rubrica: De Statutis et Eorum Observantia, no. 7, in Hermann Kantorowicz, *Albertus Gandinus und das Strafrecht der Scholastik*, 383 (Berlin: J. Guttentag, 1926).

An independent and important problem with the standard account is that it attends solely to the origin of the scheme's rule-bound aspect. As noted in the Prologue, however, the scheme exhibited a mixture of constraints and flexibility in treating evidence from its cradle to its grave. The source of this mixture calls for explanation.

THE ROMAN-CANON FACT-FINDING SCHEME AS A RESPONSE TO INHERENT TENSIONS

There are good reasons to think that evidentiary arrangements for the inquisitorial process emerged from the confluence of three factors. Two of them favored a rigid, rule-bound approach to evidence, while the third opposed it. Favoring the former approach were the late-medieval centralization of criminal justice and, in a limited but important area, a particular aspect of Christian moral theology. Favoring the latter approach was the harsh criminal policy that evolved as of the thirteenth century. It attributed great importance to the prevention of impunity for crimes committed, and required flexibility in the hunt for the truth.

Rise of the Centralized Judicial Organization

Tracing the roots of this organization leads one again to the Church of Rome. Although the popes became de facto secular rulers of a substantial part of central Italy as early as the eighth century, they were for a while not interested in organizing an efficient machinery of government. This nonchalant attitude began to change in the late eleventh century, in the wake of the Church's retreat from apocalyptic otherworldliness. Following reforms instituted by Pope Gregory VII, the Church's interests turned earthward: protecting Christian values and improving the social order became important parts of the Church's mission. In order to implement the tasks included in this mission, the leaders of the Church began to build the rudiments of hierarchical-bureaucratic state structures in the midst of the still-dominant feudal environment. A prominent part of these structures was a multilayered judicial apparatus. It was designed to be multilayered, since more than one echelon of authority was needed to assert hierarchical control and ensure that the policy of the Roman center was implemented by ecclesiastical courts scattered all over Europe. The propriety of first-instance decisions had to be made amenable to audits by superiors, and ultimately by the pope. To this end, judges were required to maintain a written record of all their official activity: those who failed to maintain it become subject to disciplinary proceedings. This innovation assured that traces of official activity could be preserved for possible audit. The resulting case file turned into the lifeline of the process, integrating all procedural segments into a meaningful whole. The needs of the evolving hierarchical apparatus induced canon lawyers as of the late eleventh century to produce treatises on procedure and evidence unprecedented in previous Western history. Their

20   *The Origin of Roman-Canon Legal Proof in Criminal Cases*

ordines iudiciarii are the true nurseries of important parts of Roman-canon evidence law.[24] And as the result of their groundbreaking work, many features of Roman-canon evidence law were already in place when the inquisitorial procedure was officially recognized in the early thirteenth century.

It is important to note for the aims of this book that the supervision of decision-making in the judicial apparatus called for legal constraints on the evaluation of evidence. Wide distribution of unregulated freedom in the exercise of this activity would have strained the animating assumptions of the centralized judicial organization. As an astute thirteenth-century French jurist remarked, if the judge "could adjudicate according to his conscience, all the avenues of appeal would be excluded, because he could always say that he decided according to conscience."[25] But the connection between constraints on the judge's fact-finding freedom and the impulses of the hierarchical apparatus for supervision are most clearly reflected in opinions expressed by some late medieval founders of the Roman-canon fact-finding scheme that lower judges must follow rules on the sufficiency of evidence, while the top of the judicial hierarchy is permitted to disregard them.[26] In contrast to the Church of Rome, late-medieval city states of Italy seldom adopted appeals as an instrument of supervision. Their small size made a single level of authority feasible. Yet, as a substitute for appeals, most of them established a special court for the purpose of reviewing the proper exercise of authority by the foreign magistrate (*podestà*) invited to administer the city for a period of time. The so-called "syndicate" procedure instituted by this court also welcomed rules constraining the judge's freedom in evaluating evidence. In their absence, the magistrate would have lacked a normative basis for justifying the propriety of judgments rendered by him in the capacity of criminal judge (*iudex ad maleficia*).[27]

Briefly, then, the emphasis on the review of judicial decisions characterized the administration of justice in countries following the Church's pattern of organizing judicial authority. The emphasis favored subjecting fact-finding activity to rules,

---

[24] See Linda Fowler-Magerl, "'*Ordines Iudiciarii*' and '*Libelli de Ordine Iudiciorum*'," 23.

[25] Quoted in Knut Nörr, *Zur Stellung des Richters in gelehrten Prozess der Frühzeit*, 87 (Munich: C.H. Beck, 1967).

[26] Early expositors of the view that ordinary judges are "*sub lege*" and the hierarchical top "*super legem*" will be mentioned later in this study. Unreviewable decision-making by ordinary judges was even associated with tyranny. See, e.g., Bartolus, Tractatus de Tyrannia, in *Bartoli a Saxoferrato Consilia, Questiones et Tractatus*, 321–327 (Basilae 1589).

[27] For a description of syndicate procedure, see Woldemar Engelmann, *Die Wiedergeburt der Rechtskultur in Italien durch dir wissenschaftliche Lehre*, 514–583 (Leipzig: K.F. Koehlers, 1938). In city states which adopted the appellate mechanism, the convict had a choice between lodging an appeal and moving for the institution of syndicate procedure. This alternative mode of checking the proper exercise of power spread beyond the borders of Italy, reinforcing the perception that proof sufficiency rules were needed for various decisions in the inquisitorial process, including, as we will see, the justification of judicial torture. For the seventeenth-century law of Saxony on this subject, see Benedict Carpzov, *Practica Nova Rerum Criminalium Imperialis Saxonica, Pars III, qu.* 217 (Wittenberg, 1635).

The Roman-Canon Fact-Finding Scheme as a Response to Inherent Tensions   21

including those on the sufficiency of evidence for decisions. Thus, rather than springing from lack of confidence in the reasoning power of judges, Roman-canon legal proof rules emanated from concerns about the unchecked exercise of judicial powers, especially in making momentous and irrevocable decisions affecting life and limb.[28] These concerns fitted nicely the desire for order widely recognized as characteristic of the Italian *Duecento*.

The Safety of the Soul

In regard to punishments entailing the spilling of blood (*poenae sanguinis*), the idea of rigid application of proof sufficiency rules was reinforced by Western Christian moral theology. According to its tenets, imposing blood punishment, or even participating in proceedings leading to their imposition, could turn into mortal sin, and ordering death into murder.[29] Because mutilating corporal punishments and the death penalty were regular criminal sanctions in the waning Middle Ages, the doctrine implied that judges were routinely exposed to spiritual dangers in the performance of their duties. In order to remove these dangers, theologians held that judges ought to be shielded from the bloody consequence of their decisions by a cocoon of outcome-determinative rules. If they sentenced the defendant to death or a mutilating punishment by applying these rules, they could then save their souls by claiming that they had acted as mere instruments of the law, rather than in a personal capacity. In James Whitman's felicitous phrase, binding evidence rules were useful to accord "moral comfort" to the judge.[30]

Yet, while the theological doctrine regarding blood punishments offered frequently overlooked support to strictly binding proof sufficiency rules, its influence on the shape of the Roman-canon fact-finding scheme should not be overstated. Even in the domain of the harshest punishment to which it was solely applicable, it did not completely displace judicial discretion.[31] Some late medieval founders of the scheme maintained that highly placed judges were allowed to decide criminal cases according to "conscience." In discussing numerical theories it was also pointed out that the founders left the resolution of testimonial conflict to judicial discretion even in capital cases. They realized that many procedural activities, including this one, could not properly be performed by mechanical application of rules. Most

---

[28] A similar conclusion was reached by Richard Fraher. See Richard M. Fraher, *Conviction According to Conscience*, 57, 59. Thirteenth-century Europeans, Fraher remarked, were not suffering from critical lack of faith in human reason. What concerned them was not the use of human judgment, but its abuse.

[29] For a richly documented account of this theological teaching, see James Whitman, *The Origins of Reasonable Doubt*, 46–49, *passim* (New Haven: Yale University Press, 2008). For a much older and shorter discussion of this issue, see Stephan Kuttner, *Kanonistische Schuldlehre*, 252–253 (Rome: Biblioteca Apostolica Vaticana, 1935).

[30] See Whitman, *The Origins of Reasonable Doubt*, 10.

[31] Outside of this domain, canon lawyers inveighed against forcing judges to decide against the dictates of their conscience.

important, as Chapter 6 will demonstrate, a minority of legal scholars held from the earliest history of the inquisitorial process that blood punishment could be imposed on highly compelling circumstantial evidence whose evaluation required the exercise of personal judgment. Pressures of effective law enforcement – about which we will say more in a moment – induced them to tolerate judicial activities that appeared spiritually risky when viewed through the theological lens. All in all, the progenitors of the Roman-canon fact-finding scheme seem to have heeded Averroes' advice that lawyers should drink only shallow drafts from the chalice of theology.[32]

It would be a mistake to think, however, that theological compunctions about the imposition of sanguinary punishments disappeared with the passing of the Middle Ages. Although the force of living faith may have weakened in quotidian affairs, religiously based discomfort about imposing the death sentence or mutilating punishments without two eyewitnesses or the defendant's confession did not dry out like ancient muddied waters. We will see that early modern jurists warned judges about spiritual perils entailed in administering sanguinary punishments on circumstantial evidence whose sufficiency they themselves determined. To borrow a phrase from Hamlet, "the dread of something after death, the undiscovered country from whose bourn no traveler returns,"[33] still exerted an influence on the administration of justice.

The Impact of Harsh Criminal Policy

Prior to late medieval times, deviant behavior was subject to societal reaction whose principal aim was the prevention of clan warfare and the resolution of local enmities. The accord between the perpetrator and the victim – or their respective clans – was the preferred mode of dealing with issues arising from the commission of crime: as attested by the medieval adage that settlement outranks the law and love outranks the sentence (*"pactum vincit legem et amor judicium"*), consensual arrangements eclipsed the recourse to courts. At the same time, the Church was not seriously interested in suppressing what it considered deviant behavior due to its original posture of otherworldliness.[34] In this climate of opinion, the high barrier to conviction resulting from the requirement for two eyewitnesses was not experienced as a pressing problem. After all, the original purpose of the requirement was to make malicious or false prosecutions of prelates more difficult. But as the Church's involvement with mundane matters increased, and the centralization movement advanced, ecclesiastical authorities were no longer prepared to treat the prosecution of crime as a local peace-upholding endeavor. Henceforth, they insisted, deviant behavior must be

---

[32] For late medieval warnings against the excessive influence of theology on the law, see Susanne Lepsius, *Der Richter und die Zeugen*, 111 (Frankfurt: Vittorio Klostermann, 2003).

[33] Shakespeare, *Hamlet*, III, 1, 70.

[34] This applied especially to secretly committed crimes. Alexander I, one of the earliest popes, justified this attitude by saying that "if all crimes in this century were adjudicated nothing would be left for divine justice" (*Si omnia crimina in hoc seculo iudicata essent, locum divina iusticia non haberent*). See *Decretum Gratiani*, C. 15, qu. 6, c. 1, para 3.

The Roman-Canon Fact-Finding Scheme as a Response to Inherent Tensions   23

repressed for the sake of protecting the values that united Christians, and crimes should be punished in the public interest, transcending narrow local concerns.

On the heels of this attitudinal change, new offenses were added to the catalog of criminal behavior. What distinguished them from early medieval misdeeds was that they often included consensual conduct. The emergence of such "victimless" crimes was facilitated by the Church's understanding of crime as sin, so that the commission of these crimes made God, so to speak, the aggrieved party. Given this new understanding of criminality, early medieval patterns of prosecution became inadequate. The view that secretly committed misdeeds should be left to divine punishment (*ecclesia de occultis non iudicat*) was rejected, and *crimina occulta* became regular targets of criminal prosecutions. Nor was it any longer considered appropriate to make criminal prosecutions dependent on the initiative of crime victims as private prosecutors. As pointed out in the Prologue, the old accusatorial type of Church proceeding, relying on private initiative, was no longer adequate, and the inquisitorial process became the ordinary mode of proceeding, giving public authority the right to initiate and prosecute criminal cases on its own initiative.[35]

These events had a bearing on attitudes toward legal proof. So long as the Church was not seriously interested in the repression of crime, exacting proof sufficiency rules were not perceived as a problem. But when the mission of the Church came to encompass the protection of orthodox Christian values from threats, these rules turned into hindrances to effective criminal prosecution. This was particularly the case in the prosecution of heretics, who were believed to threaten the established social order as international terrorists do today. The difficulties generated by the two-eyewitnesses rule came to be debated against the background of a hypothetical whose variations were destined to be repeated in Roman-canon legal literature from the thirteenth until the late eighteenth century.[36] Probably inspired by the Talmud, the hypothetical imagines a man seen exiting a room with only one way in and out. He is pale and grasps a bloody sword in his hand. Immediately after his exit from the room, a person slain by sword is found there in a pool of blood. With no eyewitnesses to the act of killing, there is no way to sentence the suspect to blood punishment – even if the victim turns out to be the suspect's mortal enemy. Should the Roman-canon full proof standard be maintained, late medieval jurists wondered, in this case of obvious guilt? Although the majority held that the standard should still stand, we will see that they weakened it by exceptions and softened its application by a protective layer of reviewable discretion. They felt impelled to do so in order to satisfy strong punitive urges engendered by the new criminal policy. Pope Innocent III famously expressed these urges by proclaiming that "public utility requires that crimes should not remain

---

[35] The flimsy biblical justification for the introduction of proceedings without a private accuser was God's statement to Abraham that the outcry against grave sins in Sodom and Gomorrah induces him to go down and see whether the outcry is justified. See Genesis 18:16.

[36] Michel Foucault still used it in his description of French eighteenth-century criminal justice. See Michel Foucault, *Surveiller et Punir*, 40 (Paris: Flammarion, 1975).

24 *The Origin of Roman-Canon Legal Proof in Criminal Cases*

unpunished" (*publicae utilitatis intersit, ne crimina remaneant impunita*).[37] In developing the fact-finding scheme for the developing inquisitorial process, its designers were thus impelled to navigate the tension arising between the requirements of old proof sufficiency rules and the demands of the harsh new criminal policy.

Projecting modern attitudes toward changes in the law, the reader might wonder why old proof sufficiency rules were not abandoned as too demanding in light of the new criminal policy. The reason this was not even contemplated was that these rules were firmly anchored in venerated legal sources. The two-eyewitnesses rule was supported by Roman law, treated at the time as reflecting the divine light of reason. How highly respected Emperor Justinian's codification of this law was can be seen in the example of Dante, the contemporary of jurists who shaped Roman-canon evidence.[38] Not only did he place Justinian in heaven, but his *Divine Comedy* includes passages in which he expounds on why Roman law provides the best model for government. And since the codification included an order of Emperor Constantine that "the response of a single witness should not be heard, even if it radiates the splendor of the Church,"[39] this text alone made the two-eyewitnesses rule entrenched in the law. Nor should we neglect the importance of several biblical texts referring to the need for two eyewitnesses for conviction.[40] The probative value of confessions also enjoyed powerful support. We will see that some passages in Justinian's codification went so far as to treat confessions as dispositive acts of self-condemnation. But confessions were also highly valued by the Church. They suited its concern for the safety of the soul – a concern that extended from the judge to the defendant. A final reason for retaining the demanding proof sufficiency standard despite its frustrating effects on effective criminal law enforcement was supplied by legal doctrine. Abandoning the requirement for two eyewitnesses or a confession appeared to mainstream legal doctrine as opening the floodgates to the imposition of blood punishment on circumstantial evidence, which, as we will presently see, was considered categorically inferior to direct evidence.

Conclusion

The preceding pages suggested that Roman-canon legal proof rules were not fashioned in response to the papal prohibition of ordeals, nor was the reason for their appearance skepticism about the capacity of humans to adjudicate serious criminal

---

[37] In the later history of the inquisitorial process, his statement was used as the standard justification and argumentation-stopper when defensive guarantees, including exacting proof standards, had to be weakened or abandoned. For a study of the origin and expansion of Pope Innocent's catchphrase, see Richard Fraher, The Theoretical Justification for the New Criminal Law of the High Middle Ages, 1984 *University of Illinois Law Review*, 577–595.

[38] He was the friend of the famous jurist and poet Cynus de Pistoia, the teacher of Bartolus.

[39] "*Et nunc manifeste sanctimus, ut unius omnino testis responsio non audiatur, etiamsi praeclarae curiae honore praefulgeat.*" C. IV. XX, 9.

[40] See Deuteronomy 17:2–7. For supporting passages in the New Testament, see Matthew 18:15–20 and John 8:12–18.

The Roman-Canon Fact-Finding Scheme as a Response to Inherent Tensions   25

cases. The demanding standard of full proof (*probatio plena*) was adopted by the Church of Rome long before the papal prohibition of ordeals, and most other proof sufficiency rules were crafted in response to the needs of the Church's multilevel judicial apparatus. The tendency of this apparatus to subject fact-finding activity to legal rules arose from the Church's ambition to ensure uniform decision-making on all its levels, and from its desire to prevent possible abuses of authority if the decision-making of lower-level judges remained unregulated. Where death or mutilation sentences were contemplated, this legalistic tendency was reinforced by theological strictures against spilling blood. But as the worldly activity of the Church gave rise to a harsh new policy toward crime, the observance of old legal proof rules became a source of frustration: high legal barriers to conviction proved serious impediments to the efficient prosecution of crime.

As a result, Roman-canon judges were subjected to the antithetical pressures described in the Prologue. While the realization of new criminal policy favored the imposition of blood punishment on compelling evidence of the kind illustrated by the bloody sword hypothetical, the old proof sufficiency standard prohibited this from happening. The resulting tension, inherent in the Roman-canon judicial apparatus, caused characteristic vacillations between emphasis on rigid rules and emphasis on flexibility in their implementation. And when the Roman-canon fact-finding scheme for criminal cases was completed in the thirteenth century, judicial discretion emerged as the central instrument for mediating the tension. It softened the rigidity of legal rules on the one hand, but was not free from them on the other. Purloining a metaphor from Dante, who probed the limits of the law in the juridical otherworld, the resulting fact-finding scheme was like a boat drawn up on the beach, with one end of its keel in the water and the other in the sand.

It is true that many medieval jurists, especially those in the secular variant of the Roman-canon evidentiary system, stressed the paramount importance of following rules. Small wonder, since the image of rule-bound trier of fact fitted the ideal of the decision-maker in hierarchically organized judicial organizations. The history of criminal procedure offers many examples of similarly unrealistic institutional preferences.[41] Some of the greatest jurists resisted the inclination to idealize reality, however, and provided a more accurate assessment of procedural goings-on in the criminal process. Bartolus, the most celebrated medieval jurist, remarked that in investigating crime the judge had "much more free rein than one might think."[42]

---

[41] In many continental criminal procedures, for example, the defendant was until quite recently subjected to evidence producing judicial interrogation at the outset of the trial, before any evidence was presented by the prosecution. This did not fit the institutional ideal according to which the prosecution must present incriminating evidence before the defendant can be used as a source of information. So legal doctrine passed over the fact that the defendant's responses were used as evidence, and interpreted his initial interrogation as a weapon accorded him to answer by his own assertions and arguments the assertions and arguments of the prosecutor.

[42] "*Iudex inquirendo habet magis habenas quam credatis.*" Bartolus ad D. lib. 48, tit. 5, lex 2, 11, in Bartolus a Saxoferrato, *In Primam Digesti Noui Partem* (Venice, 1580).

26 *The Origin of Roman-Canon Legal Proof in Criminal Cases*

In early modern times, Benedict Carpzov was more specific. Strict legal rules that hamper the punishment of criminals, he wrote, need not always be adhered to, because "public safety requires that crimes should be uncovered and defendants punished."[43]

---

[43] "*In processu criminali tam stricte regulis juris non fit inhaerendum quam salus publica requirat crimina manifestari, reos puniri.*" Benedict Carpzov, *Practica Nova Rerum Criminalium Imperialis Saxonica*, Pars III, qu. 114, no. 16.

2

Epistemic Foundations

Before setting out on the quest for mixtures of freedom and constraint in the fact-finding system of the inquisitorial process, its epistemic underpinnings should be examined. Leafing through the secondary literature on this subject, one comes across views that the late medieval founders of the scheme were ignorant of the epistemic issues informing modern criminal justice. Consider a few examples. The founders were unaware of limitations on human knowledge, we are told, and believed that certain types of evidence reveal objective truth. They were innocent of intermediate levels of knowledge short of absolute certainty, and conflated claims of objective truth and claims based on evidence.[1] They thought that knowledge is acquired by following authoritative rules, rather than by firsthand observation and sensory perception. The idea that fact-finders can estimate the probative value of evidence by themselves was rejected, and the victory of this idea had to wait for the delayed impact of sixteenth-century scientific discoveries and seventeenth-century philosophers.[2] Before their time, factual findings were made by judges in disregard of the actual impact of evidence on them.[3] And the medieval scholastic predilection for constructing overarching ordering schemes led Roman-canon jurists to establish a hierarchy of evidence in terms of its probative value, a hierarchy that is deeply alien to our present understanding of the matter.[4]

Although a degree of support for these statements can be found in the lush profusion of thirteenth-century scholarly literature, on the whole they grossly distort the Roman-canon fact-finding scheme for criminal cases. Being an obstacle to the

---

[1] See, e.g., Ian Hacking, *The Emergence of Probability*, 22–23 (Cambridge: Cambridge University Press, 1971); Paolo Marchetti, *Testis contra se: L'imputato come fonte di prova nell' processo penale dell'età moderna*, 164 (Milan: Giuffrè Editore, 1994).

[2] See, e.g., L. Jonathan Cohen, Freedom of Proof, in William Twining (ed.), *Facts in Law*, 16 *Archives for Philosophy of Law and Social Philosophy*, 10–11 (Stuttgart: Franz Steiner, 1983); Barbara Shapiro, *Beyond Reasonable Doubt and Probable Cause*, 7 (Oakland: University of California Press, 1991); John D. Jackson and Sarah J. Summers, *The Internalization of Criminal Evidence*, 34 (Cambridge: Cambridge University Press, 2012).

[3] See Michel Foucault, *Surveiller et Punir*, 42 (Paris: Flammarion, 1975).

[4] See Jean Philippe Lévy, *La Hiérarchie des Preuves dans le Droit Savant du Moyen Age depuis la Renaissance jusqu'à la Fin du XIV Siècle*, 26–31 (Paris: Librairie du Recueil Sirey, 1939).

28   *Epistemic Foundations*

proper interpretation of the scheme, their problematic nature must be brought to light.

LEGAL PROOF AND TRUTH-DISCOVERY

At the time of the Roman-canon scheme's gestation, leading theologians and philosophers followed Aristotle's opinion that the same degree of certainty cannot be obtained in all disciplines. Those who believed otherwise were derided as *indisciplinati*.[5] In commenting on Aristotle, Thomas Aquinas remarked, for instance, that in judging human conduct "demonstrative certainty" cannot be obtained, and mere "certitude of probability" must suffice.[6] By virtue of this statement of the Angelic Doctor alone it becomes difficult to maintain that thirteenth-century theologians and philosophers failed to recognize lesser levels of knowledge than full certainty, or "objective truth," and that they believed that absolute truth is established when prescribed legal proof is assembled. But what about late medieval jurists? Were they vulnerable to being lampooned as *indisciplinati*? A negative answer to this question can be derived from the writings of Bartolus, whose authority was for several centuries so formidable that it used to be said "nobody is a jurist who is not a Bartolist" *(nemo iurista nisi bartolista)*. True knowledge *(vera scientia)*, Bartolus wrote, can be obtained in two ways. One is pursued in the sciences and arts, where reasons and demonstrations are used, things are stable, and can be apprehended through their causes *(ut in scientiis contigit)*. The other way is pursued when contingent and variable things must be established, as is the case with establishing human behavior.[7] But then the judge can acquire true knowledge or "demonstrative certitude" only when he directly perceives things which must be established. Where direct sensory apprehension is not available – as is typically the case in adjudication – he has no claim to true knowledge.[8] Obviously, then, it is mistaken to think that authoritative medieval jurists were so naïve as to believe that legally required proof establishes objective truth. The intellectual distance between them and us on this particular matter is smaller than is often thought. Their

---

[5]   Etienne Gilson, *Etudes sur le Rôle de la Pensée Mediévale dans la Formation du Système Cartésien*, 253 (Paris: Vrin, 1930).

[6]   "*In actionibus enim humanis super quibus constituuntur indicia et exigent testimonia non potest haberi certitudo demonstrativa, ideo sufficit probabilis certitudo.*" Thomas Aquinas, *Summa Theologica, Secunda Secundae*, qu. 70, art. 2. In the next article Aquinas went on to remark explicitly that evidence is not "infallible," and that it can yield only "probable knowledge."

[7]   "*Scientia vera habetur duobus modis: uno modo in rebus que sunt artis seu scientiae, alicuius per rationes et demonstrationes: et istud etiam scire est rem per causam cognoscere, ut dicit philosophus. Secundo modo ista scientia habetur in his que sunt facti et tunc illud scire dicimus ad quod movemur per sensum.*" Bartolus, *Commentaria in Secundum Digesti Veteris Partem, ad D.* 12.2.31, fol. 33rb, nos. 17–18 (Lyons, 1523). This distinction comes close to that between a priori and empirical methods of finding out about the world.

[8]   "*Ad hanc autem scientiam iudex non posset perduci in his que habent actum transeuntem, sed bene posset perduci in his que sunt actus permanentis.*" Bartolus, *ibid.*

Legal Proof and Truth-Discovery

pronouncements that evidence in criminal cases should be clearer than the midday sun (*luce meridiana clarior*) expressed their *aspiration* to establish the truth in criminal cases, as well as the idea that in criminal cases proof ought to be superior to that in civil litigation.[9]

What Bartolus wrote on the ways of ascertaining human behavior also indicates how mistaken it is to say that late medieval jurists neglected the role of sensory perception in fact-finding and unreflectively followed authoritative rules. Actually, sensory perception occupied pride of place in their epistemic scheme. To understand why, consider that two schools of thought on the foundational problems of forensic fact-finding were available to them. One was the rhetoric in its Ciceronian variant. Developed in the classical period of Roman history, when court decisions were made by choosing the better of the arguments presented by two altercating orators, this school of thought tended to associate proof with proper argumentation.[10] But in the inquisitorial procedure, where the judge monopolized the development of evidence, the rhetorical concept of proof was not suitable. Aspects of Aristotelian epistemology as popularized by Averroes, stressing the primacy of sensory perception in cognition, appeared more appropriate. The resulting preference for perceptual evidence over arguments was reinforced by passages from Justinian's codification dealing with adjudication in the Roman post-classical apparatus of justice. The increased bureaucratization of this apparatus resembled processes taking place in the judicial organization of the Church of Rome following Gregorian reforms.

We should therefore not be surprised to find pronouncements in the writings of late medieval jurists asserting the cardinal importance of sensory perception.[11] Early on, it is true, some jurists thought that witnesses could report only what their eyes had apprehended of the facts of consequence.[12] The opinion soon prevailed, however, that vision was a generic term embracing all the senses, so that witnesses could also report what they had heard or perceived by the rest of their sensorium.[13] Baldus was especially resolute in emphasizing the value of sensory perception in fact-

---

9   It is true that medieval jurists – Baldus being one of them – would sometimes write, "this is how the judge comes to the knowledge of the truth." But present-day lawyers use similar shorthand expressions, even if they are epistemic realists aware of the fact that truth transcends evidence.

10 See G. Pugliese, La Preuve dans le Droit Romain de l' Epoque Classique, 17 *Recueils de la Société Jean Bodin, Partie I*, 227, 300 (Brussels: De Boek,1965).

11 Bartolus wrote, for example, that a witness can prove only those matters he perceived through his corporeal senses. "*Testis non probat nisi per sensum corporeum perceperit.*" Bartolus, *Commentaria in Secundum Digesti Veteris Partem*, ad D. 12.2.31, fol. 35vb, no. 57 (Lyons, 1523).

12 On the medieval emphasis of vision, see Katherine Tachau, *Vision and Certitude in the Age of Ockham*, 127 (Leiden: Brill, 1988), and on medieval attitude to sensory experience generally, M. Dal Pra, *Nicola di Autrecourt*, 66, 96 (Milan: Fratelli Bocca, 1950).

13 "*Unde potest dici, quod visus sit sicut genus, quod repraesentur in qualibet species sensum.*" Baldus, *In Quartum et Quintum Cod. Lib. Commentaria*, lib.4, tit. 20, lex 18, fol. 51, no. 13 (Venice, 1599). What remained controversial, however, was the question whether all facts can be proven by auditor witnesses. A titillating case for scholarly debate was the question whether sexual intercourse can be proved by sounds of amorous activity.

30   Epistemic Foundations

finding. "Requiring rational arguments where sensory information is available," he wrote in one of his expert opinions, "is intellectual infirmity."[14] And in his comments to the *Decretals*, he illustrated the superiority of knowing on the basis of perception over knowing on the basis of rational argument by using the then-popular comparison of knowledge with sunlight. When no clouds appear between our eyes and the sun, he waxed poetically, truth can be apprehended visually. But when clouds come between our eyes and the sun, truth can be apprehended only "speculatively and argumentatively."[15]

The importance of sensory perception in cognition induced late medieval jurists to establish a distinction between finding facts by evidence and finding facts by direct sensory apprehension. If a fact-finder perceives a thing directly, they argued, he needs no evidence: perception allows him to know immediately and with certitude that a thing exists. If he notes a scar on the face of the victim, he needs no proof that the scar exists. It is only when the judge cannot observe a thing directly – as is most of the time the case in adjudication – that he must seek knowledge from those who perceived it and rely on evidence. This reasoning led most medieval jurists to refuse to treat what the judge perceived directly in the performance of his official duties as a mode of proof. Immediately evident matters, they argued, are in no need of proof – "*notoria non sunt probanda.*" In thus distinguishing two separate modes of finding facts in litigation, the founders of the Roman-canon fact-finding scheme exhibited – long before Bentham[16] and Wigmore[17]– considerable analytical sophistication. It is true that their distinction can be subjected to criticism in terms of contemporary epistemology. It is now generally accepted that sensory perception can mislead and that it includes a degree of inferential elaboration.[18] But this criticism is not fatal to the distinction when used for the classificatory purposes of legal doctrine, or as a basis for organizing sources of

---

[14] "*Quarere rationem ubi habemus sensum est infirmitas intellectus.*" Baldus, *Consilia, vol. III*, consilium 364, no.3 (Venice, 1630).

[15] "*Nam lux corporalis solis interdum lucet nobis intuitive, quando inter oculos nostros et solem sunt nullae nebulae. Quandoque speculative et argumentative ut, quando videmus aliquid per rationem intellectus. Quandoque obtenebratur nobis sol, ut quando inter veritatem et intellectum nostrum sunt tenebrosissimae nubes, licet sol et veritas semper in se luceant.*" See Baldus, *In Decretalium Volumen Commentaria*, ad X 2.19 (Venice, 1580). In the text, I rendered Baldus's adverb "*intuitive*" as "visually," because "intuition" was used at the time to refer to sensory perception generally.

[16] According to Bentham, perception of facts obtained by the judge himself could legitimately be regarded as a decision without evidence, or as the most reliable means of fact-finding, since no cognitive dangers exist in transmitting observations of other people to the judge. See Jeremy Bentham, *Rationale of Judicial Evidence*, vol. 1, 250–252 (Colorado: Fred B. Rothman & Co, 1995).

[17] Wigmore excluded what he called "autoptic preference" from the concept of evidence in the strict sense of the word, on the ground that it requires no inference which he regarded as essential to evidence. See John Wigmore, *Evidence in Trials at Common Law*, vol. 1a, para. 24, p. 944 (Tillers' revision), (Boston, MA: Little, Brown, 1983).

[18] See Tiller's remarks in *Evidence in Trials at Common Law*, 944. This is not to say, however, that the need for inferential elaboration of matters apprehended by senses was not noted before. For perceptive remarks of the Angelic Doctor on this issue, see Hans Meyer, *Thomas von Aquin: sein System und seine geistesgeschichtliche Stellung*, 458 (2nd ed.)(Bonn; Peter Hanstein, 1961).

knowledge. If a trier of fact must find out whether a victim has been disfigured, for instance, the most reliable way for him to establish whether this is true is to inspect her body. His senses can deceive him, of course, and the inferential ingredient in his apprehension can be inaccurate. Yet he is still in a better cognitive position than when he must rely on the sensory perceptions of other people. Even if they honestly report their observations, they face the same cognitive risks. In other words, when the trier of fact depends on the observations of other people, additional sources of factual distortion emerge.

The distinction between the two modes of finding facts is important to bear in mind in preparation for our tour of Roman-canon evidence. For it explains why species of evidence listed by scholarly jurists did not include all kinds of evidence we now recognize as such. Material objects, for example, were not treated by jurists as evidence (*species probationum*), but as objects for the judge's immediate sensory apprehension. This has misled some commentators into believing that late medieval jurists failed to recognize material evidence as a source of information, and relied solely on the testimony of witnesses as evidence.[19] Lacking modern police science techniques, jurists did, in fact, rely mainly on the testimony of witnesses. But to the extent that their limited scientific knowledge permitted them to recognize traces left in the material world after a suspected criminal event, they attributed great importance to establishing these traces by judicial view.[20] Yet, in their classificatory scheme, this judicial activity (*inspectio ocularis*) represented direct sensory observation rather than an evidence-producing activity.

RESTRICTION ON THE USE OF HEARSAY

The importance which Roman-canon jurists attributed to sensory perception in the acquisition of knowledge was extended from judges to witnesses: witnesses could testify only about what they apprehended by their senses.[21] There was an additional requirement, however. They could convey only their own observations of material facts: if they transmitted other people's observations of these facts, they were not considered true witnesses (*vere et propriae testes*). By relying on their testimony, wrote Farinacci (quoting Baldus), the judge can obtain no more than an "indirect indication of the truth as revealed by the senses."[22]

---

[19] See, e.g., Ian Hacking, *The Emergence of Probability*, 34.

[20] The trace of the defendant's footprint, for example, constituted circumstantial evidence. See Benedict Carpzov, *Practica Nova Imperialis Saxonica Rerum Criminalium, Pars III*, qu. 120, no. 30 (Wittenberg, 1652). In homicide cases the judge was required to visit the crime scene and observe the corpse. If taking a view was embarrassing to the judge – establishing loss of virginity for example – the judge would delegate the activity to the forerunners of our experts and rely on their testimony as evidence.

[21] See Bartolus, *Commentaria in Secundum Digesti Veteris Partem, ad D.* 12.2.31, fol. 33rb, nos. 17–18.

[22] "*Per auditum auditus non percipiatur veritas sensum, sed solum quaedam relatio veritatis.*" Prospero Farinacci, *Tractatus Integer de Testibus*, qu. 69 no. 5 (Osnabrück, 1678).

Epistemic Foundations

Rather than giving credence to the carriers of these "indirect indications," the judge was supposed to seek the testimony of persons from whom the indications originated. When these persons testify in court, learned jurists pointed out, the consistency of their testimony and the bodily indications of their veracity can be observed by the judge – especially when they are confronted by witnesses who contradict them. Original declarants are also under oath and motivated to tell the truth by the awe-inspiring presence of the judge.[23] These guarantees of reliable testimony evaporate like mist on summer mornings, jurists believed, if the judge relies on witnesses who merely repeat statements of out-of-court declarants, or follow the "dead voice" of writings.[24] In brief, Roman-canon jurists not only relied on the sensory experience of witnesses, but also insisted that witnesses relate their own sensory perception of matters subject to proof.

Both secular jurists and Church lawyers were familiar with provisions prohibiting or disparaging oral hearsay in Roman law.[25] But on the basis of fragmentary passages on this subject in Justinian's codification, they developed an original and elaborate hearsay doctrine, complete with hearsay exceptions which we will review later in this book. We will note the remarkable similarities between this doctrine and the strictures against hearsay that crystallized in England several centuries later. Unlike common law judges, however, Roman-canon lawyers failed to develop an explicit doctrine relating to hearsay in its written form. Part of the reason for this omission, aside from the fact that Roman sources focused solely on hearsay witnesses, was their abiding disagreement about whether writings can be used as evidence in criminal cases. On the deep waters of this convoluted subject, scholarly jurists launched their great armadas.[26] No wonder, then, that the use of derivative written evidence remains to this day a darkly shadowed and easily misunderstood corner of Roman-canon criminal evidence. But when the question of hearsay comes up for special consideration, we will see that the fragility of written hearsay did not escape the attention of jurists who crafted the Roman-canon fact-finding scheme. Their awareness of hearsay dangers in this form will be demonstrated in rules that were not considered part of hearsay doctrine, but

---

[23] See Baldus, *Consilia sive Responsa*, V, consilium 492, no. 5 (Frankfurt, 1589).

[24] Prospero Farinacci *Tractatus Integer de Testibus*, qu. 69, no. 85. For an early, lucid articulation of reasons for banning oral hearsay, see Pillius Tancredus, *Gratia, Libri de Iudiciorum Ordine*, 3. 9. 2, at 239–240 (Aalen: Scientia Verlag, 1965).

[25] See Frank R. Herrmann, The Establishment of a Rule against Hearsay in Roman-Canonical Process, 36 *Virginia Journal of International Law*, 1, 3–22 (1995). See also Charles Donahue, Jr.,Proof by Witnesses in the Church Courts of Medieval England, in M. S. Arnold et al. (eds.), *On the Laws and Customs of England, Essays in Honor of Samuel Thorne* (Chapel Hill: University of North Carolina Press, 1981).

[26] In the late sixteenth century Farinacci still bemoaned that on this particular subject scholars tormented themselves (*doctores se multum torquent*). See Prospero Farinacci, *Variarum Quaestionum Liber Quintus*, qu. 158, no. 30.

The Nature of Factual Inquiry   33

produced the same limitations on derivative evidence as would rules on oral hearsay.[27]

THE NATURE OF FACTUAL INQUIRY

Did late medieval jurists conceive of fact-finding as an activity consisting of adding up evidence of predetermined value until the legally prescribed evidentiary standard had been reached, and then rendering judgment according to this standard, regardless of their subjective assessment of the assembled evidence? [28] That this was not the case has already been alluded to, and will be amply demonstrated in the forthcoming chapters. Observe how clearly this view clashes with what Roman-canon jurists had to say about the road the judge must travel in arriving at a verdict. Take Bartolus again as an example. Inspired by the theologians' division of four stages on the path from ignorance to moral certainty, he maintained that the judge's mental operations unfold in a succession of stages. The first was "doubt," although it was not yet accorded probative character in the strict sense of the word: it did not involve any proof-taking activity, but only induced the judge to begin the inquiry. The second stage was "suspicion." It meant that the judge's inquiring mind was already moving in one direction, but the evidence collected was not sufficiently strong to seriously dislodge the initial doubt. If the judge then acquired "stronger arguments," his mind reached the "opinion" stage. This mental state meant that he had acquired knowledge that was more secure, but not compelling enough to dispel his doubts entirely. If on obtaining further information he could "firmly adhere to one part without any doubt as to something contrary," he reached the end stage of the mental process – perfect credulity (credulitas), or perfect proof (probatio).[29] Yet, adhering to his already-mentioned epistemic position, Bartolus did not associate this final state of mind with cognizance of the truth, or the realization of scientia vera. This follows from his statement that credulitas is located between the extremes of ignorance and full knowledge.[30] That a subjective assessment of evidence inhered in this mental

[27]   It is a seldom recognized legacy of Roman-canon evidentiary doctrine that specific references to hearsay are in continental jurisdictions still limited to its oral form.

[28]   This is how Foucault imagined fact-finding activities in France's ancien régime criminal procedure. See Foucault, Surveiller et Punir, Paris: Flammarion 42. Concerning criminal procedure in German lands, some scholars nurse the belief that the mechanical ("objective") process of finding facts prevailed until the nineteenth century. See Rudolf Stichweh, Zur Subjektivierung der Entscheidungsfindung im deutschen Strafprozess des 19. Jahrhunderts, in André Gouron et al. (eds.), Subjektivierung des justiziellen Beweisverfahrens, 265–297 (Frankfurt: Vittorio Klosterman, 1994).

[29]   "Post istam opinionem, si iudici appareat tantum, quod firmiter adhereat uni parti abseque aliquo dubio alicuius contrarii, tunc dicitur perfecta credulitas seu perfecta probatio, nec est tunc causa dubia." See Bartolus, Commentaria in Secundum Digesti Veteris Partem, at Dig. 12.2.31, fol. 33va, no. 23. In his Treatise on testimony (Tractatus de testimoniis), Bartolus used the term fides – rather than credulitas – to designate this final mental state.

[30]   "Inter ista duo extrema secundum nescientiam et scientiam est quoddam medium, videlicet credulitas sive fides." Bartolus, Commentaria in Secundum Digesti Veteris Partem, ad D. 12.2.31, fol. 33rb, no. 18 in fine.

34 Epistemic Foundations

state is indicated by Bartolus's remark that a matter is said to be fully proven when the judge is "prompted to trust and believe" in the factual proposition subject to determination. [31] This subjective understanding of decision-making is especially visible in the work of Baldus. Consider how he interpreted the distinction between "half proven" and "fully proven" indications – two legal concepts that are often attributed an objective meaning independent from the judge's belief. The half-proven indication (*indicium semiplenum*), he wrote, moves the judge's mind forcefully to believe or disbelieve a proposition, while the fully proven indication (*indicium plenum*) induces such a peace of mind that he feels no need to further investigate a matter.[32] For our purposes, it is important to bear in mind that these reflections of Bartolus and Baldus on the mental processes involved in finding facts were echoed by legal authorities in several contexts at least as late as the seventeenth century.

The jurists' focus on the subjective state of credulity is sometimes understood as indicating that they had abandoned the quest for objective truth.[33] This understanding seems unwarranted. As shown at the outset of this chapter, jurists realized that truth transcends evidence, and that forensic proof does not guarantee "demonstrative certainty" or unveil true knowledge. But this realization did not preclude them from demanding that criminal convictions, especially those entailing sanguinary punishments, be based on the strongest possible evidence of guilt. Their awareness of the fallibility of judgments concerning human behavior was not incompatible with their aspiration to establish the facts of the case accurately. Then as now, the absence of guarantee that truth would be ascertained was not perceived as an argument against pursuing it. In the context of the medieval love for avian creatures, truth may have appeared to the jurists as a rarely seen bird, whose presence could only be inferred from the trembling of the branch from which it had flown.

THE RANKING OF INFORMATION SOURCES

Inclined to construct comprehensive ordering schemes, medieval jurists ranked evidence in terms of its supposed probative value. A noted French legal historian, Jean-Philippe Lévy, presented this ranking as a pyramid, with obvious facts (*notoria*) at its top. *Notoria* included in-court confessions and facts the judge observed in the performance of his duties.[34] Ranked below notoriety was full proof (*probatio plena*) –

---

[31] "...*quando dicatur plene probatum. Respondeo breviter quando est facta iudicis plena fides, hoc est quando iudex, per ea, que sunt sibi ostensa, est adductus ad fidem et credulitatem eius quod intenditur.*" Bartolus, *Commentaria in Secundum Digesti Veteris Partem*, ad D. 12.2.31, fol. 33rb, no. 15.

[32] "*Indicium semiplenum est praesumptio fortiter movens animum ad aliquid credendum vel discredendum. Indicium plenum est demonstratio rei per signa differentia, per que animus in aliquot tamquam existente quiescit et plus investigare non curat.*" Baldus, as quoted in Jacobus Menochius, *De Praesumptionibus, Coniecturis, Signis et Indiciis Commentaria*, Lib. I., qu. 7, no 14 (Geneva 1670).

[33] See Susanne Lepsius, *Von Zweifeln zur Überzeugung*, 186 (Frankfurt: Vittorio Klostermann, 2003).

[34] J. P. Lévy, *La Hiérarchie des Preuves*, 26–31. Considering what has been said earlier in this chapter, it would have been closer to the thinking of great medieval jurists if Lévy removed facts the judge observed from the evidentiary pyramid, and treated them as a mode of fact-finding different from and

The Ranking of Information Sources

the most valued evidence in the strict sense of the term – consisting of the testimony of two unimpeachable eyewitnesses (*testes omni exceptione maiores*). Next in rank came half proof (*probatio semiplena*), including the testimony of a single witness, widespread rumor (*fama*), and some species of evidence important mainly in civil cases.[35] At the bottom of the hierarchy was circumstantial evidence. Issues this hierarchy raises for the judge's fact-finding freedom will be taken up in subsequent chapters. At this point we will address only the ranking of circumstantial evidence below direct evidence, and the exalted place accorded to courtroom confessions. Both questions pertain to the essential epistemic underpinnings of the Roman-canon fact-finding scheme.

Circumstantial Evidence

In approaching this theme the objection must be anticipated that it is anachronistic to use the term *circumstantial evidence* in discussing Roman-canon evidence, because this generic concept does not appear in medieval legal sources. Influenced by ancient rhetorical texts, in particular Quintilian's *Institutes of the Orator*, medieval jurists distinguished presumptions, conjectures, signs, indications, *adminicula*, and a few additional species of evidence, without devising an umbrella term for them. But they recognized that all of these species had one feature in common: all required that a fact had to be proven first, and then an inference made from it to *factum principalum* – that is, fact material in the case. The realization of this dual nature of presumptions, signs and similar rhetorical concepts is visible even in the work of the earliest expositors of the Roman-canon fact-finding scheme – notably in their distinction between *factum a quo* and *factum ad quem*.[36] Owing to the realization of commonality, the drafters of the sixteenth-century *Constitutio Criminalis Carolina* were able to simplify evidence law by using the generic term *indication* (*indicium*) for all rhetorical species of indirect evidence.[37] And since the idea of circumstantial evidence was thus

---

    superior to evidence. For a thoughtful criticism of Lévy's hierarchy on other grounds, see Susanne Lepsius, *Von Zweifeln zur Überzeugung*, 32–39.

[35] *Semiplena probatio* originally designated the testimony of a single eyewitness, but acquired a more encompassing meaning in the context of criminal procedure. In subsequent chapters we will have occasion to refer to this change in several places.

[36] In talking about presumptions Tancred stated already in the early thirteenth century that "presumption is an argument to believe a fact that arises from the proof of another" (*praesumptio est argumentum ad credendum unum factum, surgens ex probatione alterius*). See Tancred as quoted in Wilhelmus Durantis, *Speculum Iudiciale*, II, 2, para. "Quod sit Praesumptio," no. 1, p. 590 (Venice, 1566).

[37] The simplification was the brainchild of the ingenious German lawyer Johann Freiherr zu Schwarzenberg. See August Kries, *Lehrbuch des deutschen Strafprozessrechts*, 25 (Tübingen: Mohr, 1892). Yet the realization of the dual nature of *indicia* does not mean that Roman-canon lawyers were always able properly to distinguish direct and circumstantial evidence. Even the greatest among them were not entirely free from confusion on this issue. In discussing a hypothetical, for instance, Carpzov treated as *indicium* – rather than direct proof – the testimony of a witness in an adultery case who saw a couple copulating "*pudenda in pudendis posita.*" See Benedict Carpzov, *Practica Nova Rerum Criminalium Imperialis Saxonica*, Pars III, qu. 122, no. 74 (Wittenberg, 1652).

36 *Epistemic Foundations*

present in the mind of astute medieval lawyers – although the term was absent from their vocabulary – the reader can be spared exposure to antiquated species of circumstantial evidence whose relationships were often as tangled as the strands of yarn in an old sweater.[38] The words *circumstantial evidence* and *indicium* will henceforth be used to designate all of these concepts.

The decision to place circumstantial evidence at the bottom of the proof hierarchy was an enduring feature of mainstream Roman-canon doctrine. Even in its crepuscular phase, it was still capable of inducing lawgivers of several continental states to include the preference for direct evidence into statutory provisions. As late as the nineteenth century, we will see, the death penalty, and sometimes even long prison terms, could not be imposed in some continental lands on less than direct Roman-canon full proof.[39] The low ranking of circumstantial evidence was especially salient in sporadic provisions requiring automatic review of all judgments based on *indicia*.[40] How can this persistent feature of the scheme be explained? An important reason stemmed from the recognition of the dual nature of circumstantial evidence. Jurists realized that the *factum probans* had to be proven by perceptual evidence, and the *factum probandum* by inference. The presence of the defendant at the crime scene had to be proven by witnesses, for instance, and an inference then drawn from his presence at the scene to the fact that the crime charged had been committed by him. But as has already been pointed out, evidence based on sensory perception was believed to be superior to inferences.[41] Inferences were generally regarded as fallible.[42] In one of his commentaries on the Code, Baldus illustrated the fallibility of inferences by a variant of the bloody sword hypothetical. A man is seen entering a house, and a cry is heard from within by witnesses. The man is then observed running from the house with a bloody sword, and a woman is found inside the house with a cut on her face. Although the circumstantial evidence in this hypothetical is compelling, Baldus opined, it could still be misleading since the women could have inflicted the wound.[43] When capital and mutilating punishments were at stake, another ground for the

---

[38] On the convoluted distinctions between presumptions, indications, conjectures, signs, suspicions, and *adminicula*, see Jacobus Menochius, *De Praesumptionibus, Coniecturis, Signis et Indiciis Commentaria*, Tomus I, qu. 7–38 (Geneva, 1670). Even a single concept – the concept of presumption, for example – could be confusing, as will be shown later in this study.

[39] As noted in the Prologue, similar rules survived in some countries well into the twentieth century.

[40] See Austrian Penal Code of 1803, art. 435 (a).

[41] Occasionally, philosophers voiced the opinion that information provided by our sensorium does not deceive. See Katherine Tachau, *Vision and Certitude in the Age of Ockham*, 127. But jurists recognized that reports of this information could purposely be misrepresented.

[42] Farinacci wrote, for example, "*indicium esse coniectura ex probabilibus et non necessariis ortem.*" Prospero Farinacci, *Praxis et Theoreticae Criminalis, Pars Prima, Tomus Secundus, de Indiciis et Tortura*, Tit. 5, qu. 36, no. 28 (Lyon, 1634).

[43] See Baldus, *In Codicem Commentaria*, libri IV, ad C. 4,19,25, lex 15, 6, fol. 45 rb ((Venice, 1519). Even so, for reason to be discussed in due course, he wrote that assault could be proven on this evidence. "*Tamen dicendum est sufficienter esse probatum, quia non presumitur ipsam et sibi vulnus inflixisse, sed passam esse ab inimico.*"

The Ranking of Information Sources

low ranking of circumstantial evidence stemmed from theological concerns about the spilling of blood. The judge's inferences from an *indicium* implicated him deeply in the decision-making process, so that the excuse "the law convicted the defendant, not the judge" was not available to him. With direct evidence the situation was assessed differently: the blame for the possible false bloody outcome could be attributed to the two eyewitnesses.

The low ranking of circumstantial evidence by Roman-canon jurists is often criticized as wrongheaded. Critics point out that circumstantial evidence emanating from reliable witnesses can have greater probative value than direct evidence emanating from unreliable ones. While this is certainly true, it should not obscure the fact that direct evidence is indeed more probative from an abstract theoretical standpoint – when viewed as a class. This viewpoint was dear to scholarly jurists who breathed the late medieval university air, redolent with the passion for ordering generalizations. In this intellectual atmosphere, direct and circumstantial evidence were compared *ceteris paribus* – that is, assuming that they both spring from equally credible witnesses.[44] And when the same credibility is attributed to a witness who testifies about a fact in issue and one who testifies about a fact from which the existence of the fact in issue can only be inferred, the additional risk of cognitive error in the testimony of the latter witness is readily observable. In comparing premodern and modern views on the probative value of evidence, it is also worth noting that the belief in the lesser value of circumstantial evidence has not disappeared, despite the rejection of the formal ranking of evidence by modern legal doctrine. The disparaging remark that "this is only circumstantial" can still be heard not only from the mouths of ordinary people in the street, but also from the mouths of lawyers in the courtrooms of some contemporary states. As this study progresses, the distance between Roman-canon and our views on circumstantial evidence will be further reduced. We will see that some jurists and many judges believed that circumstantial evidence can, in some constellations of circumstances, be so highly persuasive as to justify even the imposition of capital and mutilating punishments.

Courtroom Confessions

Moving now from the bottom of the Roman-canon proof hierarchy to its top, let us examine the exalted position of the defendant's courtroom confession.[45] As already noted, some legal historians maintain that courtroom confessions were originally assimilated to notorious facts – that is, facts so obviously true that no evidence was

---

[44] The inclination to treat circumstantial and direct evidence as equally credible appealed to lesser minds, which only gradually liberated themselves from the earlier medieval inclination to assume that all witnesses competent to testify were reliable. But great jurists like Azo, Tancred, and Cynus de Pistoia, and especially Bartolus and Baldus, did not equate legally qualified with credible witnesses. See Susanne Lepsius, *Von Zweifeln zur Überzeugung*, 176.

[45] Chapter 5 will address the status of out-of-court confessions.

38   *Epistemic Foundations*

needed to establish their veracity.[46] That this is not correct follows, however, from the insistence of Roman-canon law that confessions made in criminal cases ought to be verified. Facts actually notorious needed no verification. Rather than treating them as notorious, some Roman-canon legal authorities maintained that they are on the same level of reliability as the testimony of two eyewitnesses.[47] Yet mainstream Roman-canon doctrine and legal practice treated them as the most precious species of evidence. That they were more eagerly sought than the testimony of two eyewitnesses is clearly reflected in the structure of those inquisitorial processes whose formal investigation began with the interrogation of the defendant aimed at obtaining incriminating information from him, rather than with the examination of witnesses aimed at obtaining the required testimony of two eyewitnesses.

Although the exaltation of confession as the queen of proofs (*regina probationum*) is now regarded as an idiosyncrasy of the Roman-canon system, the distance between attitudes toward confessions that prevailed then and those that prevail now is another subject in regard to which the contrast between premodern and modern procedural systems is not nearly as pronounced as is often believed. Whether acknowledged or not, defendants are still treated as precious sources of information, and their confessions are still eagerly sought in practice. As this claim may sound heretical to some ears, a digression to substantiate it is in order. Consider first criminal justice systems in the continental legal tradition. They retained the defendants' *legal* duty to truthfully answer questions long after the abolition of judicial torture. The invocation of this duty was routinely used by criminal law enforcers to pressure defendants into making self-incriminating statements. Well into the nineteenth century, a consequence of this duty was that the defendants' obstinate taciturnity, or the established falsity of their responses to the investigator's questions, was sanctioned by disciplinary punishments (*poenae inobedienciae*), including stricter forms of preliminary detention, denial of food and in some jurisdictions even flogging.[48] After liberal nineteenth-century legislators outlawed these punishments, other procedural devices were employed to pressure defendants to speak and possibly confess to crimes. One measure was to order or extend preliminary detention of defendants who refused to speak, justified on the ground that defendants might, if released, tamper with evidence.[49] Another was the permission to draw inferences of guilt from the defendants' silence. Only in the early twentieth century did liberal

---

[46] See J. P. Lévy, *La Hiérarchie des Preuves*, 38.

[47] See Carpzov, *Practica Nova Imperialis Saxonica Rerum Criminalium*, Pars III, qu. 114, no. 1 (*"Paria sunt, convictum quem esse, aut confessum: quorum alterum ad condemnationem sufficit."*)

[48] It is revealing of the temper of the times that even Cesare Beccaria approved of these disciplinary punishments as morally justified. See Cesare Beccaria, *An Essay on Crimes and Punishments*, 150 (London, 1801). For an unusually frank defense of *poenae inobedienciae*, shocking to our sensibilities, see M. Vuchetich, *Institutiones Iuris Criminalis Hungarici*, 400 (Buda, 1819). "If minors can be punished for mendacity," the author mused, "why not also adults who are required to tell the truth but obstinately lie or refuse to answer questions?"

[49] If they spoke and confessed, it was argued, the danger of tampering with evidence would disappear. For an illuminating discussion of these devices, see Vladimir Bayer, La Signification de l'Aveu de

The Ranking of Information Sources 39

legislative reforms accord defendants meaningful rights to resist pressures to self-incrimination in formal judicial investigations.[50] Pressures on defendants to speak and incriminate themselves then shifted from formal judicial investigations to informal police inquiries.[51] The most effective weapons defendants have to resist psychological pressures to cooperate with authorities – the right to silence and the right to the presence of counsel at the police stage – are of relatively recent vintage on the continent. Yet even now that the defendant's right to silence has been enshrined in basic human rights documents, and is protected by the European Court of Human Rights, confessions continue to be coveted – if not in proclamations of lawyers who occupy the *piano nobile* in the mansion of justice, then by police in its basement.

Criminal justice in the common law tradition rightly enjoys the reputation of being less oriented toward relying on confessions. Although, as we will see, important historical aspects of the role of defendants as evidentiary sources are only partially elucidated, it is clear that the common law trial structure makes it easier for defendants to avoid being interrogated than is the case with defendants in the traditional continental criminal procedure.[52] This being said, there is little doubt that confessions are highly valued evidence in Anglo-American criminal procedure as well. Even here psychological pressures are often exerted on defendants in the pretrial phase of proceedings to admit criminal responsibility. It is true that these pressures are no longer focused on obtaining confessions: what police and prosecutors now seek is to persuade defendants not to contest charges and plead guilty. But although the legal nature of confessions and guilty pleas differs, both involve admissions of guilt. And it can scarcely be denied that the prosecutor's promise to drop some charges in exchange for a guilty plea can produce powerful psychological pressure on defendants not to oppose the prosecution's case.

Yet the question remains: why were confessions so exalted in the Roman-canon fact-finding scheme that even judicial torture – euphemistically termed "painful interrogation"– was recognized as a permissible procedural instrument for obtaining

---

l'Inculpé dans la Procédure Pénale de Certains Etats Occidentaux Européens, *Rivista Italiana di Diritto e Procedura Penale*, no. 3, 732 (1959).

[50] In a few continental jurisdictions the defendant's duty to truthfully testify survived till the middle of the twentieth century. For the state of the law in some Swiss cantons, see H. Pfenninger, Die Wahrheitspflicht des Beschuldigten im schweizerischen Strafverfahren, in K. Bader (ed.), *Probleme des schweizerischen Strafprozessrechts*, 116–120 (Zurich: Schulthess, 1966).

[51] Here crucial incriminating evidence was often obtained before the opening of formal judicial investigations, with their promise of defensive safeguards. These safeguards were therefore like a comb given to persons after they have lost their hair. For the French example of this shift to police inquiries following the passage of a liberal statute, see R. Vouin and J. Léauté, *Droit Pénal et Procédure Pénale*, 255–256 (3rd ed.)(Paris: Presses Universitaires de France, 1969). For an early critique of this practice, see H. Donnedieu de Vabres, *Traité de Droit Criminel*, vol. II, 1312 (Paris: Sirey, 1947).

[52] An important step toward recognition of the defendant's right to silence in England was the Sir John Jervis Act (1848), requiring the police to caution defendants that they have no duty to answer questions put to them.

40 *Epistemic Foundations*

them? The following explanation is usually advanced: instruments we now use for discovering traces of crime did not exist, so that crime detection was almost entirely dependent on witnesses. Witnesses who provided circumstantial evidence could not support blood punishments, and eyewitnesses required for the imposition of those punishments were a rare commodity. Consequently, obtaining the defendant's confession was often the only way to produce the legal proof necessary for the imposition of punishment believed at the time to be the only appropriate penal response to serious crime. While this explanation captures some of the reasons for the emergence of torture, it falls short of providing the complete answer. As our voyage through the Roman-canon evidentiary landscape progresses, it will become apparent that the requirement for two eyewitnesses was not consistently observed. Important exemptions existed from its application – especially in regard to the most serious crimes. Besides, a minority doctrine held that sanguinary punishment may be administered on compelling evidence short of the testimony of two eyewitnesses.[53] And where full proof was not necessary for the use of coveted blood punishments, other reasons must have existed for the allure of confessions and the tolerance of judicial torture.

Insufficiently recognized are reasons that drew nourishment from religious sources, such as the belief that obtaining confessions is salutary to the soul of the judge. As has repeatedly been mentioned, judges were reluctant to impose sanguinary punishments on circumstantial evidence, since establishing its sufficiency required their personal assessment of its probative force. This assessment was disturbing to pious and ethically sensitive judges, because the theological alibi that the law – not the judge – condemned the defendant failed to shield them sufficiently from moral responsibility for causing the spilling of blood. Confessions could provide an antidote to their mental discomfort: self-incrimination could be interpreted as the defendants' acceptance of the procedural outcome, and perhaps even as their assumption of responsibility for the bloody procedural outcome.[54] In addition to being considered of value to the soul of the judge, confessions were viewed as salutary to the soul of the criminal. The reason for this belief has also been touched upon earlier. Remember that in the beam of the theologian's lamp, crime appeared as a mortal sin calling for confession and repentance. Given the existing worldview, it became easy to associate the attitude toward confessions in the confessional with the attitude toward confessions in the courtroom: in both settings the confession implied repentance and seemed useful to the soul.[55] This provided

---

[53] As we will see, this doctrine was followed by courts in some jurisdictions.

[54] Supportive of this *volenti non fit iniuria* rationalization were some texts of the Justinian codification, associating courtroom confessions with self-condemnation. Chapter 5 will refer to them. Foucault rightly attributed the importance of confessions in the criminal procedure of the *ancien régime* to the belief that they amounted to an acceptance of the accusation. See Michel Foucault, *Surveiller et Punir*, 43.

[55] Nor was this association limited to medieval law. Late in the sixteenth century, Damhouder still declared that "confession is the savior of the souls, the destroyer of vice, the restorer of virtue, the expurgator of demons: it closes the mouth of hell and opens the gate of heaven." See Josse de

The Ranking of Information Sources

a seldom-noted alibi for torture. Given the belief that admission of guilt could save a sinning defendant from eternal torments in hell, immersing him temporarily in the absolving sea of pain lost some of its abhorrent nature. It was clear, of course, that repentance expressed by the courtroom confession would not save the defendant from death or mutilating punishment – except perhaps in a prosecution for heresy. Yet repentance could still be precious to him in the hereafter. Some may be tempted to dismiss this excuse as a cynical attempt to justify torture by lacing it with religious sauce. This would be a mistake, however, revealing the absence of sufficient cognitive empathy with the then-dominant worldview.

Terrestrial reasons also fostered the tolerance of torture. Consider that the possibility of members of the upper social strata being subjected to torture – and especially to its severest forms – was quite remote, so that the social elite did not recognize itself in the tormented individual. This can easily be inferred from legal provisions relating to the exemptions from torture. To be sure, some of these provisions were independent of social class. As dictated by Christian morality, minors, pregnant women, the old and the insane were spared from being subjected to torments. Discrimination on the basis of the defendant's station in society was obvious, however, in regard to exemptions from torture based on the "dignity of the defendant" (*dignitas rei*). Since dignity cutting across the social spectrum was not yet recognized, total or partial immunity from torture was accorded only to defendants belonging to upper social strata.[56] In addition to this obvious discrimination a less visible one existed as well, manifested in the prosecution of people who were not exempted from painful interrogations. Chapter 5 will show that in considering evidence sufficient for torture the judge was supposed to inquire, *inter alia*, into whether the defendant was a person capable of criminal activity. In the then-existing social environment, and as a consequence of this requirement, the same evidence was sometimes found insufficient for the torture of a socially established commoner, but sufficient in the prosecution of a less respectable one.

Social class also played a role in the decision whether to order torture based on the judge's belief in the defendant's guilt, or at least his strong suspicion of guilt.

Damhouder, *Sentenciae selectae pertinentes ad materiam praxios rerum criminalium et aliarum partium iuris scientiarumque*, 27 (Antwerp, 1601). For a similar, but less eloquent, laudation of the confession in the forensic context, see Joannes Kitonicz, *Processus Consuetudinarii Incliti Regni Hungariae*, Cap. 6, qu. 10 (Trnava: Fredericus Gall, 1724).

[56] In medieval times exemptions from torture were designed primarily for the hereditary nobility. For an example of this tendency, see the Spanish *Siete Partidas*, partida 7, tit. 30, ley 2. In lands where hereditary nobility was powerful, the emphasis on noble descent in granting immunity from torture lasted well into the eighteenth century. For Poland, see Z. Kaczmarczyk and B. Leśnodorski, *Historia Panstwa i Prawa Polski*, vol. 2, 195, 207 (Warsaw: Państwowe Wydawn. Naukowe, 1957). In early modern times, immunities from torture were also granted to persons who occupied elevated positions in the military and the government, or practiced respected professions. Most of these immunities were only partial, however, and inapplicable to the most serious crimes (*crimina infanda*). For a description of the state of law on this subject in German lands, see Carpzov, *Practica Nova Imperialis Saxonica Rerum Criminalium*, Pars III, qu. 118, nos. 65–105.

42 *Epistemic Foundations*

Although, as we will see, the prevailing legal doctrine required that torture orders be based on evidence capable of generating belief in guilt, strong suspicion appears to have sufficed in regard to persons from the bottom of the social pyramid, especially if they were of ill repute. This tendency is noticeable in sources dating from the earliest history of the inquisitorial process. In his thirteenth-century treatise on crime, Gandinus commented, for example, on the "frequently occurring" cases of persons of low status and bad reputation against whom rumors circulate that they have committed crimes, but the evidence normally required for torture is missing. Having laid down various views on the subject, he concluded that these persons may nevertheless be subjected to painful interrogations. They have no valid claim to be protected by the legal order, he wrote, since they flouted the law by the manner in which they led their lives and made a bad example of themselves.[57]

Nor should internal procedural reasons be overlooked that contributed to the allure of confessions. In some of these reasons, as in the dark glass of the past, we can recognize harbingers of the contemporary proclivity to consensual justice and trial avoidance. Consider that in-court confessions could heal not only antecedent procedural error and bar appellate review in some cases, but also reduce the burdens of investigative activities and be useful to judges as a labor-saving device. The importance of these mundane reasons increased at an equal pace with the decrease of the intensive and pervasive fear of hell – the *basso continuo* of medieval life.

The Probative Value of Coerced Statements

Coercive measures to obtain incriminating statements from defendants in the inquisitorial process are usually discussed only in regard to torture ordered by the judge upon completion of the investigation and for the specific purpose of obtaining their confession. But this particular form of torture – *tortura ad eruendam veritatem* – was only the most draconian coercive device available for the extraction of self-incriminating information.[58] The infliction of physical pain on defendants for this purpose was also permitted *before* the completion of the judicial investigation. If they refused to talk, were caught in contradictions, or if the judge concluded that they pretended not to remember or know the answer, the infliction of physical pain on them was permitted. "This form of torture," Julius Clarus stated, "is inflicted not in order to discover the truth, but in order to obtain an answer."[59] This was

---

57 See Albertus Gandinus, Tractatus de Maleficiis, Rubrica: A quo vel a quibus possit fama incipere et ex quo tempore, no. 5, in Hermann Kantorowicz, *Albertus Gandinus und das Strafrecht der Scholastik*, Band II, pp. 67–68 (Berlin: J. Guttentag, 1926).

58 Damaging statements short of a confession could be precious to investigating judges in order to locate possible witnesses to the crime, or to acquire circumstantial evidence. As we will see, they could also be useful in acquiring circumstantial evidence needed for ordering torture *ad eruendum veritatem*.

59 "*Et talis tortura non datur reo ad eruendam veritatem sed datur ad extorquendam responsionem.*" Julius Clarus, *Practica Criminalis*, lib. 5, qu. 45, no. 6 (Lyon, 1672). Similarly Carpzov, *Practica Nova Imperialis Saxonica Rerum Criminalium*, Pars III, qu. 113, nos. 56–57.

The Ranking of Information Sources

a slippery distinction, of course, especially from the standpoint of guilty defendants, for it suggested that they were being subjected to pain not in order to make them confess guilt, but because they lied in denying it. In addition to physical compulsion, psychologically coercive measures were also employed. In *ancien régime* France, defendants were required prior to the beginning of interrogations to take the promissory oath to tell the truth. This confronted guilty but pious defendants with the agonizing choice between admitting guilt and exposing themselves to blood punishment in this world, or committing the mortal sin of perjury and exposing themselves to divine punishment in the next. In German lands, defendants could be required to swear the so-called purgatory oath to assert their innocence. If they agreed to take the oath they were acquitted, and if they refused they would be tortured. This also created a painful choice for pious but guilty defendants. If they falsely swore innocence, they could escape torture but remain haunted by the fear of divine retribution for perjury.[60] Enlightenment critics of the inquisitorial process were right in referring to these psychologically coercive measures as "mental torture."

In order to determine the epistemic foundations of the Roman-canon fact-finding scheme, it is important to inquire whether coerced statements obtained from defendants possessed probative value. This can best be examined through torture ordered at the end of the investigation for the explicit purpose of obtaining a confession. Was this torture a rational instrument, capable of yielding accurate information? Despite growing shelves of essays written on this subject, the question remains shrouded in a fog of uncertainty, and is still capable of fomenting passionate controversy. The main obstacle to approaching this subject *sine ira et studio* is the reprehensible character of torture. In our moral landscape it represents such an odious behavioral extreme, and is subject to such moral obloquy, that it becomes difficult to contemplate that it might be cognitively useful in some situations. The concession of usefulness, it is feared, could in difficult cases tempt investigators to employ physical compulsion in order to obtain needed information. The use of torture could also spread beyond difficult cases, since the sympathy for suffering as a civilizational constraint would be weakened. To dress the matter in a topical garb, could not conceding the truth-revealing capacity of water-torture (*"question à l'eau"*) – the most common form of torture in the French inquisitorial process – facilitate the acceptance of water-boarding in terrorist cases? Animating this concern is the belief that the opposition to torture on the ground that it cannot produce reliable information is more effective in discouraging its use than the emphasis on its inhumanity. And since some law enforcement officials might in fact be more hospitable to arguments stressing the cognitively useless nature of torture, or the dangers of false information obtained by it, the blanket denial of probative value to extorted information could be a wise governmental policy. But in an attempt to

---

[60]   Dante vividly depicted this predicament in *Inferno*, Canto 22, 43–54.

44   *Epistemic Foundations*

determine the epistemic basis of the Roman-canon fact-finding scheme, humanitarian revulsion to torture must be disregarded, and its probative potential examined in a temporary anesthesia of the heart.

It stands to reason that admissions of guilt extracted by torture are in and of themselves cognitively worthless. The desire to put an end to excruciating pain is the root impulse of most people, and can induce even *innocent* defendants to confess to crimes they did not commit. It is also true that some *guilty* defendants could endure torture without confessing, so that in regard to them torture produces no cognitive gain and represents useless cruelty. The epistemic worthlessness of extorted confessions is therefore clear in the case of unspecified, general admissions of guilt, and also in the case of detailed confessions induced by leading questions. Their worthlessness is less than clear, however, in regard to confessions obtained without suggestive questioning, if they lead to evidence confirming the veracity of self-incriminating statements, or provide information likely to be known only to the person who perpetrated the crime. Suppose, for example, that a coerced confession of robbery includes information about the place where the stolen item is hidden. If investigators discover the stolen item at the indicated location, the reliability of the confession is corroborated and cannot be denied probative value. The objection could be raised, of course, that the confession per se is still worthless, and that only the discovered item has probative value as circumstantial material evidence. If the defendant admits to having hidden the item in his friend's apartment, it could also be argued, the item's discovery is not circumstantial evidence against the defendant but evidence against his friend. This objection neglects to consider, however, that the extorted statement enabled the discovery of stolen property, and that the link of this statement to subsequently discovered material evidence accords at least some probative value to the extorted statement. In short, confirmation by subsequently discovered evidence can make coerced confessions reliable.

But if this is possible in principle, did Roman-canon jurists devise a scheme satisfying the conditions necessary to make extorted self-incrimination cognitively valuable? It should be recognized that they did not ignore the tendency of men and women to falsely admit commission of crime for the sake of stopping the infliction of serious physical pain. Borrowed from Roman law, the expression "torture is a fragile and dangerous matter" appears mantra-like in their writings. They were also aware of the morally problematic aspects of torture, albeit only under the then-existing torso of human dignity perceptions.[61] This induced them to craft a body of rules – the "law of torture"– supposed to contain safeguards that only reliable confessions are used as support for the administration of sanguinary punishment. As we examine these rules in Chapter 5, it will emerge that, as *designed*, they do not deserve outright dismissal

---

[61]   "*Nihil tam crudele et inhumanum esse,*" wrote Carpzov, "*quam hominem at imaginem Dei constitutum tormentis lacerare*" (Nothing is as cruel and inhumane as by torture to mangle humans created in God's image). See Carpzov, *Practica Nova Imperialis Saxonica Rerum Criminalium,* Pars III, qu. 117, no. 3.

The Ranking of Information Sources

as being irrational. This being said, two aspects of this macabre "law of torture" were indeed cognitively worthless, and deserve to be recognized as such at this early point. One concerns the verifications of confessions extorted to prove mental states, such as intent, or pure belief crimes, such as heresy. For if the tormented defendant responded affirmatively to the question whether he intended to commit a crime, the effective verification of his statement was either impossible, or, as we will see, did not extend beyond evidence used to justify the torture order in the first place.[62] And since verification of confessions in cases of this kind failed to provide a noticeable cognitive gain, it was in the epistemic sense useless. It made sense only as a psychological facilitator of the judge's decision to send the confessing defendant to the gallows. The other cognitively useless verification of confessions related to the crime of witchcraft (*crimen magiae*). The crime was defined by medieval theologians and scholastic philosophers as a contract with the devil. Witches were believed to enter into contract with the devil in the male body (*incubus*), and sorcerers with the devil in the female body (*succubus*). In exchange for promising to engage in sexual intercourse with these denizens of the underworld, witches and sorcerers were believed to acquire special harmful powers. Since this theological and philosophical understanding of the crime was accepted by late medieval jurists, the successful prosecutions of witches and sorcerers required, *inter alia*, proof that the contract with the devil was actually concluded. In the understandable absence of eyewitnesses to this imaginary crime, the confession of the witch or sorcerer remained the only available path to conviction. But since the law of torture required that the truthfulness of confessions should be confirmed, how could one verify the accuracy of the extorted statement that the contract with the devil was actually concluded? The solution was found in the belief that contracting with demons – even sexual intercourse with them – leaves traces in the outside world. This belief enabled the elaboration of rules on how these traces could be identified by witnesses, or by the ocular observation of the judge.[63] In the lifeworld of societies in which the supernatural and the human interpenetrated, the discovery of these imaginary traces made witchcraft confessions believable to many contemporaries. Yet, the culprit for the reliance on false confessions of witchcraft was not the absence of the rational need for their verification. Rather, responsibility must be assigned to social illusions concerning the existence of an imaginary crime, and the companion belief in nonexistent traces the crime supposedly leaves in the external world, traces capable of providing verification of the reliability of confessions.

---

[62] Cognitively worthless questions such as "Did you commit the crime intentionally?" were asked of tormented individuals as late as the eighteenth century. See Jodocus Beck, *Responsa Juris Criminalis et Civilia*, responsio 7, p. 95 (Nuremberg, 1736).

[63] A catalog of these imaginary outward signs is included in a ghastly fifteenth-century manual for witchcraft prosecutors. See Henricus Institutoris and Jacobus Sprenger, *Malleus Maleficarum*, vol. I, pars III, qu. 10 (Christopher Mackay ed.) (Oxford: Oxford University Press, 2006). A somewhat different collection of these imaginary signs appears in Carpzov, *Practica Nova Imperialis Saxonica Rerum Criminalium*, Pars III, qu. 122, no. 60.

46   *Epistemic Foundations*

CONCLUSION

As this chapter has revealed, the epistemic views of the founders of the Roman-canon fact-finding scheme were not as distant from our views as standard accounts suggest. In the first place, late medieval jurists were aware of limitations on what can be established in criminal proceedings: they recognized intermediate levels of knowledge short of absolute certainty. As an astute commentator has noted, their thinking on this subject has in no important way been improved upon by modern treatment of evidence in the law.[64] Second, the founders' understanding of the nature of factual inquiry indicates their awareness of the importance of direct sensory perception of dispositive facts, rather than a blind acceptance of authority. The greatest among the founders, we noted, went so far as to maintain that when the judge is capable of directly perceiving dispositive facts in the performance of his office, he engages in a mode of cognition superior to the reliance on evidence. The importance which the founders attributed to direct sensory perception of material facts induced them to develop limitations on the use of derivative evidence and elaborate a hearsay doctrine. Their ranking of evidence, while often dismissed as a senseless scholastic obsession, expressed attitudes toward the probative value of information that have still not completely disappeared. Circumstantial evidence is still claimed to be inferior to the direct variety, and, if equal credibility is assigned to the carriers of direct and indirect evidence, this view is correct as a theoretical proposition. The defendant's confession is also still greatly valued in criminal justice systems. If this tends to be denied, it is in major part due to the concern that the acknowledgment of the great importance of defendants as sources of information might weaken the salutary impact of the privilege against self-incrimination. It is only in regard to torture that a gap between us and premodern jurists yawns at our feet. Yet the law of torture they devised, no matter how repulsive it is to our sensibilities, cannot be dismissed out of hand as irrational. Chapter 5 will take a close look at this law in order to establish whether observance of its provisions, which should not be taken for granted, could have yielded accurate information.

---

[64] See James Franklin, *The Science of Conjecture*, 43 (Baltimore: Johns Hopkins University Press, 2002).

3

Orientation in the Labyrinth

Roman-canon law of evidence contained proof sufficiency rules for a variety of decisions. Rules existed relating to proof needed for launching formal investigations, ordering judicial torture and entering judgments of conviction. Even rules pertaining to conviction were not uniform, but varied depending on the severity of punishment. Most prominent, we know, were sufficiency rules for the imposition of blood punishments, requiring two eyewitnesses or the defendant's confession. Whenever serious crime was the object of prosecution, judges struggled to gather evidence required for the imposition of *poenae sanguinis*, although they could from the inception of the inquisitorial process meet more easily the less demanding standard for the use of milder criminal sanctions. In our time too, the helix of the commentary on Roman-canon legal proof winds around the stem of the evidentiary requirement for the imposition of the death penalty and mutilating punishments. In order to understand the prominence of proof sufficiency rules for these punishments, it should be borne in mind that death and maiming were viewed as the only appropriate punitive reactions to serious crime. Quite unsurprisingly, they were usually referred to as "regular punishments" (*poenae ordinariae*). Nor was this attitude to criminal sanctions limited to medieval times. As late as the seventeenth century, legal authorities still maintained that serious corporal punishments were the only practically effective and legally valid responses to crime.[1] When a century later the Austrian empress Maria Theresa, influenced by her Enlightenment advisors, ruled that penal servitude could be used as a substitute for blood punishments, she ordered that it should periodically be accompanied by flogging "so that criminals experience that penal servitude is actually criminal punishment."[2] The close association of corporal punishment and the criminal law during five centuries of Western legal history is reflected even in etymology. During most of the *ancien régime*'s history,

---

[1] See Benedict Carpzov, *Practica Nova Rerum Criminalium Imperialis Saxonica*, Pars III, qu. 102, no. 60 (Wittenberg, 1652).

[2] For references to relevant documents, see Vladimir Bayer, Kazna batina u kontinentalnoj Hrvatskoj (Flogging punishment in continental Croatia), 23 *Collected Papers of the University of Zagreb Law School*, 41, n. 39 (1973).

48   *Orientation in the Labyrinth*

criminal jurisdiction was referred to as "jurisdiction of the blood" (*jurisdictio sanguinis*) or "the law of the sword" (*ius gladii*). In German lands, criminal courts were called *Halsgerichte* (noose courts), and the Russian term for criminal law is still *ugolovnoe pravo* (capital law). It was only in the late eighteenth century, when the sun was already setting on the *ancien régime*, that the infliction of physical pain gradually ceased to be regarded as a quintessential ingredient of punishment.[3]

Because it is often overlooked, it deserves to be noted that not all constitutive elements of serious crime had to be proven by two eyewitnesses or a confession. Mental elements, such as intent, could be established on compelling *indicia*. It is only because their precise character remained controversial that seeking confessions of mental states was often the safer path to conviction. Exonerating circumstances or affirmative defenses – such as self-defense – could be proven by the corroborated testimony of a single eyewitness.[4] Traces remaining in the physical world after the crime had to be established whenever possible by "ocular inspection" of the judge, rather than by two eyewitnesses or a confession.[5] Nor did the exacting Roman-canon full proof standard apply without exceptions, or in regard to all crimes, as will be revealed in Chapter 6.

As a consequence of the close association of criminal law and severe corporal chastisement, lesser punishments than death and maiming did not satisfy the prevailing urge to punish. Where by reason of failure to assemble evidence required for ordinary punishments judges were forced to fine or banish a criminal whom they considered guilty of serious crime, they felt that he escaped genuine criminal sanctions. Prosecutions for *crimen magiae*, treason, or heresy spring to mind as salient examples of cases in which the inability to impose the blood sanction was experienced by law enforcers as a serious problem. But the inability to satisfy their *furor puniendi* was not limited to imaginary demonic offenses, or those we would now classify as political. Theft, adultery, various transgressions of the prevailing sexual code – even activities that are nowadays not criminal at all – were perceived as so heinous that they appeared to require serious corporal punishment as a reaction to their commission.

Although the proof sufficiency standard for the imposition of punishments was most visible and still tends to monopolize attention, the question of what proof was sufficient for ordering torture also exercised Roman-canon jurists. The issue was of great practical importance, since confessions obtained by painful interrogations

---

[3]   This retreat from corporal punishment became the *idée maîtresse* of Foucault's famous book. See Michel Foucault, *Surveiller et Punir*, 16 (Paris: Flammarion, 1975).

[4]   Even circumstantial evidence and unsworn testimony of incompetent witnesses could in some courts prove facts favorable to defendants. See Benedict Carpzov, *Practica Nova Rerum Criminalium Imperialis Saxonica*, Pars III, qu. 115, nos. 74–75 and 78.

[5]   In the Italian variant of the inquisitorial process, establishing these traces was treated as of such great moment that establishing them was a prerequisite for initiating a formal criminal investigation. See Julius Clarus, *Receptarum Sententiarum Opera Omnia*, Liber V, paragraph: Finalis, qu. 4 (Frankfurt, 1596).

ordered on insufficient proof were considered null and void. In jurisdictions in which defense counsel were permitted to participate in criminal proceedings, contesting torture on this ground became their most important activity, offering the best, though still meager, chances of helping their clients. Discussion of the Roman-canon law in this area will temporarily be postponed, however, and be taken up in Chapter 5, devoted to legal requirements for the use of coerced confessions. The present chapter will only organize our survey of the Roman-canon mainstream views on the use of sanguinary punishments in a way suitable to revealing how legal proof affected the judge's decision-making freedom.

TENSION IN THE FACT-FINDING SYSTEM AS A GUIDE

We have already noted the widespread belief that the value of evidence in the Roman-canon fact-finding scheme was established by applying legal proof rules mechanically, so that the judge acted as an automaton or an accountant of pre-scribed items of evidence. A well-known nineteenth-century French historian likened the judge to a harpsichord responding to keys that are struck.[6] The endurance of this belief is reflected in legal writing on the subject in both continental[7] and common law countries.[8] But not all legal historians agree. Some maintain that no late medieval legal sources leave the impression of demanding that judges depart from ordinary reasoning processes for the sake of adhering to rigid proof rules. A few historians go so far as to maintain that evaluation of evidence free from legal constraints was already the tenet of medieval legal scholars and court practice.[9] Sandwiched between these two radically opposed views is an intermediate position holding that mainstream Roman-canon legal doctrine required for convic-tion not only that the demanding proof standard be satisfied, but also that the judge

---

[6] Adhémar Esmain, *Histoire de la Procédure Criminelle en France*, 251 (Paris: Larose et Forcel, 1882).

[7] Of great influence for the persistence of this belief in our time was the work of Jean-Philippe Lévy. See J. P. Lévy, Le problème de la preuve dans les droits savants du Moyen Age, in: *La Preuve II: Moyen Age et Temps Modernes, Recueils de la Société Jean Bodin XVII* (1965). For an overview, see Susanne Lepsius, *Der Richter und die Zeugen*, 23–28 (Frankfurt: Vittorio Klostermann, 2003). See also Vergès et al., *Droit de la Preuve* (citing Faustin Hélie), 57 (Paris: Presses Universitaires de France, 2015).

[8] Early subscribers to this view, Bentham and Wigmore, were mentioned in Chapter 1. John Langbein seems to have adopted this view in regard to early Roman-canon evidence law for criminal cases. See John Langbein, *Torture and the Law of Proof*, 6 (Chicago: University of Chicago Press, 1976). A similar understanding of Roman-canon legal proof is that of Barbara Shapiro, *Beyond Reasonable Doubt and Probable Cause*, 3 (Oakland: University of Chicago Press, 1991).

[9] An early expositor of this theory was Walter Ullmann. See W. Ullmann, Medieval Principles of Evidence, 62 *Law Quarterly Review*, 85 (1946). James Franklin has recently articulated a similar position. See James Franklin, *The Science of Conjecture*, 19 (Baltimore: Johns Hopkins University Press, 2001). Also departing from the rigid understanding of late medieval Roman-canon rules of proof is the richly documented study of Richard M. Fraher, Conviction According to Conscience: The Medieval Jurists' Debate Concerning Judicial Discretion and the Law of Proof, 7 *Law & History Review*, 23–64 (1989).

50 — *Orientation in the Labyrinth*

be convinced of the defendant's guilt.[10] A variety of views also prevail in regard to the internal evolution of the Roman-canon fact-finding scheme. According to some commentators, observance of legal proof was initially rigid and acquired flexibility only in early modern times, when blood punishment was no longer felt to be the only appropriate punishment for serious crime.[11] Others believe, by contrast, that the scheme was pliable in its late medieval form, and acquired a degree of rigidity only in its twilight phase.[12]

Our guide in establishing the degree to which the Roman-canon fact-finding scheme limited judicial freedom will be the tension between outcomes the judge found warranted in a given case, and outcomes mandated by proof sufficiency rules. The tension will be used as Ariadne's thread in steering us through the labyrinth of procedural and evidentiary issues that must be addressed in order to determine the actual constraining force of Roman-canon legal proof. It is not difficult to understand why the tension is a valuable guide, since the judge was tempted to depart from the proof sufficiency rule only when it prevented him from reaching the decision he considered substantively correct. But if one approaches the constraining force of the Roman-canon fact-finding scheme from this angle, two possible procedural situations must be distinguished. The observance of Roman-canon legal proof rules could have required that the defendant be subjected to blood punishment even though the judge believed that he might be *innocent*, or it could have required that the defendant be spared this punishment even though legally insufficient evidence persuaded the judge that he was *guilty*.

In what follows, the discussion of Roman-canon legal proof will be organized around these two disparate judicial reactions to convicting the innocent and acquitting the guilty. Aspects of legal proof capable of obligating the judge to *impose* blood punishment irrespective of his personal assessment of its value will be examined separately from aspects of legal proof capable of obligating him to *abstain* from imposing this punishment irrespective of his views on the cogency of legally insufficient evidence. The former will be called "positive," and the latter "negative" legal proof. The meaning of the latter term should not be equated with negative "statutory" proof as understood by nineteenth-century German lawyers.[13] To them, negative statutory proof related to situations in which the absence of Roman-canon full proof prevented the judge from imposing capital and other extremely harsh punishments, irrespective of whether other evidence in the case persuaded him of the defendant's guilt. Our understanding of negative legal proof will be somewhat broader. It will also apply to situations in which legal rules, other than those of

[10] See Mathias Schmoeckel, *Humanität und Staatsraison*, 193, 294 (Vienna: Böhlau, 2000).
[11] See John Paul Lévy, Le problème de la preuve dans les droits savants du Moyen Age; John Langbein, *Torture and the Law of Proof*, 43–44; Paolo Marchetti, *Testis contra se: l'imputato come fonte di prova nel processo penale dell'età moderna*, 44, 160 (Milan: Giuffrè, 1994).
[12] See Mirjan Damaška, The Death of Legal Torture, 87 *Yale Law Journal*, 860, 870–872 (1978).
[13] They talked about "statutory" rather than "legal" proof, because Roman-canon evidence law was, in German lands of the period, already in statutory form.

proof sufficiency, prevented the judge from making factual determinations he thought were substantively warranted. A legal rule could have prohibited him, for instance, from using a specified item of evidence in decision-making even though he found it convincing. This second form of negative legal proof will be important in comparing the fact-finding freedom of the judge in the inquisitorial process with that of judges in modern systems of criminal justice.

LEGALLY MANDATED AND SUBSTANTIVELY WARRANTED FACT-FINDING

The contention may be challenged that Roman-canon judges were torn by conflicting demands of legal proof and their personal assessment of evidence. Premodern judges, it may be objected, were either unaware of the discord between legally required and substantively correct outcomes, or followed the legally required outcome without being bothered by it. Consider first the objection that judges were unaware of the discord.[14] In late medieval and perhaps even in early modern times, a critic may protest, people failed to realize that the sworn testimony of two unimpeachable eyewitnesses could be false. They believed that observance of the legally prescribed procedural order and strict testimonial incapacity rules guaranteed accurate verdicts. Now, there is no denying that evidence sufficient for the imposition of blood punishment possessed great probative force in the eyes of medieval and early modern lawyers – as it also would to contemporary triers of fact. Where two legally qualified eyewitnesses swore something on their immortal souls, judges seldom had reason to believe that a conviction based on their testimony could produce a miscarriage of justice. "What is testified by two," Goethe's Mephisto famously said to Martha, "is everywhere known to be true."[15] But to concede that Roman-canon full proof possessed great probative force is not to imply that medieval and modern lawyers were unaware of the possibility that two legally competent eyewitnesses might testify falsely. Our discussion of the origin of the Roman-canon fact-finding scheme revealed that even ordinary medieval folks realized the dangers of forensic perjury.[16] And we will soon see that greatly similar testimonial accounts raised the suspicion of collusion in late medieval courtrooms.

---

[14] For references to the opinion that prior to the eighteenth century people did not realize that sworn eyewitnesses can provide false information, see Paolo Marchetti, *Testis contra se*, 178, 209 (1994). The opinion may seem plausible to those familiar with the longstanding confusion between legal and credible witnesses in English administration of justice. See Barbara Shapiro, *Beyond Reasonable Doubt and Probable Cause*, 6. That direct evidence left little room for disbelief also seems to be the opinion of Isabella Rosoni. See I. Rosoni, *Quae Singula non Prosunt Collecta Iuvant*, Introductory notes, vii (Milan: Giuffrè, 1995).

[15] "*Durch zweier Zeugen Mund wird allerwegs die Wahrheit kund.*" Goethe, *Faust*, Part I, *Neighbor's Home*, no. 3015.

[16] Note that the realization of the discord between legal and right decisions is unmistakable in Gratian's twelfth-century *Decretum*. See Raffaele Balbi, *La Sentenza Iniusta nel Decretum di Graziano*, 185, 189 (Paris: Dalloz, 1990). Although perhaps ahead of his time, Bartolus discussed even unintended

If medieval and early modern judges were aware of the possibility that legally mandated outcomes need not be substantively accurate, were they bothered by this realization? The answer depends on whether factual accuracy of outcomes was important to them. If the basic objective of premodern criminal procedure was not to establish whether a crime was actually committed and who its perpetrator was, then the discrepancy between legally mandated and accurate verdicts was not a serious concern. This conclusion could follow from James Whitman's theory about the influence of Christian moral theology on premodern criminal procedure. As we noted in considering the origin of the Roman-canon fact-finding scheme, Whitman rightly pointed out that pressure to strictly abide by the proof sufficiency standard for blood punishment emanated from theologians' claim that the spilling of blood constitutes mortal sin. According to them, the judge could safely administer *poenae sanguinis* only by acting as a mere instrument of the law and mechanically following proof sufficiency rules, rather than by exercising personal judgment in the implementation of these rules. This particular pressure favoring *rigor canonum* Whitman persuasively demonstrates. But he then goes on to contend that relieving judicial anxiety about imposing blood punishments was the main preoccupation of premodern continental criminal procedure. Its strong focus on accurate fact-finding, he thinks, dates only to the eighteenth or nineteenth centuries.[17]

Here Whitman presses his theory too hard. While worries about the safety of the judge's soul (*salus animae*) persisted for a long time in continental criminal justice, they were not nearly strong enough to displace the deepest impulse of inquisitorial procedure – that of detecting and punishing crime. In introducing this procedure in the early thirteenth century, Pope Innocent III proclaimed that its objective was to ensure efficient crime control. He stressed the importance of accurate fact-finding by insisting that the commission of serious crime should be clearly established.[18] And from the thirteenth century onward, it was generally understood that proceeding "*per inquisitionem*" was preferable to using other forms of prosecution precisely on the ground that judicial investigations facilitated truth-discovery.[19] If preventing the moral nausea of judges in pronouncing blood punishment were the main concern of the inquisitorial criminal process, it would be difficult to explain the insistence of law enforcement authorities on dogged prosecution of all crimes and avoiding impunity. As Chapter 1 noted, Pope Innocent III's pronouncement that it is

---

inaccuracies in the assertions of qualified witnesses. See Susanne Lepsius, *Der Richter und die Zeugen*, 317, *passim*.

[17] See James Whitman, *The Origins of Reasonable Doubt*, 210 (New Haven: Yale University Press, 2008).

[18] See O. Hageneder et al., *Das Register Innozens III*, 2 Pontifikatsjahr, 1199 (Rome/Vienna: A.A. Strnad, 1979).

[19] Consider the following statement by Gandinus: "*Per inquisitionem procedatur, per quam facilius veritas invenitur. Inquisitio maioris est efficatie tam ratione iudicis quam cause veritatis.*" See Albertus Gandinus, Tractatus de Maleficiis, in Hermann Kantorowicz, *Albertus Gandinus und das Strafrecht der Scholastik, Rubrica: Quo Modo de Maleficiis Cognoscatur per Inquisitionem*, 16, p. 47 (Graz/Cologne, 1926).

in the public interest that crimes should not remain unpunished (*publicae utilitatis intersit, ne crimina remaneant impunita*) became an inspirational catchphrase circulating in continental literature on criminal justice until the late eighteenth century.[20] It seems safe to conclude that the search for substantively accurate outcomes – the quest for "substantive truth"– was the animating spirit and primary objective of inquisitorial procedure from its inception, and the safety of the soul only a factor shaping the modalities by which this basic procedural aim was pursued.

Since reaching accurate outcomes was the desideratum of inquisitorial procedure, the dissonance between outcomes required "*naturaliter*" and outcomes required "*juridice*" was experienced by judges as a frustrating problem. It is true that open complaints about the matter multiplied only in the eighteenth century. Writing in this period, a German judge lamented how much "sadness and tumult to the soul and conscience" judges experience who cannot impose blood punishment in the absence of legal proof when legally insufficient evidence is so strong that it appears "almost impossible" that the defendant might be innocent.[21] But the concern with the discord between legally mandated and substantively warranted verdicts – albeit not articulated as an annoyance – can already be detected in late medieval sources. The famous fourteenth-century canonist Butrio, for example, pondered over the issue of what the judge should do when legally required proof for conviction is missing, but his "conscience" tells him that the defendant is guilty.[22]

For the purposes of this study the suspicion must also be laid to rest that by assuming different degrees of mental discomfort in convicting the innocent and acquitting the guilty, current moral intuitions are attributed to distant societies with less refined moral sensibilities. Should not equal insouciance in regard to these two situations be inferred from the teachings of medieval theologians that judges are under obligation to convict a person on full Roman-canon proof even if they have extrajudicial knowledge of his innocence? Did late medieval and early modern judges not adopt this brainchild of the theologians and treat the conviction of the innocent with evenness of temper? Assuming such a nonchalant attitude would be a mistake. In the first place, even theologians did not contemplate with equanimity the conviction of a person known to the judge to be innocent, simply because two legally competent eyewitnesses testified that he committed a crime. For reasons noted below, such a conviction was acceptable to them only if various expedients devised to avoid this regrettable outcome failed. And as far as jurists are concerned, their unequal attitude toward convicting the innocent and acquitting the guilty can easily be demonstrated. From the thirteenth to the eighteenth century, their writings

---

[20] See Chapter 1, *supra*, n. 37.

[21] "*Triste hoc iudici est cui tunc necessitas imponitur, reum, quem nocentem esse, non opiniatur, sed pro ea, quae in rebus humanis esse potest, certitudine, certo scit, absolvendi.*" See Augustino Leyser, *De Malefico Convicto sed non Confesso*, 10–11 (Wittenberg, 1742).

[22] See, Antonious a Butrio, *Super Secunda Primi Decretalium Commentarij*, ad X 1,31,1, n. 21, fol. 69rb (Venice, 1578). Only in the eighteenth century did the word *conscience*, to which we will soon return, cease to refer to knowledge, rather than to an inner sense of wrong.

54 *Orientation in the Labyrinth*

proclaimed that it is better to acquit the guilty than to convict the innocent.[23] This insistence often assumed the form of what lawyers in countries following the common law tradition refer to as "Blackstone's principle" – namely, that it is better to acquit a large number of guilty persons than to convict a single innocent person. An eighteenth-century jurist went so far as to claim that it is better to acquit 1,000 guilty defendants than to convict a single innocent one.[24] Although exaggerated, proclamations of this kind clearly evince an unequal attitude toward the two types of miscarriage of justice. All things considered, we are justified in considering the question of obligating the judge in the inquisitorial process to *impose* blood punishment when he does not believe in a defendant's guilt separately from the question of obligating him to *refrain* from imposing blood punishment when he believes that a person is guilty.

PRIVATE KNOWLEDGE OF THE JUDGE

In order to facilitate orientation in the Roman-canon legal landscape, a potential source of tension between legally required and substantively warranted verdicts will be noted but then left out of further consideration. Responsible for this source was the idea that the judge is prohibited from deciding cases by using knowledge he acquired out of court. The knowledge could point to an outcome different from the outcome based on evidence collected in the investigation, and thereby create a dissonance between the verdict the judge believed was correct and the verdict warranted by law. Medieval theologians predicated this prohibition on the familiar ground that the judge should refrain from exercising personal judgment in cases involving sanguinary punishments, and mechanically follow the dictates of legal proof. The standard example was that of a judge who, while looking out of the window, observed the defendant kill a person. Consistently following this train of thought, influential theologians maintained that a judge cannot be morally blamed even if he convicted a defendant of whose innocence he was persuaded on the basis of what he knew "privately." Moral blame for the miscarriage of justice, they wrote, would attach not to him, but to false witnesses who asserted that the defendant was guilty.[25] Closer to decision-making responsibilities, jurists were reluctant to accept

[23] A medieval example inspired by Roman law comes again from Gandinus. "*Sanctius est facinus nocentis impunitum relinqui*," he penned, "*quam innocentem damnari.*" See Albertus Gandinus, Tractatus de Maleficiis, in Hermann Kantorowicz, *Albertus Gandinus und das Strafrecht der Scholastik*, Rubrica: De presumptionibus et indiciis indubitatis ex quibus condemnatio potest sequi, 1, pp. 93–94.

[24] "*Satius est mille nocentes absolvere, quam unum innocentem condemnare.*" See Matia Bodo, *Jurisprudentia Criminalis*, Pars I, art. IX, para. 2 (Bratislava, 1760).

[25] An influential early proponent of this theological view was Abelard. See Pierre Abelard, Know Yourself, book 1, no. 81, p. 17, in P. Abelard, *Ethical Writings* (Indianapolis: Hackett Publishing, 1995). The view was somewhat later popularized by the Angelic Doctor. See *Thomas Aquinas, Summa Theologica, Secunda Secundae*, qu. 64, art. 7. As noted above, however, sending an innocent man to the gallows was regarded even by these theologians as a last resort.

Private Knowledge of the Judge 55

this teaching. So they either argued that the judge is not under an obligation to order the imposition of blood sentences he believes are unjust,[26] or advanced the modern solution that the case should be remitted to another judge.[27]

Observe, however, that the quandary of what the judge ought to do with his private knowledge was devoid of practical significance. Throughout the history of the inquisitorial process, the issue was discussed mainly as an intellectually intriguing subject, gratifying the doctrinal writers' itch of mentation.[28] One reason for the practical insignificance of the quandary was that the Roman-canon ban on the use of private knowledge rested on a broader foundation than the aversion of Christian moral theology to the spilling of blood. Judges in secular courts were prohibited from using knowledge acquired out of court even in cases of minor crimes, where nonsanguinary punishments were the proper criminal sanction. Nor was the judge of the Church, who was often also the father confessor, permitted to use what he learned in the confessional, although he was not authorized to impose capital and mutilating punishments. The appearance of this broader ban was prompted by the realization that the use of private knowledge conflicted with the understanding of the office of the judge (*officium iudicis*), which had evolved in the judicial apparatus of the Church since the late eleventh century. In this increasingly hierarchical setting, witnessing and adjudicating had to be separated because the separation facilitated the supervision of first-instance judgments by higher judicial authority.[29] Another cause was the related idea that the judge ought to consider only information presented in court, according to rules for the acquisition of knowledge (*ordo iudiciarius*). The judge who possessed private information relevant to criminal prosecution could only become a witness in a case tried by another judge, and convey to him what he had perceived out of court. A final reason why the ban on the use of his private knowledge was without practical significance was that it rested on the premise that the Roman-canon full proof rule was mechanically applied: if two legally competent eyewitnesses incriminated the defendant, the judge had to convict him even if he privately knew that the witnesses had testified falsely. But as the next two chapters will show, the Roman-canon fact-finding scheme did not work in

---

[26] See James Whitman, *The Origins of Reasonable Doubt*, 113–114.

[27] For an early example of this solution, see Antonio Padova-Shiappa, Sur la conscience du juge dans le *Ius Commune* européen, in Jean-Marie Carbasse and Laurence Depambour-Torride (eds.), *La Conscience du Juge dans la Tradition Juridique Européenne*, 113 (Paris: Presses Universitaires de France, 2008).

[28] The intellectual fashion lasted for a long time. As late as the closing decades of the eighteenth century, a French legal authority wrote that the judge must convict a defendant of whose guilt he is "legally persuaded," even if he is convinced of the defendant's innocence "as an individual and out of court" ("*come particulier et hors de justice*"). See Daniel Jousse, *Traité de la Justice Criminelle en France*, Tome II, livre 25, no. 147 (Paris, 1771).

[29] On this point a stark contrast exists with old English administration of justice, where these two functions remained fused until early modern times. Some jurors were both witnesses and adjudicators. As late as early modern times, English lawyers still argued that the fusion of functions was superior to their separation.

56 *Orientation in the Labyrinth*

this way. For all these reasons the problem of the judge's private knowledge will be disregarded as we confront the complexities of Roman-canon evidentiary arrangements.

DECISION ACCORDING TO CONSCIENCE

In contrast to the agreement that the judge could not use knowledge he gained out of court, premodern legal sources reveal a difference of opinion about the use of knowledge the judge acquired in court on his own initiative and in satisfaction of his own cognitive needs. Much of the disagreement stemmed from different interpretations of the Roman-canon maxim that the judge ought to adjudicate according to allegations and proof, rather than according to conscience (*"iudex iudicat secundum allegata et probata, non secundum conscientiam"*). Since the word *conscience* referred at the time both to moral sentiment and to the knowledge of facts, some jurists interpreted the maxim as demanding that the judge abstain from using not only what he learned as a private person out of court, but also whatever he learned in court as a result of his own independent activity. The issue of whether the judge was permitted to use knowledge he obtained by departing from the list of questions to be asked of witnesses was especially contested.[30] The majority of jurists did not hold this view, however. No less a figure than Bartolus opposed extending the ban on the use of personally acquired knowledge from the extrajudicial to the intrajudicial context. "What the judge has in his conscience," he remarked in a gloss to the Digest, "is known to him either as a judge, or as a private person. In the first case he judges according to conscience informed by acts done before him. Otherwise, if something is known to him as a private person, he cannot judge according to conscience, but rather according to proofs made before him."[31] Having said this, Bartolus then mentally genuflected before the position of moral theologians, arguing that when the judge learns something as a private person, he does not sin if he ignores what he has learned and decides "knowing the contrary."[32]

Some legal historians expressed the opinion that Roman-canon jurists interpreted the maxim *"iudex iudicat secundum allegata et probata"* as requiring that the judge decide criminal cases according to what legally competent

---

[30] The list was formulated on the basis of initial informal inquiries into the case, the first stage of the inquisitorial process to be discussed in Chapter 4.

[31] *"Allegatur quod iudex debet iudicare secundum allegata et probata, non autem secundum conscientiam. Solutio. Aut id quod iudex habet in conscientiam est notum sibi ut iudici, aut tamquam private personae. Primo casu secundum conscientiam suam iudicat informatus ex actis coram eo, et ita potest intelligi hic. Alias si ut private personae est sibi notum, tunc non potest iudicare secundum conscientiam, sed secundum probationes sibi factas."* See Bartolus, *Commentaria in Primam Digesti Veteris Partem*, ad D.1.18.6.1, fol. 72v (Venice, 1538).

[32] *"Et de hoc nota in c. secundo extra de officio ordinarii* [reference to Pope Gregory X], *ubi si iudex iudicat secundum legem, non peccat, licet contrarium cognoscat."* See Bartolus, *ibid.*

Decision According to Conscience

witnesses asserted, and abstain from evaluating their assertions independently.[33] As far as the inquisitorial criminal process is concerned, however, this opinion is unsustainable. For one thing, the maxim was addressed to the issue of what evidence should be admitted in a case, rather than how admitted evidence ought to be evaluated.[34] For another, the maxim was developed against the background of civil proceedings and the variant of the criminal process (*processus per accusationem*) in which the private prosecutor and the defendant submitted allegations and evidence to the judge. The *processus per accusationem* attracted scholarly jurists by its complexity – especially the burden of proof problems it generated – so they devoted much attention to it in their writings. But as the Prologue noted, it was almost without significance in the life of the law, being overshadowed by the dominant inquisitorial process. And while the maxim that the judge ought to decide according to allegations and proof could apply in the bipolar structure of *processus per accusationem*, it obviously could not acquire proper footing in the unilateral inquisitorial process in which the judge engaged in self-propelled and probing activity. His investigative duties were patently unreconcilable with the passive acceptance of allegations and probative material submitted to him by the parties. Our tour of Roman-canon fact-finding arrangements can therefore proceed without being diverted by glints of doubt that even in the inquisitorial process of the *ancien régime* the judge was prohibited from acquiring knowledge on his own.

Our exploration of the Roman-canon standard of proof for the imposition of blood punishment (*poena ordinaria*) will be organized in a way that facilitates the understanding of how legal proof affected the judge's freedom to ascertain the probative value of evidence. To this end, the positive and negative aspects of Roman-canon legal proof will be examined separately. The positive aspect will come up first for consideration. We will seek to determine whether the Roman-canon fact-finding scheme actually obligated the judge to administer the *poena ordinaria* mechanically when the prescribed legal proof was assembled. Chapter 4 will address the question of whether the imposition of blood punishment was required when the testimony of two properly qualified eyewitnesses was obtained, and Chapter 5 will then explore whether this punishment had to be imposed when the defendant's courtroom confession was available. Having completed the review of the positive aspects of the Roman-canon proof sufficiency standard, we will turn in Chapter 6 to its negative aspects. Was the judge obligated to abstain from imposing sanguinary punishment, we will inquire, when legally required proof

---

[33] In their opinion, the judge's independent evaluation of evidence would have constituted decision-making on the basis of *conscientia* prohibited by the maxim. Influential in disseminating this view was Jean Philippe Lévy. See J. P. Lévy, *La Hiérarchie des Preuves dans le Droit Savant du Moyen Age*, 8 (Paris: Librairie du Recueil Sirey, 1939). See also Bernard Schnapper, Testes Inhabiles, 33 *Revue d'Histoire du Droit*, 575 (1965).

[34] See also Susanne Lepsius, *Der Richter und die Zeugen*, 35.

was missing, but legally insufficient evidence persuaded him that the defendant committed the crime? Chapter 7 will then look at the other form of negative legal proof and consider cases where Roman-canon law prohibited the judge from using certain items of evidence in support of conviction even if they persuaded him of the defendant's guilt.

4

The Two-Eyewitnesses Rule

Beginning our tour of the Roman-canon fact-finding scheme, let us closely examine the widespread opinion that the judge was bound to impose blood punishment on the sworn testimony of two legally competent eyewitnesses even if he was unpersuaded by their assertions. The opinion is based on the assumption that Roman-canon rules of testimonial competency were conceived by their progenitors as an objective filter to screen reliable from unreliable witnesses, and that the judge's subjective assessment of their credibility, or the cogency of their statements, was not permitted to override the postulated objective criteria. While some scholars believe that this situation prevailed only in medieval times, others maintain that it constituted the distinctive feature of the Roman-canon fact-finding scheme throughout its lifespan. The present chapter will demonstrate that this understanding of the Roman-canon full proof rule (*probatio plena*) is untenable in light of institutional features of the inquisitorial process and its procedural realities.[1] Approaching the full proof rule from this angle requires, however, that the procedural setting in which the judge both investigated the case and rendered the judgment should be examined apart from the setting in which he was entrusted only with the collection of evidence, while the task of rendering the ultimate decision was the responsibility of a body of judges.

THE JUDGE AS INVESTIGATOR

Understanding how the judge established full proof requires awareness that his investigation was divided into two stages. The objective of the first stage, the so-called general inquisition (*inquisitio generalis*), was to ascertain whether sufficient information existed that a crime had been committed and that a designated person

---

[1] A caveat is in order about the meaning of "full proof." Originally, the term designated only the requirement for two eyewitnesses, while courtroom confessions were associated with notorious facts. In the later history of Roman-canon evidence, the term came to encompass in-court confessions as well. See Josse de Damhouder, *Praxis Rerum Criminalium, Opus Absolutissimum*, Caput 49, no. 1, p. 90 (Antwerp, 1601). This chapter will use the term in its pristine sense.

59

was its likely perpetrator. If these two preconditions (*fundamenta inquisitionis*) were met, the judge opened the special inquisition (*inquisitio specialis*) to gather the evidentiary material needed for the judgment. The initial general inquisition was informal: the judge did not interrogate witnesses under oath, and could structure the interrogation process by freely deciding what questions to ask.[2] Formal evidence rules became applicable only in the course of the special investigation: here witnesses had to be examined under oath, and were required to answer questions (*articuli inquisitionales*) formulated by the judge on the basis of information obtained in the course of the general investigation. Important to observe for our purposes is that knowledge obtained by him informally seeped into subsequent formal proceedings. To disregard this seepage distorts the reality of the inquisitorial process, much as the reality of modern criminal procedures would be distorted by focusing solely on evidence obtained in formal proceedings, neglecting the role of information obtained by the police.

The influence of informal on formal fact-finding activities can be illustrated by the example of Roman-canon rules designed to determine who is qualified to testify. In the course of the general inquisition, the judge could easily acquire credible information from persons legally incompetent to be witnesses.[3] If this information appeared believable to him he was quite understandably tempted to let the incompetent person testify. In Chapter 7 more will be said on this issue, and it will become obvious that succumbing to this temptation was not a rare event in the inquisitorial process.[4] But even if the judge resisted the temptation, items of information imparted by incompetent witnesses were still useful. They could help him, for instance, in articulating questions to be put to qualified witnesses in formal proceedings, most notably for the purpose of exposing possible weaknesses in their testimony. This leakage of information from general inquisition to subsequent formal proceedings is by itself capable of casting doubt on the opinion that testimonial incapacity rules functioned as an objective filter, screening credible from incredible testimony without subjective judicial input.

---

[2] A few formal rules existed on judicial views (*constatatio de corpore delicti*) undertaken in order to establish traces left in the physical world after the crime had been committed. In the Italian variant of the inquisitorial process they assumed considerable practical importance. Imported into Germany, they were greatly relaxed, however. See Benedict Carpzov, *Practica Nova Rerum Criminalium Imperialis Saxonica*, Pars III, qu. 108, no. 49 (Wittenberg, 1635).

[3] This could easily happen in the course of wide-ranging and legally unstructured examination "*ad informationem curiae.*" But some grounds for testimonial incapacity could surface also in formal interrogations conducted in the special inquisition. Enmity between a potential witness and the suspect is an example.

[4] Charles Donahue has discovered flexible attitudes toward testimonial disqualifications in medieval English ecclesiastical courts. See Charles Donahue, Proof by Witnesses in the Church Courts of Medieval England, in M. S. Arnold et al. (eds.), *On the Laws and Customs of England: Essays in Honor of Samuel Thorne*, 127, 158 (Chapel Hill: University of North Carolina Press, 1981). We will see that the attitude was not limited to English courts that followed Roman-canon evidence procedure.

The Judge As Investigator

Conflicting Formal Testimony

Let us look now at the treatment of legally qualified witnesses in the special inquisition. Their treatment is of decisive importance in ascertaining whether the assessment of their testimony excluded the exercise of the investigator's personal judgment. Conflicting and matching testimony present different problems and must be considered separately. We will first examine the case of conflicting testimony. In discussing the origin of Roman-canon legal proof we came across the theory that its architects developed a self-executing, mechanical system for the resolution of testimonial conflict.[5] They listed factors to be considered in deciding whose testimony should be credited, and these factors were followed without examining the content of what witnesses asserted. This was possible, we were told, because the weight of testimony was associated with the abstractly determined status of witnesses: the focus on status removed the need to scrutinize the probative value of what witnesses asserted. And if witnesses were all of the same status or dignity, the judge followed larger numbers.

Now, it is true that at one phase in the history of Western procedures, the personal status of witnesses was the primary factor in determining the probative value of their testimony. But at the time the inquisitorial criminal process was instituted, judges were already supposed to consider not only the status of witnesses, but also what they were asserting – their *dicta*. And when the status and statements of witnesses were considered in tandem, the mechanical crediting of testimony became well-nigh impossible.[6] This can easily be grasped by looking closely at factors usually listed by jurists as relevant to the evaluation of testimony. As noted in Chapter 1, while some of these factors may appear on the surface as having been outcome-determinative, on closer examination they turn out to have functioned like rules of thumb for average cases, or like checklists of matters the judge ought to bear in mind when confronted with conflicting testimony. For how could he unreflectively decide whose testimony to credit, for example, when conflicting assertions were made by people belonging to the same station in society? Or how could he automatically decide whose testimony to follow if assertions of a woman of honorable estate but living in vice conflicted with the testimony of a man of low status but exemplary virtue? The exercise of personal judgment was quite obviously indispensable in deciding how to resolve testimonial conflict in these and similar situations.

Late medieval awareness of the need for personal judgment in evaluating testimonial conflicts is obvious in the writings of Baldus. Consider his expert opinion in a case in which the testimony of three men conflicted with the testimony of four women. According to abstract rules for the evaluation of testimony, men were considered more credible than women. But should not the greater number of women prevail? The famous jurists did not seek to obtain an answer to this question

---

[5] See Chapter 1, text following note 4.
[6] Cf. Susanne Lepsius, *Von Zweifeln zur Überzeugung*, 176 (Frankfurt: Vittorio Klostermann, 2003).

62   *The Two-Eyewitnesses Rule*

from the abstract ranking of probative value indicated by factors listed as relevant. The conflict of testimony, he penned, was for the judge to decide on the basis of what appears to him evident. When faced with conflicting evidence, he said, judges should follow their conscience.[7] In support for this position he then quoted a passage from Justinian's Digest, saying that "the judge knows best when credit is due witnesses."[8] In early modern times, treatise writers regularly insisted that the number of witnesses and similar abstract criteria cannot compensate for the lack of credibility in testimonial assertions.[9] And even the sixteenth-century codification of evidence law for the German Empire – the *Constitutio Criminalis Carolina* – granted judges leeway in resolving testimonial conflicts, although the evidentiary system of the codification was more rigid than the one developed by learned late medieval jurists.

Matching Testimony

If mechanical approaches to the evaluation of *conflicting* evidence were well-nigh impossible, the possibility remains that *concordant* testimony of legally competent eyewitnesses was mechanically credited. But as intimated above, premodern judges were not so naïve as to think that miscarriages of justice could not arise from the matching testimony of witnesses who swore that they had seen the defendant perpetrate the crime.[10] Although presumptively valuable, concordant testimony was not accepted unreflectively. The determination whether a person was an eyewitness in itself required some attention to and analysis of what he or she asserted. If a witness alleged, for example, that he saw the defendant break into the desk where the victim kept a valuable piece of jewelry, and that a few minutes later he observed the jewelry in the defendant's possession, was he reporting eyewitness information, although he did not actually observe the "taking" of the jewels – the fact constituting one of the defining elements of larceny?[11] Assuming that the judge found that the testimony constituted an eyewitness account, he was then supposed to establish whether it was sufficiently similar to the testimony of another eyewitness to satisfy the full proof rule. Were the variances between the two accounts insignificant, or were they so substantial that the full proof standard remained unsatisfied? The difficulty involved in resolving this issue prompted Baldus to develop two elaborate schemes

---

[7]   "*Inter probationes adversantes, sequi conscientiam suam.*" See Baldus, *Consilium sive Responsorum Volumen Quartum*, consilium 455, p. 103 verso (Venice, 1590).

[8]   The remark "*tu [iudex] magis scire potest quam fides sit testibus adhibenda*" was included in Justinian's codification from a letter of the Roman emperor Hadrian addressed to one of his officials. More will be said below on this letter, frequently referred to by Roman-canon jurists.

[9]   For a widely influential statement, see Prospero Farinacci, *Tractatus Integer de Testibus*, Tit. VI, qu. 65, no. 148 (Osnabrück, 1678).

[10] See *supra*, Chapter 3, text above note 16.

[11] Issues of this genre were debated in Roman-canon theory and disputed in practice until the end of the legal proof system. See Carl Mittermaier, *Die Lehre von Beweise*, 363 (Darmstadt, 1834).

The Judge As Investigator   63

designed to assist judges in determining what he termed "unity" or "singularity" of eyewitness testimony.[12] It is true that these problems were legal in nature, but their resolution needed factual determinations that frequently called for credibility assessments. This can best be seen by the example of eyewitness accounts that were so similar as to provoke concerns of collusion. Far from being credited unreflectively, such highly synchronized testimonial *pas de deux* were greeted with skepticism. "When witnesses use the same speech in one and the same discourse," Baldus warned the judge, "suspicion exists that they have spoken to each other, or were suborned."[13] Dispelling the suspicion necessitated subtle credibility assessments rather than mechanical application of rules.

But the conclusion that the testimony of legally competent witnesses was not credited unreflectively follows with greatest clarity from the manner in which they were interrogated in the inquisitorial criminal process, not only in its initial informal stage but also in the formal special inquisition.[14] Rules on the subject are so strongly suggestive that one wonders why the regulation of the interrogation process does not stand out in high relief in all accounts of the way in which the Roman-canon full proof rule was actually applied. Consider a few of these rules. In his role as *"discussor testimoniorum,"* the judge was required to watch carefully for signs of possible falsity in the assertions of witnesses. If he detected contradictions in a testimonial account, its accuracy came under a cloud and was unlikely to be credited. If a witness was caught lying on one point, his entire testimony could be rejected.[15] But the judge was required not only to scrutinize the content of what witnesses asserted, but also to observe their demeanor for possible signs of falsity. He was expected to note, for example, if the witness blushed, stuttered, hesitated in answering questions, or in some other way produced signs of possible falsity.[16] Yet the most dramatic indication that legally competent witnesses were not blindly taken at their word was the rule adopted by several continental jurisdictions that those witnesses who were caught lying could be subjected to a form of mild torture.[17]

---

[12]   One scheme was inspired by Aristotle's *predicamenta*, and the other by Aristotle's four types of causation (formal, material, efficient and final). See Baldus, Comment on D.22.5.2.3, made *In Quartum et Quintum Cod. Lib. Commentaria*, Lib. IV, tit. 20 (de Testibus), lex 18, fol. 51va. no. 21 (Venice, 1599).

[13]   "*Nam quando testes loquuntur uno et eodem sermone, est ibi suspicio, ne inuicem se sint allocuti, vel sint subordinati.*" Baldus, *ibid.*, comment to Dig. 22.5.3.7.

[14]   The manner of interrogation was accorded so much importance that some manuals for investigating judges attributed the rules of proper interrogation to divine law. See, e.g., Flaminio Cartari, *Praxis et Theoreticae Interrogandum*, Lib. 1, cap. 1, no.13 (Rome, 1618).

[15]   "*Testis in parte falsus,*" Roman-canon jurists used to say, "*regulariter in totum reputatur falsus.*"

[16]   This attention to demeanor evidence can already be traced in thirteenth-century literature. See, for example, Gulielmus Durandus, *Speculum Iuris*, 1. 1 p. 4, para. 7 (Basel, 1574).

[17]   The duty of witnesses to testify was already established in most Italian jurisdictions in the late Middle Ages. See Albertus Gandinus, Tractatus de Maleficiis, Rubrica: De Questionibus et Tormentis, no. 8, in Hermann Kantorowicz, *Albertus Gandinus und das Strafrecht der Scholastik, Zweiter Band*, 157 (Berlin: Guttentag, 1926). On the permissibility of witness torture in German political units, see Carpzov, *Practica Nova Rerum Criminalium*, Pars III, qu. 113, n. 56 and qu. 119 nos. 47–49.

64   *The Two-Eyewitnesses Rule*

The fact that eyewitnesses were competent to testify, that they were *testes idonei*, was in and of itself insufficient for using their testimony to satisfy the Roman-canon full proof standard. What was needed in addition was that the judge found them credible. Only after this credibility assessment did they became witnesses "above all exception" (*omni exceptione maiores*), as required by the Roman-canon full proof standard. That legal and credible witnesses were not confused even in the late Middle Age follows plainly from what Baldus had to say on the subject. The judge, he remarked, must consider four factors before crediting eyewitness testimony. In the first place, he should establish whether they are "suitable" (*idonei*), that is, legally competent to testify. Second, he must determine whether what each of them asserted was "said simply or duplicitously, that is variously." In the third place, he must find that their accounts are concordant and "premeditated." Finally, he must establish that they are credible and that what they assert exhibits the appearance of truth.[18]

Given that the sworn testimony of legally competent witnesses was not accepted automatically, how much freedom did the judge possess to reject it? Some medieval jurists suggested that the judge was entirely free from legal constraints in assessing the value of evidence. In support, they referred to a letter of the Roman emperor Hadrian included in Justinian's Digest, stating that "no true and certain rule can be handed down on the credibility of arguments, or witnesses, because of the variability of men, the multiplicity of their transactions and the unknown trustworthiness of witnesses."[19] Commenting on this passage, Baldus remarked that "the mind of the judge should not be bound, so that he can exercise his own judgment about what facts are true."[20] In a similar vein, Bartolus wrote that full proof is obtained when the judge is "led to trust and believe in the matter subject to proof."[21] As mentioned in Chapter 3, these and similar statements led some legal historians to the conclusion that free evaluation of evidence already prevailed in medieval times.[22] Whether this conclusion is warranted depends on how free evaluation of evidence is understood.

---

[18] *Iudex ergo quator considerat. Primum in teste, an sit idoneus. Secundum an id, quod dicitur a teste, dicitur simpliciter, an dupliciter, id est varie. Tertium inter testimonia, an sit unita et premeditata. Quartum circa testimonia, an sit credibilia, et verisimilia.*" See Baldus, *In Quartum et Quintum Cod. Lib. Commentaria*, ad Cod. 4.20.18, fol. 51va, no.7.

[19] See Dig. 22.5.3.2. "*De fide argumentorum seu testium non potest tradi vera et certa regula propter hominum varietatem et negotiorum multiplicatem et incognitam testium fidelitatem.*"

[20] See Baldus, *In Quartum et Quintum Cod. Lib. Commentaria*, Lib. IV, tit. 20, lex 18, no. 30, fol. 52rb. "*Et ideo mens iudicantis non debet esse ligata, quin possit discurrere per sententiam verorum.*" In no. 29 he elaborated that "*ex iudicis motu eliciendam probationem utilitatem vel defectuitatem, ibi cum [Hadrian] dixit ex sententia animi tui estimare oportet quid aut credas, aut parum probatum tibi opineri.*" Under no. 38 of lex 18 he advised the judge to follow those testimonial assertions to which the light of verity adheres ("*lux veritatis adhaerat*").

[21] "*Quando dicitur plene probatum? Respondendum breviter quando ex facta iudici plena fides, hoc est quando iudex per ea que sunt sibi ostensa est adductus ad fidem et credulitatem eius quod intenditus.*" See Bartolus, ad Dig. 12.3.31, in *In Ius Universum Civile Commentaria, Concilia, Tractatus et Repertorium* (Basel, 1562).

[22] See Chapter 3, note 9 and related text.

This is a theme, however, whose consideration must be postponed until our voyage through the Roman-canon evidentiary landscape ends, and we compare Roman-canon to modern evidentiary concepts. For now it is enough to note that medieval jurists did not believe that the judge may base his disbelief in the testimony of legally qualified witnesses on inscrutable personal grounds. Freedom of this kind would have been incompatible with the values of the hierarchical Roman-canon judicial apparatus. That the decision was supposed to rest on externally verifiable factors can be gathered from the jurists' suggestions that the judge ought to indicate in the file of the case the reasons for his disbelief in the assertions of legally competent witnesses. Bartolus thus remarked that it is "prudent" for the judge to write down reasons for the suspicion which led him to reduce his trust in a witness, because the file of the case could be examined on appeal.[23] Stemming from canon law, suggestions of this kind can easily be understood: the freedom of the judge in rejecting legal proof had to be circumscribed for the sake of possible supervision by superior authority.

DECISION BY A BODY OF JUDGES

What will occupy us next is the implementation of the full proof rule in the functionally more complex variant of the inquisitorial process that emerged as of the sixteenth century in the wake of increased centralization and bureaucratization of the state apparatus. In this new institutional environment the collection of evidence was entrusted to the investigating judge, while the decision based on this evidentiary material became the responsibility of a body of judges, who assessed the value of evidence as recorded in the file of the case by the judge or a notary.[24] The first point to be made about this new institutional setting is that the approach to evidence of judges composing the decision-making body differed from the approach of the judge in whom investigative and adjudicative functions merged. The difference relevant for our present purposes was due to the fact that assessing the probative value of testimony on the basis of the cold file differed – as it still does – from assessing its value following direct contacts and interactions with testifying witnesses. In the latter case, the judge was exposed not only to verbal information conveyed by witnesses, but also to the nonverbal impressions gained in the course of the interrogation process. And as was pointed out in talking about the general inquisition, he was capable of obtaining reliable information even from

---

[23] "Tamen quia acta quandoque sunt examinanda in causa appelationis, tutius est quam causam suspicionis, propter quam fides testi miniatur iudex faciat apparere in actis." See Bartolus, ibid., ad Dig. 22.3. Ideoque.

[24] A variant of this institutional setting developed in jurisdictions in which the authority of the German Constitutio Criminalis Carolina was recognized. Here the judge was required to send the file of the case to legal experts, or Law Faculties, for advice. See Carolina, article 219. The opinion of legal experts or learned institutions was binding on the judge. And while this "transmissio actorum ad iuris peritorum," or "Aktenversendung," was originally provided for difficult cases, it became routine practice in most German political units.

incompetent witnesses, and using this information in assessing the probative force of assertions made by legally qualified witnesses. Judges who evaluated evidence on the basis of the case file, by contrast, were exposed to a more limited range of information, and came to the decision by studying and analyzing recorded testimony. This difference made the application of the full proof standard necessarily less flexible than it was in the environment in which the judge was in direct contact with information sources. If the file contained relevant statements of two competent eyewitnesses, and if their statements were sufficiently in agreement on the gravity of the crime, the body of judges was often left with little choice but to rule that the full proof standard was satisfied.[25] Following the increased centralization of government, a degree of rigidity in the law of proof was also introduced by princely legislation in the field of evidence. As rules enacted by the authority of the prince came to replace the often discordant voices of learned jurists, an atmosphere developed conducive to reducing the leeway of judges in applying evidence law.

But even when these sources of greater rigidity are taken into account, it is still mistaken to imagine that incriminating testimony of two legally competent eyewitnesses was mechanically accepted as being true in the new milieu. For starters, the investigating judge was capable of signaling to the decision-making panel the dubious credibility of eyewitness testimony simply by recording their inconsistent or improbable assertions in the file of the case. In some jurisdictions he was even able to record their suspicious demeanor. Knowledge the judge gained in the general inquisition could also find its way to the decision-making panel in circuitous ways. He could use this knowledge, for example, in formulating questions (*articulos*) addressed to witnesses in the special inquisition so as to expose the unpersuasive character of their responses. Preserved in the file of the case, these responses could provide the panel of judges with clues about the probative value of testimony. The panel also retained considerable freedom in rejecting eyewitness accounts on the ground that they were insufficiently matching. All told, then, the functionally differentiated procedural environment did not turn judges into sentencing automatons, impelled to surrender the defendant to the executioner on the basis of eyewitness testimony even if it appeared questionable to them.

Even so, the opinion kept spreading as of the eighteenth century that Roman-canon full proof obligated judges to automatically convict the defendant on the basis of the testimony of two eyewitnesses. A widely respected Italian legal theorist famously bemoaned how barbarous it was for the law to force the judge to betray his conscience by declaring true an accusation based on legal proof he had reason to

---

[25] Judges were not unaware that they were missing demeanor evidence. The saying "files do not blush" (*acta non erubescunt*) must have originated in this institutional setting. As a palliative, some courts began to require that the file of the case be accompanied by a special dossier containing information on the comportment of testifying witnesses. On this so-called *Gebärdenprotokol* of courts in German political units, see Alexander Ignor, *Geschichte des Strafprozesses in Deutschland, 1532–1846*, 38 (Paderborn: Schöningh, 2002).

Decision by a Body of Judges 67

doubt.[26] Laments of this kind persisted despite the Enlightenment luminaries' contemporaneous lament that judges of the *ancien régime* were unconstrained by law and administered justice arbitrarily. Did these judges really follow strictly only the law on full proof, disciplined like monks in a scriptorium, while disregarding the law in other respects, uninhibited like the faun in Debussy's afternoon?

What caused the dissemination of the belief that the Roman-canon full proof rule was blindly applied in criminal cases? Two conjectures are plausible. One reason might have been that this belief was shared mainly by academics in nineteenth-century German political units still clinging to Roman-canon evidence law. Cloistered in seraphic doctrinal spheres, these academics parsed legislative texts on Roman-canon proof sufficiency rules in isolation from their implementation, and especially in ignorance of the interrogation process and the manner in which eye-witness testimony had actually been acquired. When approached in this abstract fashion, the statutory definition of the two-eyewitnesses rule lent itself easily to the interpretation that the judge ought to follow "objective" criteria formulated by the sovereign, rather than his "subjective" assessment of probative worth.[27] The other reason might have been intentional misrepresentation of the full proof rule by progressive, reform-minded German lawyers, who exaggerated the rigidity of the rule in the hope that it would precipitate the demise of the repressive inquisitorial criminal process and lead to the adoption of the increasingly popular French criminal procedure modelled upon English criminal justice.

Despite these effusions about the mechanical character of Roman-canon full proof, judges did not feel impelled to impose capital punishment on unconvincing testimony of legally competent eyewitnesses. They lamented only that Roman-canon full proof deprived them of authority to impose the harshest punishments on compelling but legally insufficient evidence.[28] If they felt bound to sentence defendants to death on unconvincing statutory proof, they certainly would have criticized this positive effect of the Roman-canon full proof, and criticized it more forcefully than its negative effect impeding them from convicting defendants whom they believed to be guilty. Carl Mittermaier, the great nineteenth-century German

---

[26] "*Il giudice non sarebbe neppure nella barbaria coazione di tradire la sua conscienza col dichiarar vera l'accusa perchè accompagnata dalle giuridiche prove, malgrado tutto questo, egli avessse ragioni di dubitare della sua verità.*" See Gaetano Filangieri, *La Scienza della Legislatione*, Lib. III, capo XIV, 154 (Paris: Derriey, 1853).

[27] For a sampling of such abstract interpretations, see J. F. H. Abegg, *Lehrbuch des gemeinen Criminalprozesses mit besonderer Berücksichtigung des preussichen Rechts*, 141 (Königsberg, Bornträger, 1833); Sebastian Jenull, *Das österreichische criminal Recht nach seinen Grundlagen und seinem Geiste dargestellt*, Teil 4, p. 4 (Vienna, 1837) and especially Anselm Feuerbach's *Betrachtungen über das Geschworenengericht*, 24 (Landshut, 1813). Some scholars still believe that these interpretations reflected German procedural reality prior to the legislative reforms that took place in the middle of the nineteenth century. See R. Stichweh, *Zur subjektivierung der Entscheidungsfindung*, in Andre Gordon et al. (eds.), *Subjektivierung des justiziellen Beweisverfahrens*, 269 (Frankfurt: Klostermann, 1994).

[28] Remember the Jeremiads of the German judge Leyser, quoted in Chapter 3.

68 The Two-Eyewitnesses Rule

lawyer, rightly observed that anyone who spent even a short time in courtrooms knew how remote from truth was the belief that judges working under the statutory proof system were compelled to convict a defendant simply because two eyewitnesses had testified against him.[29] This observation could have been made with equal validity several centuries earlier, in regard to the court practice of most continental jurisdictions that adopted the functionally differentiated variant of inquisitorial procedure.

CONCLUSION

Although the Roman-canon proof sufficiency standard for the imposition of sanguinary punishments required two legally competent and unimpeachable eyewitnesses to testify to the commission of the crime, the preceding pages have shown that the judge had to perform so many activities in checking the reliability and consistency of their testimony that he found the standard satisfied only when he also found no reason to doubt their testimony. His belief in the defendant's guilt became one component of the full proof requirement. To put this conclusion differently, the legal demand for the testimony of two unimpeachable eyewitnesses had to be accompanied, or chaperoned so to speak, by the judge's subjective belief that they asserted the truth. Both requirements had to be met for the Roman-canon full proof rule to become operative.

The theory was mentioned in the Chapter 3 that full proof suffered a mortal blow as of the seventeenth century due to the spreading of noncorporal punishments.[30] Thereafter, the theory propounds, full proof continued to lead only the phantom life of laws on the books: an evidentiary revolution occurred, ushering in the era of normatively unconstrained evaluation of evidence. This chapter put forth an alternative theory.[31] It proposed that no revolutionary transformation occurred in the Roman-canon fact-finding scheme as of the seventeenth century, despite the outlined changes in the institutional setting of the inquisitorial process. Rather than losing its vitality, or becoming comatose, the full proof standard even became somewhat more rigid. Only the incidence of its use was reduced, since the number of cases was shrinking in which blood punishment appeared to law enforcers as the only proper penal response to serious crime. If a revolution occurred, it took place in penology rather than in the law of evidence.

---

[29] See Carl Mittermaier, *Die Lehre von Beweise*, 85 (*"Jeder Richter, der in deutschen Gerichtshöfen auch nur kurze Zeit lebte, weiss wie wenig wahr ist das ein deutscher Richter, sobald er zwei Zeugen übereinstimmend in ihrer Aussage findet, auch diese Aussage für wahr halten muss."*)

[30] See John Langbein, *Torture and the Law of Proof*, 10–12 (Chicago: University of Chicago Press, 1976) and Richard Evans, *Rituale der Vergeltung. Die Todesstrafe in der deutschen Geschichte*, 152 (Berlin: Kindler Verlag, 2001).

[31] Similarly also Arnd Koch, *Denunciatio, Zur Geschichte eines strafprozessualen Rechtsinstituts*, 205–207 (Frankfurt: Vittorio Klostermann, 2006).

5

The Probative Impact of Confessions

Although confessions were accorded pride of place in the Roman-canon fact-finding scheme, only those made in court (*coram iudice*) constituted full proof and provided support for sentences of blood punishment. Extrajudicial confessions were treated as circumstantial evidence (*indicia*) insufficient for this purpose. Nor were courtroom confessions admissible as proof of all relevant facts. In some jurisdictions their role was limited to answering the question who perpetrated the crime. The proof of the logically antecedent issue that a crime has been committed – the proof of *corpus delicti* – was not supposed to come from the defendant's lips. It had to be established by judicial views or witnesses, and in their absence by widespread rumor (*fama*).[1] Courtroom confessions were classified as either spontaneous or coerced. Treated as spontaneous were all those that were made prior to torture ordered *after* the completion of the special investigation. Although labeled "spontaneous," they often stemmed from pressures and promptings by the psychological and even physical means described in Chapter 2. But despite such pressures, these confessions were accepted most of the time without proper checking of their accuracy. Some legal historians attributed this practice to the belief of premodern judges that confessions made without judicial torture cannot be false. This opinion is refuted, however, by frequent references to voluntary but false confessions in medieval and early modern sources, frequently illustrated by the example of an impotent man confessing to having raped a woman.[2] Other historians think that premodern jurists viewed confessions obtained without torture as a species of forensic transaction,

[1] The separate regime for proving the existence of crime and the culpability of its perpetrator was the result of the separation of the investigation into the general and special parts. Remember that the primary role of the former was to establish whether a crime had been committed and who its likely perpetrator was, while the task of the latter was to determine whether he had in fact committed the crime. Only where the separate objectives of these two stages of investigation were not strictly observed, or were unknown, could the *corpus delicti* be proven by courtroom confessions, provided that certain safeguards were observed. On these safeguards, see Benedict Carpzov, *Practica Nova Imperialis Saxonica Rerum Criminalium*, Pars III, qu. 16, no.31 (Wittenberg, 1652).

[2] Damhouder stated more broadly that confessions of impossible things and those openly repugnant to nature are without probative value. See Josse de Damhouder, *Praxis Rerum Criminalium, Opus Absolutissimum*, Caput 54, no. 33 (Antwerp, 1601).

69

70   *The Probative Impact of Confessions*

transferring to criminal cases attitudes developed in civil litigation.[3] Whatever the reasons for the routine acceptance of "spontaneous" confessions, judges were not legally bound to credit them if they found them unreliable. Nor did their routine acceptance remain unchallenged: some influential jurists urged the judge to examine them carefully, and refuse to credit them if their falsity was suggested by "the very substance of innocence."[4] It might be tempting to liken this nonchalant attitude to spontaneous confessions to the current practice in some jurisdictions of accepting guilty pleas without meaningful inquiry into whether their factual basis corresponds to reality. But while a degree of similarity may exist, contemporary judges would certainly not fail to carefully examine the factual basis of guilty pleas in death penalty cases, which constituted the staple of inquisitorial procedure.

Coerced confessions were subject to a different regime. Chapter 2 revealed that the designers of the inquisitorial process were aware that self-incriminating statements obtained by the infliction of serious physical pain can be false, and that this awareness induced them to craft a body of rules meant to ensure that only reliable confessions could lead to the pronouncement of blood punishment. The resulting law of torture should now be examined in order to establish whether its rules – if observed – were capable of reducing the danger of false self-incriminations and preventing innocent people from being executed or maimed. Thereafter, the question central to our concerns will be addressed: did the Roman-canon system obligate judges to automatically credit confessions obtained in observance of the rules of torture, irrespective of whether they considered these confessions truthful?

THE LAW OF TORTURE

At the end of the special investigation evidence assembled by the judge often strongly supported the hypothesis of guilt. Some of this evidence was provided by the defendant as a result of aggressive judicial questioning, despite sporadic talismanic proclamations of the doctrine that nobody was required to convict himself out of his own mouth (*nemo prodere se ipsum*). While refusing to confess, the defendant often would still be led to disclose potential witnesses or reveal incriminating information.[5] Yet the assembled evidence, whether coming from defendants

---

[3]   "*Confessio spontanea*," observed Farinacci, "*facit reum manifestum, inducit notorium, habet vim rei iudicatae, et iis est similis.*" See Prospero Farinacci, *Praxis et Theoreticae Criminalis*, III, qu. 81, n. 4 (Frankfurt, 1611).

[4]   Baldus wrote, for example, that spontaneous confessions should not be credited unless "*indicia verisimilia et probabilia vel ipsa innocentiae substantia in contrarium appareat.*" See Baldus, *Consilia*, Liber Quintus, consilium 479, no. 3 (Venice, 1658). Although Farinacci attributed great probative force to spontaneous confession, even he was opposed to their blind acceptance in some situations. In one of his expert opinions he argued, for example, that a spontaneous confession of homicide was "too general" to be trusted. See Prospero Farinacci, *Responsorum Criminalium, Liber Secundus*, consilium 143, qu. 6 (Rome, 1615).

[5]   In early modern times manuals for practitioners appeared, instructing judges about the best methods of examining defendants and detecting their possible lies. In regard to informal interrogations of suspects,

The Law of Torture

or witnesses, seldom included the testimony of two properly qualified eyewitnesses. In secretly committed crimes, this was almost *ex definitione* the case. When evidence required to satisfy the full proof was missing, the task of the judge became to decide whether the collected evidence, although insufficient for the imposition of blood punishment, was strong enough to warrant subjecting the defendant to torture in the hope of extracting a confession from him and obtaining the *probatio plena* necessary for the use of sanguinary punishment.

Evidence Needed for the Torture Order

The law required that torture orders rest on strongly incriminating evidence. If this requirement was not met, and the defendant was tortured on insufficient evidence, his confession, if obtained, was invalid and could not be used for conviction.[6] Evidence necessary for the order was usually referred to as half proof (*probatio semiplena*). As pointed out in Chapter 2, the term was invented by twelfth-century glossators to designate the testimony of a single unimpeachable eyewitness. If two such witnesses produced full proof, glossators said, a single witness produced half truth.[7] But when torture was introduced into the criminal process, the term came to embrace all types of evidence other than Roman-canon full proof: not only testimony of a single unimpeachable eyewitness, but also powerful circumstantial evidence. The starting point for this extension of the meaning of *probatio semiplena* was a maxim discovered by medieval jurists in the Digest. The maxim stated that the use of torture is allowed only when evidence in the criminal case is so strong that nothing more than a confession is needed for conviction.[8] Especially in early modern times, the term "indubitable indications" (*indicia indubitata*) became common as an alternative designation for the mixture of direct and circumstantial evidence needed for torture.

The doctrinal discussion of what evidence satisfies half proof or indubitable indications bristled with references to presumptions, signs, conjectures, dubitable indications, and a few other types of circumstantial evidence.[9] Much midnight oil

---

these manuals recommended, for instance, that the interrogation of suspects should begin with queries distant from the incriminating event, and then only gradually turn to questions about ultimate facts. Maintaining consistency in fabrication under this method is, in fact, more difficult. Two seventeenth-century manuals illustrate these lie-detecting strategies with great clarity. See Flaminio Cartari, *Praxis et Theoreticae Interrogandum Reorum Libri Quattuor* (Rome, 1618), and Ioanus C. Frölich, *Nemesis Romano, Austriaco, Tyrolensis* (Innsbruck, 1696).

[6] See Carpzov, *Practica Nova Imperialis Saxonica Rerum Criminalium*, Pars III, qu. 126, no. 3. The qualifier "if obtained" is justified, because not all defendants subjected to torture confessed.

[7] Seizing upon statements of some pre-modern lawyers that "half proof" equals "half truth," Enlightenment critics of the *ancien régime* attributed this belief to Roman-canon jurists generally, and exposed them to ridicule. Foucault followed their example. See Michel Foucault, *Surveiller et Punir*, 46 (Paris: Flammarion, 1975). The ridicule is undeserved, because sophisticated medieval jurists like Baldus, and post-modern ones like Cujas, emphasized that "truth cannot be split" (*veritas scindi non potest*).

[8] "*Nihil aliud deesse videtur quam rei confessio.*" D. 48,18,1,1.

[9] An often-used one was "*adminiculum,*" referring to information capable of corroborating weak indicia.

72 *The Probative Impact of Confessions*

was burned in attempts to reach consensus on the meaning of these terms, and especially on the question of their mutual relationships. Often debated, for example, was the distinction between *indicia* and presumptions. Some jurists argued that indications were inferences from specific proven facts, while presumptions were inferences from what happens most of the time (*quod plerumque fit*). Many others disagreed.[10] Anybody contemplating reading the mountainous literature on this subject must be prepared, like Laocoön, to grasp a slippery tangle: while the literature is insightful in some respects, much of it is overly casuistic and ultimately confusing. As already mentioned, the drafters of *Constitutio Criminalis Carolina* recognized that all these terms indicate that a fact may be true because another one has been proven. This enabled them to simplify the law by using the generic expression *indicia* for all these rhetorical concepts, and classifying them as either "dubitable" or "indubitable."

To provide the reader with an idea of what *indicia* were used for torture orders, it is worth taking a glimpse at Carpzov's catalog of this evidence. He first addressed *indicia* which by themselves were insufficient for ordering torture, but could be useful in combination with others to justify torture in the prosecution of all crimes. Indicia of this kind included a common belief (*fama*) in a community that the defendant committed the crime, his hostility toward the victim, his socializing with criminals, his flight from the jurisdiction, and certain lies, such as a false alibi, detected in his testimony.[11] Next on Carpzov's list were *indicia* sufficient in themselves for a torture order in all kinds of crime. They included, for instance, the testimony of a single unimpeachable eyewitness and the defendant's bragging that he committed the crime.[12] Enumerated thereafter were *indicia* relevant in prosecuting specific crimes. In murder prosecutions, for instance, an *indicium* was the fact that the defendant was seen at the crime scene at the time of commission with a weapon in hand, or with blood-soaked clothing.[13] In prosecutions for adultery, an *indicium* was that the defendant was discovered hiding at the home of a beautiful woman,[14] or that a man and a woman were seen having sexual intercourse ("*pudenda in pudendis posita*").[15] In larceny cases, the typical *indicium* was the

[10] As noted in Chapter 2, the distinction was convoluted – so much so that it confused even Menochio, the most famous expert on these floating signifiers. In Liber I of his treatise he described the difference between them in great detail, for example, only to declare in Liber IV that there is no difference between them. See Jacobus Menochius, *De Praesumptionibus, Coniecturis, Signis et Indiciis Commentaria Libri VI* (Geneva, 1670). Compare Menochio's Lib. I, qu. 89, no. 2, with his Lib. IV, praesumptio 89, no. 15

[11] See Carpzov, *Practica Nova Imperialis Saxonica Rerum Criminalium*, Pars III, qu. 120, nos. 17, 35, 60 and 71–76.

[12] *Ibid.*, qu. 21, nos. 10 and 41.

[13] *Ibid.*, qu. 122, no. 2.

[14] *Ibid.*, qu. 122, no. 70.

[15] *Ibid.*, qu. 122, no. 74. This particular "*indicium*" was actually direct evidence. Even great pre-modern jurists like Carpzov were not always able to distinguish direct from circumstantial evidence. See *supra*, Chapter 2, note 37.

The Law of Torture 73

discovery of stolen goods in the possession of a man of bad reputation.[16] It is important to note, however, that most of this evidence, and especially if it was sufficient by itself for torture, had to be proven by two eyewitnesses.

As a result of the abundance of rules on *indicia*, it superficially appears that little space was left to the judge for legally unconstrained reasoning about necessary evidence for torture. This would be a mistake, however. In the first place, consider the requirement of two eyewitnesses for the proof of important *indicia*. These eyewitnesses were supposed to be "above all exception," and, as the Chapter 4 has shown, this determination called for a subjective assessment of their credibility by the judge. Second, the investigation would often unearth both incriminating and exculpating *indicia*, and the resolution of clashing inferences from their existence eluded rigid regulation.[17] A further element of flexibility emanated from the requirement that in regard to the applicability of most *indicia* the judge should consider whether the defendant was capable of committing the crime with which he was charged.[18] This reservation was often inserted in the description of various *indicia*, meaning that they could be used only if additional corroborating information became available (*"si adminicula concurrant"*). Consider finally that the lists of *indicia* needed for torture were not exhaustive, so that judges in most jurisdictions were free to recognize new *indicia* that could easily conflict with legally articulated ones. Taking all this into account, it should not surprise us that Carpzov's list mostly consisted of guidelines alerting judges to factors to be considered in deciding whether to issue torture orders.[19]

The realization of late medieval and early modern jurists that establishing the sufficiency of evidence for torture, despite the multitude of rules on the subject, called for the exercise of personal judgment is reflected in their definitions of *indicia indubitata*. Baldus remarked, for example, that *indicia* become indubitable when they induced such "peace of mind in the fact-finder that he does not care to investigate any further."[20] In one of his expert opinions he expressed himself poetically on the subject by noting that features determining *indicia indubitata* are "posted in the heart of the judge."[21] Two centuries later, Farinacci was equally explicit in describing the subjective component of the decision to order torture. He voiced agreement with Paulus de Castro's definition that indications are indubitable when "they narrow the mind of the judge so that he completely believes and is

---

[16] *Ibid.*, qu. 122. no. 39.
[17] The drafters of Carolina acknowledged this fact in article 28.
[18] See, e.g., Carpzov, *Practica Nova Imperialis Saxonica Rerum Criminalium*, qu. 122, no. 51, 53, 67, 81, and qu. 121, no. 35.
[19] See Carpzov, *ibid..*, qu. 120, nos. 2–5, and qu. 123, nos. 27–35.
[20] *"Indicium indubitatum est demonstratio rei per signa differentia, per quae animus in aliquot tanquam existante quiescit et plus investigare non curat."* Quoted approvingly by Menochius, *De Praesumptionibus, Coniecturis, Signis et Indiciis Commentaria Libri VI*, Liber I, qu. 7, no. 15.
[21] *"Stat in pectore iudicis an indicia sint sufficientia ad torturam."* See Baldus, *Consilia*, Liber Quartum, consilium 515, no. 6, p. 138 (Venice, 1658).

74 The Probative Impact of Confessions

incapable of leaning toward a contrary decision."[22] Definitions of this kind suggest that torture orders in the inquisitorial process were supposed to rest on the judge's belief that the defendant was guilty. Evidence required for torture orders thus came close to evidence justifying contemporary judges to convict.

Old legal sources tended to express the judge's freedom from binding rules in determining the sufficiency of evidence for torture by saying that it was a matter of judicial discretion (*arbitrium*).[23] But even in this context discretion was not understood as a license to reach a decision on grounds shrouded in the mist of impenetrable personal reasons. As we have repeatedly noted, discretion exercised without outwardly discernible reasons was contrary to the values of the Roman-canon judicial apparatus, which insisted on the supervision of decisions made on lower echelons of authority. One advocate of limited discretion in this area was no less a luminary than Bartolus. He cautioned against hastily using personal judgment in finding sufficient evidence for torture, despite his strongly subjective understanding of the mental processes involved in assessing evidence. In adopting this cautious stance he may have been motivated by a painful personal experience. As a young assistant to the Italian city magistrate, the Podestà, he ordered the torture of a person who died while being tormented, whereupon the angry reaction of townspeople forced him to jump from a window to save his life. The defenestration resulted in a life-long disfiguring head injury, providing a constant reminder of the dangers involved in rash resorts to torture.[24]

The Case of Amorous Rivalry

To illustrate how the issue of sufficient evidence for torture was argued, a sixteenth-century Italian murder case merits a digression.[25] The facts of the case seem to have been lifted from the pages of Stendhal's *Chroniques italiennes*. A knight and a youthful count, both residing in Florence, vied for the favors of Isabella, a noblewoman inclined to multiple amatory associations. One night an armed brawl occurred between these two men and their followers in front of her house. The brawl resulted in the count's death, and the knight was charged with murder. Two versions of what transpired were constructed on the basis of circumstantial evidence gathered in the investigation. The incriminating version was that the knight had known that the count would pass by Isabella's house on the critical night and stationed himself there, waiting to kill his youthful rival. The exculpating

---

[22] "*Indicium indubitatum illud est quod arctat mentem iudicis, ita ut ominino credit, nec posit in cotrarium inclinare.*" See Farinacci, *Praxis et Theoreticae Criminalis, Pars I, Tomus I*, qu. 36, no. 36.

[23] A thirteenth-century example is Gandinus. "*Sed quaero,*" he asked, "*que et qualia debeant esse ista indicia, que debent procedere, ut quis possit torqueri*"? He replied: "*non possunt certo modo dici vel ostendi, nec de eis poterit dari certa doctrina, sed hoc committitur arbitrio iudicantis.*" See Albertus Gandinus, *Tractatus de Maleficiis, Rubrica: De Questionibus*, no. 14, p. 159, in Hermann Kantorowicz, *Albertus Gandinus und das Strafrecht der Scholastik*, Band II (Berlin: J. Guttentag, 1926).

[24] See Susanne Lepsius, *Von Zweifeln zur Überzeugung*, 13 (Frankfurt: Vittorio Klostermann, 2003).

[25] The case appears in Farinacci, *Responsorum Criminalium, Liber Secundus*, consilium 193. References to the text of the case will be given solely to its numbers. The actual disposition of the case is unknown.

The Law of Torture

version was that the knight went to Isabella's home *"amoris causa"* (for reasons of love) rather than *"animo occidendi"* (with intent to kill). But while he waited in front of her house to be let in for a night of love, the count unexpectedly showed up, lifted his lantern to the knight's face, and, having recognized his rival, precipitated the melee in which he was killed.

At the close of the *inquisitio specialis* the issue arose whether enough evidence had been assembled to subject the knight to torture in order to obtain his confession that he killed the count with premeditation.[26] The precursor of the modern public prosecutor, the *Fiscus*, argued that the killing was planned, and that the assembled evidence was strong enough to justify the torture order. On his telling, the amorous rivalry between the defendant and the victim constituted a powerful *indicium* of premeditated murder. Consulted in the case, Farinacci objected, claiming that the rivalry was not proven. What was established by reliable witnesses, he urged, was only that the knight loved Isabella. Proof of amorous rivalry required additional evidence that the count also loved Isabella and she him, and that their love was known to the defendant and troubled him.[27] The count did not really love Isabella, Farinacci added, since he was at the time seeing another woman. The *Fiscus* retorted by referring to what Boccaccio called the "stirrings of the flesh" (*gli stimuli della carne*). "We often see young men," he argued, "loving one woman but enjoying another, even two others."[28]

In an attempt to disprove the existence of knight's premeditation from another angle, Farinacci brought up the fact that the knight did not make preparations to flee Florence. This fact, he claimed, constituted a presumption (*praesumptio*) against premeditation. Since premeditation was an aggravating circumstance transforming the killing into an atrocious capital crime, the knight would, if guilty, have had good reason to abscond from the city. While fleeing from a jurisdiction was a recognized *indicium* of guilt, Farinacci concluded, remaining within the jurisdiction was a *praesumptio* against the finding of guilt. The *Fiscus* did not challenge the existence of this presumption, but claimed that it was invalidated, since the Florence city gates were closed for the night. Preparing horses to flee, he observed, would in this situation have done more harm than good to the knight.[29] The fact that on the night in question the knight armed himself with a pistol and stiletto was, in the *Fiscus'* opinion, another *indicium* of premeditated homicide. Reclassifying this fact

---

[26] As pointed out in Chapter 3, Roman-canon jurists provided an exception to the rule that facts constituting crime cannot be proven circumstantially, and allowed that intent, premeditation and belief can be proven by the manner in which a crime has been committed, or by other "manifest *indicia*." But since the precise character of these *indicia* remained entangled in controversy, the only safe way to establish the mental component of crimes was to have the defendant reveal in a confession what he believed or intended. The doubt that any cognitive gain was obtained in this way was expressed in Chapter 2.

[27] No. 9.

[28] No. 82. "*Saepius videmus quod isti iuvenes unam puellam amant, alia fruantur, et quod quandoque etiam utraque.*"

[29] Nos. 20 and 92.

76 *The Probative Impact of Confessions*

as a presumption, Farinacci claimed that the presumption was invalidated by the "conjecture" that the knight armed himself for defensive rather than offensive purposes.[30] A tryst in the middle of the night involving a married woman at her home, he submitted, was a potentially dangerous activity, and no sinister inferences should be drawn from arming oneself.[31] In response, the *Fiscus* invoked a litany of scholarly authority for the proposition that the killing committed at night raised a presumption in favor of premeditated killing. Farinacci responded by citing authority for the specific proposition that the presumption was inapplicable to a nocturnal killing if it was committed in a brawl, as happened in the case in question.[32] The *Fiscus* then pointed out that the knight first denied and then admitted having an intimate relationship with Isabella. Lies, he correctly remarked, were an *indicium* in support of ordering torture. But Farinacci denied the applicability of this *indicium* in the case in question, invoking the "conjecture" that the knight lied in order to protect the reputation of the woman he loved, rather than to falsely deny the motive for murder.

Put yourself now in the position of the judge called to decide the issue of sufficient evidence for torture after all these references to *indicia, praesumptiones* and *coniecturae*. It seems clear that their invocation did not produce a legal straitjacket for the judge's decision, and that he remained free to decide the contested issue by relying on logic and common sense. What the two jurists presented to him were, in fact, logical and experiential arguments, not much different from those present-day lawyers would use in the courtroom, albeit without classifying them in terms of quaint rhetorical concepts. All of which is not to deny that these concepts could have been used as *post hoc* means to dress in legal garb decisions made on independent grounds, and to create the impression that the sufficiency of evidence for torture was a rule-driven exercise.

Rules on the Application of Torture

Although the method of applying torture was left to judicial discretion, some basic features of the method were widely shared.[33] First, the defendant had to be threatened with torture – often by the display of how its instruments worked – in the hope of obtaining a confession without actual infliction of pain. If this so-called *territio* failed, the painful interrogation would begin. Since the architects of the system were aware that innocent persons might incriminate themselves for the sake of putting an

---

[30] No. 60. It is true that Farinacci emphasized the vulnerability of *indicia* and presumptions to conjectures only in regard to the proof of premeditation. "*Doctores per me elegati,*" he wrote, "*dicunt quod ad excludendum praesumptionem praemeditationis sufficient et praevanent coniecture.*"

[31] Nos. 14, 36, 52.

[32] Nos. 60 and 71.

[33] See Carpzov, *Practica Nova Imperialis Saxonica Rerum Criminalium*, Pars III, qu. 117, n. 9. A rare example of legislation containing specific instructions on ways to apply torture was the eighteenth-century criminal law codification of Empress Maria Theresa.

The Law of Torture   77

end to torments, extorted confessions were supposed to be detailed, including facts whose accuracy could be checked. The details required for valid confessions could be quite considerable. In another sixteenth-century criminal case, this one involving an archdeacon prosecuted for sexual crimes, he confessed on torture to having had sexual intercourse with 40 women. The confession was invalid, Farinacci argued, since the defendant failed to indicate the place and time of the admitted sexual encounters, as well as the names of the women involved.[34] Suggestive questions asked under torture were absolutely prohibited in order to prevent false specificity of extorted confessions. While this prohibition was indeed indispensable as a safeguard against false confessions, it underscores the inhumane disregard of the plight of innocent defendants subjected to torments.[35] If defendants withstood painful inter-rogation without confessing, the judge was permitted to order the repetition of torture, but only if new incriminating *indicia* became available.[36] The reason given for this demand was the opinion that withstanding torture "purged" evidence used in ordering it. The repetition was permitted for most crimes only once, but for some especially serious ones (*crimina infanda*), twice or even more. If defendants still refused to confess, they had to be acquitted.[37] Legal doctrine attributed major importance to what was considered another safeguard against false confessions – the so-called ratification of compelled confessions. It consisted of the repetition of extorted statements a few days after the end of torture, when the pain caused by the torments ceased or subsided. The rationale given for this prerequisite was said to be establishing the voluntariness of any self-incriminating statements that were obtained. We now recognize, of course, that the repetition was an illusory guarantee of voluntariness, especially if defendants knew – as was often the case– that their refusal to confirm the confession could lead to the repetition of torments.[38] If they refused to confirm not only the first but also the second extorted confession, they were still not acquitted, but sentenced to a milder punishment that did not entail the spilling of blood.[39]

[34] See Prospero Farinacci, *Consilia sive Responsa atque Decisiones Causarum Criminalium*, Editio Postrema, consilium 156, no. 15 (Lyon, 1610).

[35] It is easy to imagine them imploring the torturer to suggest what he wanted to hear from them, just so the infliction of pain would cease.

[36] In a treatise that was used for almost two centuries in Hungarian legal education, the author warned judges that they should be on guard against ordering repetition of torture without new evidence "as one should be on guard against fire" (*torture repetitionis iudices omnes cavere debent sicut ab igno*). See Joannes Kitonicz, *Processus Consuetudinarii Incliti Regni Hungariae*, Editio Prima, Caput VI, qu. 8, p. 244 (Trnava: fredericus Galli, 1724). See also, Carpzov, *Practica Nova Imperialis Saxonica Rerum Criminalium*, Pars III, qu. 125, no. 31.

[37] See e.g., Carpzov, *Practica Nova Imperialis Saxonica Rerum Criminalium*, Pars III, qu. 125, nos. 3, 5, 6, 9–15.

[38] It deserves to be noted that some medieval theologians and philosophers, including Roger Bacon, maintained that free will cannot be broken by the infliction of pain. Cf. Johannes Fried, Wille, Freiwilligkeit, Geständnis um 1300, *Historisches Jahrbuch*, vol. 105, 388, 420–424 (1985).

[39] In contrast to a defendant who *never* confessed and had to be acquitted because torture withstood purged incriminating evidence, a defendant who *confessed* but later refused to ratify the confession

78   *The Probative Impact of Confessions*

An epistemically meaningful safeguard was the requirement that extorted statements should match available evidence.[40] If "verisimilar and probable *indicia*" were discovered suggesting the contrary of statements extracted from the defendant, the confession was invalid and could not support a conviction.[41] Whether a ratified confession could be challenged after a judgment of conviction was handed down, but before it was executed, was the subject of controversy.[42] Much debated was the sixteenth-century *cause célèbre* – the prosecution of Bernardo, the younger brother of the legendary Italian noblewoman Beatrice Cenci. Along with Beatrice, Bernardo was charged with successfully plotting to kill their tyrannical father. Since parricide was an "unspeakable crime," Bernardo's nobleman's status did not save him from painful interrogation. Severely tormented, he confessed to the crime and ratified the confession. After his death sentence was pronounced, Farinacci collected impressive doctrinal authority for the proposition that ratification of a confession obtained in violation of torture law does not cure the violation and is still invalid.[43] For the purposes of this book the most interesting requirement was that judges were not supposed to credit ratified confessions if they found them unbelievable. "A confession extorted by torture," wrote Carpzov, echoing the widely held opinion of legal doctrine, "should not be believed unless it corresponds to the truth and is probable."[44] But the belief motivating the refusal to accept the coerced confession had to be based on ascertainable grounds.

The reader will wonder whether the need to verify coerced confessions, clearly established in legal doctrine, was observed in the brutal and messy reality of practice. Given the repressive atmosphere of the inquisitorial criminal process, it is easy to suspect that most procedural safeguards proclaimed by legal doctrine – including those relating to the verification of coerced confessions – were mere rhetorical commitments without practical significance.[45] Although far from enough is

---

could not claim that incriminating evidence against him was ever "purged." See Carpzov, *Practica Nova Imperialis Saxonica Rerum Criminalium*, Pars III, qu. 126, no. 58.

[40]   See, e.g., Frölich, *Nemesis Romano, Austriaco, Tyrolensis*, Buch III, Titul 24, no. 7, p. 227.

[41]   See Baldus, *In Codicem Libri IV*, fol. 40ra, comment to C 4. 19, 25, n. 2 (Venice, 1519). See also Carpzov, *Practica Nova Imperialis Saxonica Rerum Criminalium*, Pars III, qu. 126, no. 12.

[42]   Disagreeing with Carpzov, Frölich favored a delay in the execution of judgments based on ratified confessions, so that the possibility of their additional challenge was not precluded. See Frölich, *Nemesis Romano, Austriaco, Tyrolensis*, Buch IV, titul 3, no. 4, pp. 240–241.

[43]   "*Non obstat quod confessio Bernardi sit geminata et ratificata.*" See Farinacci, *Responsorum Criminalium*, consilium 185, no. 30. The court disagreed, and both Bernardo and Beatrice were executed.

[44]   "*Confessioni quaestione extorta fides aliter habenda non est quam si ea veritate conveniat atque probabilis sit.*" See Carpzov, *Practica Nova Imperialis Saxonica Rerum Criminalium*, Pars III, qu. 126, and qu. 120, no. 13. This position prevailed not only in the Italian strand of Roman-canon law, but also in its French variant. See, e.g., Jean Imbert, *La Pratique Judicaire et Criminelle. Receue et Obseruee par tout le Royaume de France*, III, 14, at 656 (Paris, 1627).

[45]   John Langbein referred to Carolina and a seventeenth-century author for the proposition that the corroboration of extorted confessions was not required. See John Langbein, *Torture and the Law of Proof*, 15 (Chicago: University of Chicago Press, 1975). Recently, this opinion has been persuasively

Conclusion

known about the actual treatment of coerced confessions, the blanket denial that they were verified is unjustified. The actual operation of the inquisitorial process was not always and everywhere so thoroughly callous as to be indifferent to the possibility of imposing capital and mutilating punishments on innocent people from whom false confessions were wrung by torture. Attitudes prevalent in special courts set up by the popes to eradicate heresy,[46] and in secular courts when processing crimes we would nowadays classify as political, should not be projected into the area of ordinary criminality as then conceived. Available evidence suggests that violations of the law of torture were taken seriously at least in some continental lands, and that they were sometimes also sanctioned by syndicalist tribunals set up to assess the professional responsibility of judges.[47] This is not to say that the invidious social discriminations noted in Chapter 2 in regard to the sufficiency of evidence for torture may not also have existed in regard to the verification of confessions obtained by it. Perfunctory in the prosecution of defendants of low social standing and ill repute, verification must have been more scrupulous in the prosecution of persons who did not belong to the *hoi polloi*.

CONCLUSION

A backward look at what has been said in this chapter about the legal regulation of torture in the inquisitorial procedure reveals that the defendant's confession was not unreflectively credited, and especially that the law did not obligate the judge to accept coerced confessions if he found them unreliable. The mistaken impression of mechanical crediting may have been caused by the mantra-like pronouncement of jurists that "conviction is the necessary sequel of confession."[48] To show that the sequel did not ensue mechanically, we first considered the situation of the investigating judge ordering torture. We observed that legal doctrine required him to assemble "indubitable indications" of guilt – that is, evidence leading him to believe that the defendant was guilty. If the defendant then confessed under torture, his self-incriminating statements confirmed the judge's belief. Phrased differently, the

---

questioned by a noted legal historian. See Kenneth Pennington, Torture and fear, 19 *Rivista Internazionale di Diritto Commune*, 203, 227–229 (2008).

[46] Proceedings before these special papal courts, whose rules deviated from rules of ordinary criminal courts, are often taken as representative of the inquisitorial process generally. On proceedings before these courts of Holy Inquisition, see Paul Hinschius, *System des katholischen Kirchenrechts*, vol. 5, 427 st seq. (Berlin: J. Guttentag, 1893).

[47] For a detailed discussion of the issue of judicial responsibility for disregarding torture law, see Farinacci, *Responsorum Criminalium*, Pars I, Tomus II, tit. V, nos. 112–123. In some German political units, intentional transgressors of the law of torture were threatened with serious punishment, including the death penalty. Carpzov devoted a whole subsection of his treatise to the problem. The subsection includes a reference to an opinion of a high court of Saxony dealing with the violation of torture law by a judge. See Carpzov, *Practica Nova Imperialis Saxonica Rerum Criminalium*, Pars III, qu. 127, no. 18.

[48] *"Confessionem necessario sequitur condemnatio."*

80 The Probative Impact of Confessions

confession incorporated the judge's belief in the defendant's guilt. Next we considered the attitude of judges who decided on the propriety of torture orders by leafing through and studying the case file recording the investigative activities performed by the investigating judge. Although the reviewing judges had less leeway to evaluate evidence, they were still not supposed to credit a coerced confession if they found the evidence on which it was ordered insufficient, or believed for some other reason that it was not true. As in regard to the two-eyewitnesses rule, so in regard to the defendant's courtroom confession, the conclusion is warranted that this second prerequisite for the use of blood punishment was not supposed to be credited unless the court found it reliable. Maintaining the contrary may have been useful to Enlightenment luminaries as a hand on the spade digging a grave for the inquisitorial process and preparing the soil for the adoption of jury trial, which, as we will see, was thought incompatible with legal proof rules. As a matter of accurate historical record, however, their opinion is unsustainable.

6

The Negative Effect of Legal Proof

The preceding chapters examined whether Roman-canon law exercised the positive effect by obligating the judge to impose blood punishment on the testimony of two eyewitnesses, or the defendant's confession, irrespective of his personal assessment of the probative value of evidence. It turned out that this obligation did not exist. Our inquiry switches now to the question of whether legal proof produced the *negative* effect. What was the judge supposed to do if he failed to find two proper eyewitnesses or secure a courtroom confession, while other evidence in the case persuaded him that the defendant had committed the crime? Did Roman-canon evidence law compel him to abstain from imposing sanguinary punishments? Legally insufficient evidence could have been quite compelling. To reuse the jurists' hypothetical, imagine that a reliable eyewitness testified that he saw the defendant decapitate the victim with a sword, and that another witness saw the defendant at the critical time running near the victim's home with a bloody sword. Since the second witness was not an eyewitness to the crime, the evidentiary standard for blood punishment was not satisfied, although the assembled evidence convinced the judge of the defendant's guilt. If the law now prevented him from imposing blood punishment, a discord would arise between the legally required outcome and the outcome deemed by the judge to be correct. Did the possibility of this discord induce the architects of the inquisitorial fact-finding scheme to make the proof standard malleable even in its negative aspects, and enable the judge to pass what he believed was the correct sentence?

THE MAINSTREAM DOCTRINE

Most jurists held that the strict evidentiary standard should be adhered to despite the discord. The ban on imposing blood punishment on the testimony of a single eyewitness was declared by them to be as firm as marble (*regula marmorea*), applicable even if the single eyewitness was a person of the highest stature and authority. Nor could blood punishment be imposed on circumstantial evidence,

82   The Negative Effect of Legal Proof

no matter how persuasive.[1] Where death or mutilation is at stake, they insisted, proof of guilt should be "clearer than the midday sun," and this illumination can be provided only by direct evidence. In addition to some biblical sources and Roman law passages, support for this position emanated from the now-familiar anxiety about the safety of the judge's soul. If he were permitted to impose irreparable blood punishment on the basis of mistaken inferences from circumstantial evidence, his pilgrimage to heaven could be compromised. But if he based the blood sanction on the testimony of eyewitnesses and their evidence was false, the responsibility for the execution or mutilation of innocent persons would shift from him onto them.

The demand of mainstream Roman-canon doctrine that the exacting proof standard ought to be observed sparked serious tensions with the repressive urges of the inquisitorial process. Remember its motto that no crime should remain unpunished, and the belief of premodern criminal law enforcers that only blood punishments are appropriate responses to serious crime.[2] To be sure, the demand that judges *abstain* from imposing blood punishment although convinced of a defendant's guilt was easier to accept than the demand would have been that they *impose* blood punishment on a person they considered innocent. Even so, tensions generated by the tug-of-war between the exacting evidentiary standard and pragmatic needs of law enforcement induced followers of the mainstream doctrine to vacillate in support of the negative effects of legal proof and weaken them by exceptions. A telling example of these vacillations can be found in Farinacci's work. In his treatise on crime he started off by proclaiming the principle that blood punishment cannot be imposed on circumstantial evidence, but later qualified what he had said by stating that this punishment can also be imposed on the testimony of a single reliable eyewitness, provided that it is supported by *indicia indubitata* capable of placing the facts to be found "so manifestly before the eyes of the judge that he cannot believe otherwise."[3] In one of his *consilia* Farinacci conceded that mere circumstantial

---

[1] An early and widely influential expositor of this view was Gandinus. See Albertus Gandinus, Tractatus de Maleficiis, Rubrica: De presumptionibus et indiciis indubitatis ex quibus condemnatio potest sequi in Hermann Kantorowicz, *Albertus Gandinus und das Strafrecht der Scholastik*, 93–94 (Berlin: J. Guttentag, 1926). His position on the subject continued to be invoked in continental jurisdictions well into early modern times. A sixteenth-century compilation of mainly Italian authorities for the mainstream position can be found in Hippolytus de Marsilii, *Rerum Criminalium Praxes et Tractatus Omnium Nobiliorum*, Cap. Quoniam, n. 33, 424 (Frankfurt, 1587). An influential French adherent of the mainstream view was Imbert. See Jean Imbert, *La pratique judiciaire, tant civile que criminelle, receue et obseruee par tout le Royaume de France*, lib. III, cap. XIV (Paris, 1627). Proponents of the mainstream view were especially numerous in German lands, where the sixteenth-century Constitutio Criminalis Carolina codified the Roman-canon full proof standard.

[2] See supra, Chapter 1, note 37, and Chapter 3, text above note 1.

[3] "... *quando indicia indubitata essent talia, ut manifeste ante oculos iudicis factum ponerent, ita ut idem iudex aliter credere non posset*," Prospero Farinacci, *Praxis et Theoreticae Criminalis*, Pars III, qu. 86, no. 114 (Lyon, 1634). For a similar opinion in eighteenth-century France, see Daniel Jousse, *Traité de la Justice Criminelle de France*, Tome 1, partie III, Livre I, titre III, no. 140, p. 712 (Paris, 1771).

The Mainstream Doctrine

evidence, without any direct proof, could justify the imposition of corporal punishment.[4] Wavering of this kind made the mainstream doctrine convoluted and occasionally even incoherent.

Crimes Difficult to Prove

Capable of greatly weakening the negative effect of legal proof was the idea that its demands can be ignored in prosecuting crimes that are committed secretly and are difficult to prove.[5] Various lists were compiled of crimes falling into this category: adultery, larceny, and incest are typical examples. But in addition to specific offences, departures from Roman-canon full proof were also permitted in some situations in which unspecified crimes were committed. Any crimes committed at night (*crimina nocturna*), and any crimes perpetrated collectively, were the most frequently mentioned examples.[6] Because the enumeration of crimes and situations justifying exemptions from the full proof standard was not exhaustive, the question arose what else could make crimes difficult to prove. The open-ended dispensation from full proof could deprive it of operational significance, since it could be abandoned whenever its implementation encountered practical difficulties. Aware of the problem, jurists adopted various avoidance strategies. Carpzov's solution was, for example, that full proof can be abandoned only in regard to crimes that are typically hard to prove, rather than in regard to crimes whose processing presents proof difficulty only in special circumstances that can arise in particular cases.[7]

Crimes of Exceptional Gravity

As the history of criminal justice attests, nothing is more effective in undermining procedural arrangements that complicate the realization of punitive urges than the belief that some crimes present especially grave dangers to the established order. It is therefore scarcely surprising that the view emerged in the formative years of the inquisitorial process that its rules could be disregarded in prosecuting the most heinous offenses (*crimina atrocissima, excepta* or *infanda*). Baldus was an early expositor of this view. "Because of the enormity of crime," he wrote, "what cannot

---

4   "On *indicia indubitata* the defendant can be condemned, if not to capital punishment," he opined, "then at least to extraordinary punishment, even if corporeal" (*Ex indiciis indubitatis potest reus condemnari, si no in poenam mortis, saltem in extraordinariam mitiorem etiam corporalem*). See Prospero Farinacci, *Responsorum Criminalium Liber Secundus*, consilium 108, no. 97, p. 37 (Rome, 1615). See also Jousse, *Traité de la Justice Criminelle de France*, ibid.

5   The standard Latin articulation of this exception was "*delicta occulta et difficile probationis, quando veritas aliter haberi non potest.*" Sometimes added to this exception were crimes whose traces were evanescent ("*delicta facti transeuntis*").

6   See Farinacci, *Praxis et Theoreticae Criminalis*, Pars III, qu. 86, nos. 35–36; Carpzov, *Practica Nova Imperialis Saxonica Rerum Criminalium*, Pars I, qu. 114, no. 35, and Pars III, qu. 108, no. 36 (Wittenberg, 1652).

7   Carpzov, *Practica Nova Imperialis Saxonica Rerum Criminalium*, Pars I, qu. 115, no. 37.

84 *The Negative Effect of Legal Proof*

be allowed must be conceded, and the law may be transgressed."[8] Although this view was widely shared by mainstream doctrine, the question remained unsettled what crimes were of exceptional gravity. Agreement existed only that the crime of offending divine majesty (*crimen laesae maiestatis divinae*) and the crime of offending human majesty (*crimen laesae maiestatis humanae*) belonged in this group.[9] Beyond the inclusion of these two crimes in the category of *crimina atrocissima*, only the general formula seems to have gained currency that crimes punishable by aggravated death penalty should be regarded as "most atrocious."[10]

Also remaining unsettled was the question of what rules could be set aside in processing crimes of exceptional gravity. Was the exacting evidentiary standard for imposing blood punishment among them? While there was considerable support for the position that the testimony of some technically disqualified eyewitnesses could be used to satisfy the full proof standard for *crimina atrocissima*, the standard itself was seldom questioned.[11] Nor was the issue settled whether disregard of evidence law was permitted to all judges, or only to highly placed ones. The prevailing opinion was that only "major magistrates" were authorized to disregard evidence law.[12] The tendency to bind only "minor magistrates" by proof sufficiency rules reflected the strength of hierarchical concerns in the Roman-canon apparatus of justice, and their power to override worries about the dangers to the souls of judges who imposed blood punishment without legal constraints. Judges who occupied higher echelons of authority were allowed to impose capital and mutilating punishments without the need for the protective cover of rules, while the ultimate secular authority – the prince – was believed by many to possess the power to impose punishment in the absence of any rule.[13]

---

[8] "*Propter enormitatem delicti non concedenda conceduntur et licitum est leges transgredi.*" See Baldus de Ubaldis, *In Codicem Libri IV*, ad C. 1, 19, 1, n. 1, fol. 68rb (Venice, 1519). In support of this rule Baldus mentioned a statement of Pope Innocent IV (1243–1254), from whom the license to disregard the law may have emanated.

[9] They were also considered to be the most serious form of criminality. "*Crimen laesae Maiestatis,*" wrote Carpzov, "*omnium delictorum gravissimum est.*" See Carpzov, *Practica Nova Imperialis Saxonica Rerum Criminalium*, Pars I, qu. 41, n. 1. The crime of offending divine majesty included witchcraft and heresy, while the crime of offending human majesty focused on treason. For an analysis of these two offenses, see Josse de Damhouder, *Praxis Rerum Criminalium, Opus Absolutissimum*, Cap. 61, pp. 109–142, and Cap. 62, pp. 143–145 (Antwerp, 1601).

[10] Relying on Italian legal authority, Carpzov included sodomy, arson, and forgery in his list of "the most atrocious" offenses, but noted that the list was not exhaustive. See Carpzov, *Practica Nova Imperialis Saxonica Rerum Criminalium*, Pars III, qu. 102, nos. 62 and 65.

[11] Carpzov maintained that the need for full proof could be dispensed with only in witchcraft cases. See *Practica Nova Imperialis Saxonica Rerum Criminalium*, Pars III, qu. 102, no. 60. Consider, however, that the defensive part of special investigation could be omitted in treason cases, and that even members of the high nobility were not exempted from torture.

[12] See Baldus, as quoted in Norbert Horn, *Aequitas in den Lehren des Baldus*, 42 (Cologne: Böhlau Verlag, 1968).

[13] Damhouder wrote, for example, that the prince can adjudicate according to his "true and just conscience," and that only his inferiors were bound by allegations and proof ("*Princeps potest iudicare secundum veram et iustam conscientiam suam, licet alii inferiores secundum allegata et probata*"). See

The Mainstream Doctrine 85

A well-known opponent of these departures from regular procedural order in prosecuting the most serious crimes was the sixteenth-century jurist Hippolytus Marsilius. He argued that the extreme gravity of a crime should have no place in guilt determination and could play a role only in sentencing.[14] In the next century, the German jurist Justus Oldekop attacked these departures in terms foreshadowing our present doctrinal views. "What can be more alien to pity and more distant from reason and common sense," he asked, "than to insist on the observance of law and legal order in prosecuting minor crimes and permit their violation in the most atrocious ones?"[15] Despite such isolated voices opposed to the idea that law may be disregarded in the prosecution of the most serious offenses, the idea survived until the sun began to set on the *ancien régime*. Then the contrary view gained momentum that the more serious the crime and the harsher the threatened punishment, the more demanding proof sufficiency rules ought to be.

Summation

Contrary to the widespread opinion on the mechanical nature of Roman-canon evidence, the full proof standard was not inflexible even in regard to its negative aspects. Even under mainstream Roman-canon doctrine, two eyewitnesses were not always required for the imposition of sanguinary punishments. *Testis unus* was not always *testis nullus*. This being said, it would be mistaken to conclude that mainstream Roman-canon doctrine treated the full proof standard as equally flexible in its negative as in its positive sense. In some situations negative legal proof was considered to be firm enough to prevent judges from imposing blood punishment on a defendant although they were convinced that he was guilty. Suppose that a crime processed was not atrocious, or that the doctrine of *crimina atrocissima* was not recognized in a particular jurisdiction. Suppose further that the crime did not fall into the category of offenses difficult to prove. In this situation, and in the absence of two eyewitnesses or the defendant's courtroom confession, judges had no choice but to abstain from imposing blood punishment on a defendant, even if other evidence in the case fully convinced them that he had committed a serious crime. Legally mandated and substantively accurate decisions could part company.

Damhouder, *Praxis Rerum Criminalium, Opus Absolutissimum*, Capit 82, no. 84, p. 221. See also Kenneth Pennington, *The Prince and the Law, 1200–1600*, 93, passim (Oakland: University of California Press, 1993). As we will see in examining the treatment of illegally obtained evidence, however, some support existed for the position that proof sufficiency rules for torture and blood punishments sprang from sources superior to all terrestrial powers, and could not be transgressed even by the highest ecclesiastical and secular authorities.

[14] For details, see Giorgia Alessi Palazzolo, *Prova Legale e Pena*, 76–77 (Naples: G. Jovene, 1979).

[15] " ... *quod enim magis a pietate, quid a ratione et sensu communi magis absonum, quam dicere, in criminibus levibus jura et juris ordine observari oportere, sed in atrocioribus et gravioribus delictis, jura et juris ordinem violare licere?*" Justus Oldekop, *Tractatus Duo, Contra Dn. Benedictum Carpovium*, Dec. II, qu. VII, no. 3 (Bremen, 1664).

86 The Negative Effect of Legal Proof

THE MINORITY DOCTRINE

In spite of concessions made by mainstream doctrine to the needs of effective law enforcement, a minority view emerged as early as the thirteenth century, holding that blood punishment could be imposed on highly persuasive evidence even if two eyewitnesses and the defendant's confession were not available. The earliest promotors of this doctrine offered only a few examples of such compelling evidence.[16] For the proof of murder, for instance, their favorite exhibit was the hypothetical about the defendant seen running from the victim's house with a bloody sword. Such isolated instances of departures from Roman-canon full proof were easier to accept and promote than a general theory applicable to all convincing evidence short of full proof. Isolated instances could be presented as minor additions to exceptions recognized by mainstream doctrine rather than as a competitor to its tenets.

Even so, theories of general applicability were soon propounded, maintaining that blood punishment could be administered on *indicia indubitata*, violent presumptions, or differently designated evidence less demanding than the normally required proof sufficiency standard. A widely influential expositor of this minority view was Baldus.[17] What he wrote on the subject led some historians to believe that he vacillated and was inconsistent in regard to evidence required for sanguinary punishment.[18] The criticism is not justified. It is true that in one of his comments on the Digest a passage can be found saying that corporal punishment may not be imposed on mere "presumptions."[19] A closer look at the passage reveals, however, that it does not express what Baldus thought on the matter, but reports instead the opinion of Pope Innocent IV on a slightly different subject.[20] Baldus voiced his own opinion elsewhere. In a commentary to the Code he noted that a person can be convicted on the basis of *indicia indubitata* clearer than the midday sun.[21] And referring to an example of Nicolaus Mattarellis, he added that "the multitude and quality of *indicia*" can reveal the truth to the "mental eye" of the judge as clear light can reveal the

---

[16] One of them was Thomas de Piperatta. On this ingenious Italian lawyer, see Richard Fraher, Conviction According to Conscience: The Medieval Jurists' Debate Concerning Judicial Discretion and the Law of Proof, 7 *Law & History Review* 23, 35 (1989). Another one was Nicolaus Mattarellis, a source of influence on Baldus.

[17] The ranks of the doctrine's adherents included some other well-known jurists. The poster child for the doctrine was Niccolo de Tedesci. See Palazzolo, *Prova Legale e Pena*, 68. A well-known member was Menochio. See Jacobus Menochius, *De Praesumptionibus, Coniecturis, Signis et Indiciis Commentaria*, Tomus 1, ru. 97, no. 38 (Geneva, 1670). For additional exponents of the doctrine, see Farinacci, *Responsorum Criminalium Liber Secundus*, consilium 108, nos. 74, 78, 96, 97 and 99.

[18] See Isabella Rosoni, *Que singula non prosunt collecta iuvant*, 84–85 (Milan: Giuffrè, 1995).

[19] "*Judex ex praesumptionibus non debet moveri ad impositionem poenae corporalis.*" See Baldus de Ubaldis, *In Primam Digesti Veteris Partem Commentaria*, ad Dig. 4.2.23, fol. 218vb (Venice, 1586).

[20] The pope's opinion related to a point from Liber extra. See X 2.23.10, Capitulum X, 1.5.

[21] See Baldus de Ubaldis. *In Quartum et Quintum Cod. Lib. Commentaria*, ad C. 4.19, 25, Lex 25, *Sciant cuncti* 1, fol. 45rb (Venice, 1599).

truth to his corporal eyes.[22] But his position emerges with greatest clarity from the observation made in another context that "many *indicia* can produce full proof sufficient even for capital punishment."[23] It is true that he was circumspect in advocating departures from the requirement for two eyewitnesses or a confession. The circumspection is visible in his opposition to the routine use of *indicia indubitata* for this purpose. If the judge has no other evidence than *indicia*, no matter how strong, he cautioned, it is safer to use them to order torture than to proceed to conviction.[24] Torture held the promise of obtaining a confession, and thereby also the normally required proof for blood punishment. His reluctance to impose capital punishment on less than the most demanding proof sufficiency standard is easily understood, given the then-existing epistemic, institutional and cultural concerns. Circumstantial evidence was considered categorically inferior to direct, while it was generally agreed that proof in criminal cases ought to be "clearer than the midday sun" (*luce meridiana clarior*). The reluctance stemmed also from the widespread recognition that determining the probative value of *indicia* calls for the exercise of personal judgment.[25] This implicated the judge in pronouncing sentences of lethal or blood punishments, and generated the familiar concerns for the safety of his soul. If his inferences from circumstantial evidence were mistaken, was he not building a mansion in hell for himself?

Doctrinally, the most serious challenge to adherents of the minority view was to determine what *indicia* sufficed for conviction. The distinction between *indicia* close to dispositive facts (*indicia proxima*) and *indicia* requiring several inferences to these facts (*indicia remota*) was their principal analytical tool to cope with the difficulty. Could a single very compelling *indicium proximum* suffice for conviction to blood punishment? As in many other contexts, they liked to discuss this particular issue against the background of sexual crimes that obviously titillated them. If a naked man is found in bed with a naked woman not his wife, could this *indicium* alone suffice for conviction of fornication or adultery?[26] But most frequently debated was the question whether adding *indicia dubitata* – that is, weak circumstantial

---

[22] Baldus, *ibid.*, Sciant cuncti, 4. ("*Item ponit Nic. de Mat. exemplum, ubicunque ex qualitate, et multitudine indiciorum indicatur veritas oculis mentis iudicis, sicut clara lux ostendit veritatem oculis corporis*".)

[23] "*Delictum ex pluribus concurrentibus augutur, et ex multis indicijs resultat plena probatio, et ad condemnationem capitalem, etiam contra impuberem.*" See Baldus, *In Primam et Secund. Infortiati Partem Commentaria, ad D. Lib. 29, Ad Sillanium, Lex XIII, fol.123* (Venice, 1586).

[24] "*Tutius tamen facit iudex qui non habet aliam probationem quam indicia, quamcumque sint, si extorqueat confessionem per torturam.*" See Baldus as quoted by Palazzolo, *Prova Legale e Pena*, 67, n. 65.

[25] As Clarus put it, "*secundum omnes in materia indiciorum non potest dari certa doctrina, sed totum relinquitur arbitrio boni viri, scilicet iudice.*" See, Julius Clarus, *Liber Quintus siue Practica Criminalis*, lib. 5, para. fin., qu. 20 (Venice, 1640).

[26] For a variation on this favorite hypothetical, see Menochio, *De Praesumptionibus, Coniecturis, Signis et Indiciis Commentaria*, Tomus Quintus, praesumptio 41, no. 11.

88   *The Negative Effect of Legal Proof*

evidence – could produce an *indicium indubitatum*, sufficient as support for a blood punishment sentence.[27] Could only *indicia* approved by law be used for this purpose, or could the judge also use indirect evidence he had himself identified in a case?[28] This problem exercised mainstream jurists too. For having conceded that blood punishment can in some situations be imposed on a lesser evidentiary standard, evidence comprising it became a concern for them as well. Orthodoxy and heterodoxy overlapped, and mainstream jurists were often induced to refer, be it approvingly or critically, to positions taken by followers of the minority doctrine.

The voluminous literature spawned by proponents of the minority doctrine on *indicia* required for administering blood punishments need not concern us here.[29] The only thing important to our inquiry is the degree to which rules recognized by minority doctrine affected the judge's fact-finding freedom. As the case of amorous rivalry recounted in Chapter 5 demonstrated, even prolific legal regulation of circumstantial evidence left the judge considerable wiggle room in assessing the value of evidence. Yet, some effective legal constraints on his freedom persisted. Practically most important was the requirement that some important *indicia* must be proven by two witnesses even if the judge was persuaded of the defendant's guilt in their absence.[30] Constraining his freedom were also sporadic rules prohibiting him from basing the verdict on specified *indicia* considered alone – even if proven by two eyewitnesses. Thus, for example, the verdict could not be based on the testimony of the crime victim alone, no matter how persuasive the testimony might have seemed to the judge in the context of a particular case. It is important to keep in mind that, even under the minority doctrine, a discrepancy could thus arise between outcomes legally mandated and outcomes believed by the judge to be correct.

COURT PRACTICE

Did *ancien régime* courts follow mainstream doctrine and refuse to impose sanguinary punishments on the basis of *indicia indubitata*? Primary sources and sporadic archival studies indicate that fidelity to mainstream doctrine varied. The highest legal proof standard seems to have been taken seriously in the courts of those German lands which followed the strict provisions on evidence law in the Carolina.[31] As late as the eighteenth century the full proof requirement was still

---

[27] A cautionary note is in order here. In reading the literature on this point it is often unclear whether what their authors said related to sufficient proof for sanguinary or milder corporal punishments.

[28] Baldus opined, for example, that the latter alternative is justified. See Baldus, *In Quartum et Quintum Cod. Lib. Commentaria*, Lex 25, 3, fol. 45rb ("... *non sunt talia indicia a lege approbata, sed sunt iudicis religio commissa*"). His opinion was later followed by Farinacci. See Farinacci, *Praxis et Theoreticae Criminalis*, consilium 108, no. 90.

[29] For a meticulous survey, see Isabella Rosoni, *Que singula non prosunt collecta iuvant*.

[30] Counted as such an important *indicium* was the extrajudicial confession of the defendant. Analytically, of course, it represented direct rather than circumstantial evidence.

[31] Not all German lands had to follow these provisions, although they were designed for the entire empire, because the codification contained an exemption clause ("*clausula salvatoria*"). Some

observed there, as demonstrated by the jeremiad of the German judge Leyser quoted in Chapter 3. Remember that he bemoaned his inability to impose capital punishment on *indicia*, even if they fully convinced him of a defendant's guilt. In his doctoral dissertation he illustrated his frustration with this state of the law on an actual case of robbery from a miller's home. Shortly after the robbery, the miller followed traces made by the wheels of the carriage which the robbers used to remove stolen goods, and found the carriage in front of the defendant's house. A quickly ordered search of the premises discovered some objects belonging to the miller. The defendant claimed that he bought them from a person he was unable to name, and he and his son contradicted themselves in explaining how some of these objects were acquired. On top of all this incriminating evidence came incriminating testimony of the defendant's accomplices. Yet, given the absence of full Roman-canon proof, the court could not find all this evidence sufficient for conviction, but only for ordering torture. And since the tormented defendant failed to confess, he had to be released, much to the judge's chagrin.[32]

In Italian political units, courts seem to have been much more receptive to the minority doctrine. Sixteenth-century sources reveal that in some of these courts judges regularly pronounced blood punishment for heresy, treason and the most heinous kinds of murder on *indicia indubitata*.[33] In regard to other serious crimes court practice was unsettled. In his sixteenth-century treatise Farinacci stated that Italian practice was still difficult to sum up, but that some courts imposed blood punishment in the absence of the testimony of two eyewitnesses or a courtroom confession.[34] The practice of French courts also seems to have varied. Jean Bodin claimed that French courts did not follow the prevailing Italian doctrine opposed to imposing blood punishment on mere "presumptions."[35] This implied that French courts were prepared to use even *poena ordinaria* on less than full proof. Yet, writing less than a century later, Jean Imbert remarked that French courts refused to administer capital and serious corporal punishment on *indicia* even when they were "indubitable."[36] Archival research has revealed, however, that at least one French

German political units took advantage of the exemption and permitted blood punishment sentences on indubitable indications.

[32] "*Quum, rei naturaliter per evidentissima indicia, non tamen per testes, convicti nequeant a iudice, esti de veritate criminis ab illis plenissime persuaso, ad mortem damnari.*" See Augustin Leyser, *De Maleficio Convicto sed non Confesso*, 10 (Wittenberg, 1742).

[33] For the courts of Milan, see Clarus, *Liber Quintus siue Practica Criminalis*, lib. 5, para. fin., qu. 20, no. 1. But he also informs us that legal doctrine was opposed to this practice ("*Praeterea etiam ex indiciis indubitatis in causa criminali condemnatio fieri non debet secundum communem opinionem*").

[34] "*Apud nos praxis etiam amplexa est an et quando praesumptiones seu indicia ad condemnationem sufficient.*" See Farinacci, *Praxis et Theoreticae Criminalis*, qu. 86, no. 58. Conflicting Italian court decisions on the subject are described by him in one of his *consilia*, conjuring well the tenor of arguments for and against the minority view. See Prospero Farinacci, *Responsorum Criminalium Liber Secundus*, consilium 108, no. 103 (Rome, 1615).

[35] See Jean Bodin, *De la demonomanie des sorciers*, 224 (Paris, 1567).

[36] See Jean Imbert, *La pratique judiciaire tant civile que criminelle de France, receue et obseruee par tout le royaume de France*, Lib. III, cap. XIV, p. 675 (Paris, 1627).

90 The Negative Effect of Legal Proof

jurisdiction did in fact impose blood punishment in the absence of two eyewitnesses and a confession.[37] In Spain, it was also not unprecedented that courts would impose blood punishment on less evidence than the highest standard of Roman-canon legal proof.[38]

CONCLUSION

The preceding pages revealed that the highest Roman-canon proof sufficiency standard could compel the judge to refrain from imposing blood punishment even when legally insufficient evidence convinced him of a defendant's criminal responsibility. Where the mainstream doctrine held sway, the objective demand for proof could make the judge's subjective assessment of evidence irrelevant, and tension could arise between what the law required and what the judge deemed correct in terms of criminal policy. Considering the widely proclaimed inquisitorial maxim that crimes should not remain unpunished, and considering also that blood punishment was thought to be the only proper sanction for serious crime, the tension could be quite serious. The urge quite naturally arose to lower evidentiary barriers which the exacting proof sufficiency standard raised to effective criminal law enforcement. Exceptions from the demands of full proof recognized by mainstream doctrine and the minority doctrinal view were steps in this direction. As just noted, however, even under the minority doctrine and court practice following it, legal proof could still create impediments to the use of blood punishment. In response to this problem, instruments were designed in the earliest history of the inquisitorial process to alleviate the frustrating effects caused by the negative aspects of legal proof. We will review them in due course.

The fact that two eyewitnesses or the defendant's confession were not always and everywhere required for the imposition of the coveted blood punishment leads to an implication that deserves to be underscored again before we move on. The rise of judicial torture in the inquisitorial process is commonly attributed to the difficulty of finding two unimpeachable eyewitnesses. But since this chapter has shown the widespread absence of the need for these witnesses, why was torture recognized even where the Roman-canon full proof could be disregarded? To comprehend why judges were reluctant to impose irreparable corporal punishment on less than full Roman-canon legal proof even where they were permitted to do so, one must conjure again the mental anguish of medieval and early modern judges who believed that their afterlives could be imperiled if their assessment of circumstantial evidence was mistaken and they caused the death or mutilation of an innocent person. Although not necessarily on supernatural grounds, some of this anguish persists in the sensibility of modern judges in criminal justice systems in which the

---

[37] See Bernard Durand, Arbitraire du Juge et Droit de la Torture: L'exemple du Conseil Souverain de Roussillon, *Recueuil de Mémoirs et Travaux*, Fasc. 10, 141, 179 (1979).

[38] See Paolo Marchetti, *Testis contra se*, 98 (Milano: Giuffrè, 1994).

Conclusion 91

death penalty has not been outlawed. Quite understandably, then, most premodern judges preferred to shift the responsibility for the bloody procedural result onto the defendant and order torture in the hope of obtaining his confession, rather than assume personal responsibility for the result by ruling that the assembled circumstantial evidence constituted the *indicium indubitatum* required for the imposition of blood punishment. Their desire to avoid religiously inspired anguish – *ardor animi* – is easily traceable to primary sources and is not put forward as a conjecture. Listen to Farinacci again. Having acknowledged that some learned jurists maintained that the judge could impose corporal punishment on circumstantial evidence, Farinacci warned that by doing so he could "damn his soul in perpetuity."[39]

---

[39] "*Verum tu iudex qui vides a doctoribus tibi tributum arbitrium condemnandi ex praesumptionibus adverte, ne istud arbitrium damnet animam tuam in perpetuum.*" Farinacci, *Praxis et Theoreticae Criminalis*, Pars III. qu. 86, no. 92.

7

The Rejection of Persuasive Evidence

Up to this point we have focused on Roman-canon rules concerning the question of what proof was required for the imposition of blood punishment. We have explored their potential to limit the fact-finding freedom of the judge. As intimated in the Prologue, however, a proper understanding of the degree to which the Roman-canon fact-finding scheme limited this freedom cannot be gained without looking beyond rules dealing with the quantity and quality of evidence. Also deserving of scrutiny are Roman-canon rules on testimonial incapacity, hearsay and evidence obtained by illegal means. As was also intimated in the Prologue, the objection must be anticipated that these rules had nothing to do with the judge's freedom to assess the value of evidence. They determined only the admissibility of evidence, and it was not their business to prescribe how admissible evidence should be evaluated. But this analytically correct objection is misplaced in the institutional setting of the inquisitorial process, where the judge was regularly exposed to inadmissible evidence. If this evidence happened to be persuasive, it could not fail to have an impact on his decision-making. An effective barrier to this impact would have existed only if admissibility issues and the decision on the merits were entrusted to different individuals, who separately decided issues of admissibility and the value of evidence. But courts of the *ancien régime* were not structured like the paradigmatic common law court in which the judge decides the admissibility of evidence and the jury its weight. We saw that in the original variant of the inquisitorial process the judge was charged with deciding both issues, and that in the latter form of this process a panel of judges reached the decision by reading the case file that included records of all official activities – including those dealing with admissibility issues.

In this institutional setting, space inevitably opened up for inadmissible but persuasive evidence to influence the innate information processing of the judge. When the law required him to disregard an item of evidence because of its inadmissibility, even though the item appeared convincing to him, an unspoken rule of weight emerged, obligating him *sub silentio* to attribute no value to this item, despite the fact that it had persuaded him of a relevant factual proposition. Suppose that the testimony of a legally incompetent eyewitness convinced him that the defendant was

Testimonial Disqualifications

guilty. Did he actually disregard this testimony in arriving at factual conclusions? Did inadmissible knowledge influence him at least in evaluating admissible evidence in the case? It is to these issues that we now turn. And as we do, additional tensions will come into view between legally mandated factual finding and findings which Roman-canon judges believed to be substantively correct.

TESTIMONIAL DISQUALIFICATIONS

It has repeatedly been acknowledged that the medieval founders of Roman-canon evidence attributed great importance to the personal and social status of witnesses: persons falling into certain abstractly determined categories were not allowed to testify, regardless of what they knew. Many of these testimonial disqualifications mirrored social, religious and cultural biases of the historical period. Under the rubric "infamous people," for instance, heretics, Jewish persons, and infidels were excluded from testifying. Also disqualified under the same rubric were persons engaged in "dishonorable professions," such as prostitutes, pimps and "kept women."[1] Servants could not testify in cases involving their masters, or women in cases involving their husbands. Poor people could become competent witnesses only if the judge found that they led honest lives and enjoyed good reputations.[2] Excluded as well were persons who did not fall into the abstractly determined classes of unreliable witnesses, if their relationship to the case – enmity toward the defendant, for example – raised doubts about their credibility.

Several theories crafted by legal historians claim that these rules were applied in a mechanical fashion. One theory of this kind was reviewed in Chapter 1, but found to be standing on thin ice. Another theory deserves our attention here. It proposes that rules of testimonial competency were inflexible when the inquisitorial process was in its infancy. Even if a judge happened to believe what legally incompetent persons asserted, his belief was not permitted to override the law's abstract *ex ante* assessment. The disqualifying status of persons was controlling, and the reliability of their testimony irrelevant. Only in the early modern period, this theory holds, was a degree of flexibility introduced in this area. In a reversal of preferences, the interest in accurate fact-finding gained ground at the expense of the binding nature of the law.[3] This theory is also difficult to reconcile with what late medieval jurists wrote on the subject. Nor is it plausible in light of what historical research has revealed about the practice of medieval courts.

---

[1]   See Prospero Farinacci, *Tractatus Integer de Testibus; de Oppositionibus contra Personas Testium*, Tit. VI, qu. 56, art. VIII (Osnabrück, 1617).

[2]   See Benedikt Carpzov, *Practica Nova Imperialis Saxonica Rerum Criminalium*, Pars III, qu. 114, nos. 28–34 (Wittenberg, 1652).

[3]   See, Bernard Schnapper, Testes Inhabiles: les Témoins Reprochables dans l'Ancien Droit Pénal, in Bernard Schnapper, *Voies Nouvelles en Histoire du Droit*, 146, 164–167 (Paris: Presses Universitaires de France, 1991). See also Paolo Marchetti, *Testis contra se*, 170 (Milan: Giuffrè, 1994).

94 *The Rejection of Persuasive Evidence*

As a matter of fact, late medieval jurists paid attention to what legally disqualified persons (*testes inhabiles*) related to the judge. Instructive in this regard is the statement of Baldus in one of his *consilia* that incompetent witnesses could be used in prosecuting "nocturnal misdeeds difficult to prove if truth cannot otherwise be established."[4] A flexible attitude toward them is also discernible in the writings of authorities from the earliest history of the inquisitorial process.[5] Charles Donahue discovered flexibility toward incompetent witnesses in the ecclesiastical courts of medieval England which relied on Roman-canon evidence law. He established that judges of these courts tended to defer ruling on testimonial incapacity until after the testimony of all witnesses was obtained, so that the probative force of their assertions could be ascertained.[6] An old German doctoral dissertation has revealed the same pattern of letting incompetent witnesses testify in the late medieval practice of northern Italian criminal courts operating under the statutes of city states.[7] Nor should the necessary space for flexibility in applying testimonial disqualification be overlooked springing from the circumstance that it was often impossible to mechanically establish whether a person fell into a disqualifying category. Whether a poor person was honest enough to be permitted to testify, for example, was a fact that obviously did not lend itself to unreflective determination.

The main obstacle to the mechanical application of testimonial disqualification rules was the initial stage of the inquisitorial process – the informal *inquisitio generalis*. We noted that in its course the judge questioned all persons with knowledge, including persons who were incompetent to testify in formal criminal proceedings. In so doing he was often able to determine that information related by incompetent witnesses was credible, and could in some cases even be crucial to the accurate disposition of the case.[8] Are we to believe that thirteenth- and fourteenth-century judges were incapable of realizing that a legally disqualified witness – say, a domestic servant or a Jewish person – could convey accurate information? If Baldus was incapable of realizing that statements of a disqualified witness could be of probative value, he certainly would not have advocated that these statements could be used in prosecuting crimes difficult to prove. And even if judges resisted the temptation to use disqualified witnesses in formal proceedings – and we have seen that this was not always the case – believable information imparted by these witnesses

---

[4] See *Consiliorum sive Responsiorum Baldi Ubaldi Perusini*, Vol. III, consilium 77, no. 5 (Frankfurt, 1589).

[5] Azo, Tancred, and Cynus de Pistoia come to mind. For these and additional early authorities, see Susanne Lepsius, *Von Zweifeln zür Überzeugung*, 176–177 (Frankfurt: Vittorio Klostermann, 2003).

[6] See Charles Donahue Jr., Proof by Witnesses in the Church Courts of Medieval England, in Morris Arnold et al. (eds.), *On the Laws and Customs of England*, 143, 147, 155 (Chapel Hill: North Carolina University Press, 1981).

[7] See Heinrich Himstedt, *Die neuen Rechtsgedanken im Zeugenbeweis der oberitalienischen Stadtrechtprozesses des 13 and 14 Jahrhunderts*, 120–138 (Rothschild, 1909).

[8] Observe also that some grounds for testimonial disqualification emerged only after lengthy questioning of potential witnesses.

Testimonial Disqualifications

was not necessarily disregarded, especially if the information was exonerating. At the very least, believable information was used by the judge in formulating questions to be asked of competent witnesses.

As of the sixteenth century, the flexible approach to testimonial disqualification is so unmistakable that it is no longer a matter of scholarly controversy. Early modern jurists agreed with Baldus that the testimony of disqualified witnesses could be used in processing offenses difficult to prove.[9] Also widely shared was the view that this testimony could be used in prosecuting the most serious or atrocious crimes. In some jurisdictions disqualified witnesses were simply converted from *testes inhabiles* into *testes habiles*.[10] In Italian jurisdictions where the torture of witnesses was in some situations permissible, the testimony of incompetent persons could be admitted if it was obtained by milder forms of painful interrogation, on the ground that statements obtained under torture "purged" the person's lesser credibility.[11] And although criminal cases were decided by a panel of judges rather than by the judge who conducted the investigation, assertions of disqualified witnesses obtained in the course of the general inquisition still influenced decision-making on the merits. The amorous rivalry case discussed in Chapter 5 exemplifies this possibility. Although the case file included the testimony of several incompetent witnesses, lawyers took great pains to dissuade the court from being swayed by their assertions. The testimony of Isabella, the lady who accepted nightly visits by men, was also in the file, although she was a "dishonest woman" and her statements were for this reason technically worthless.[12]

The probative effect of believable assertions made by incompetent witnesses remained vexingly uncertain, however. Early on, the view prevailed in legal doctrine that these assertions constitute *indicia* insufficient for contributing to evidence needed not only for imposing blood punishment, but also for ordering torture and imposing nonsanguinary criminal sanctions. Their only legitimate use was to challenge assertions of competent witnesses by suggesting their falsity. But in early modern times the opinion spread that the testimony of legally incompetent witnesses could be used as evidence for ordering torture, so that this brutal attempt at obtaining full proof could be justified on the basis of

---

9   Carpzov repeated what Baldus said three centuries before him: *"inhabiles quoque testes quandoque admitti, si aliter veritas haberi non possit, et praesertim in delictis et factis quae sunt difficilis probationis."* Carpzov, *Practica Nova Imperialis Saxonica Rerum Criminalium*, Pars III, qu. 114, no. 35. See also Farinacci, *Tractatus Integer de Testibus; de Oppositionibus contra Personas Testium*, tit. VI, qu. 62, no. 51. Similarly also Johann Brunnemann, *Tractatus Juridicus de Inquisitionis Processu*, Membrum II, Cap. VIII, no. 24 (Frankfurt/ Leipzig: J. Shrey & J.G. Conrad, 1714).

10 See Brunnemann, *Tractatus Juridicus de Inquisitionis Processu*, Membrum I, Cap. VIII, no. 20.

11 Julius Clarus informs us of this practice. *"Sunt etiam aliqui casus in quibus testes inhabiles admittuntur cum tortura, talis enim tortura purgat defectum testis, adeo ut fidem facit contra reum, licet alias sine tortura non probaret."* Iulius Clarus, *Opera Omnia, siue Practica Civilis et Criminalis*, Liber V, Practica Criminalis, para. fin., qu. 25, no. 1 (Lyon, 1661).

12 See Prospero Farinacci, *Responsorum Criminalium Liber Secundus*, Consilium 135, no. 35 (Rome, 1615).

96   The Rejection of Persuasive Evidence

their sworn assertions.[13] Sporadically, the opinion was also expressed that their assertions could contribute to the formation of *indicia indubitata*, especially when added to the testimony of a single competent eyewitness.[14] Here the testimony of incompetent witnesses assumed its most important form, because it could *directly* contribute to the evidentiary standard capable of supplying the basis for administering capital and mutilating punishments.

How did this treatment of testimonial disqualifications impact the judge's fact-finding freedom? According to mainstream doctrine, their most important consequence was that he could not use legally incompetent witnesses to satisfy the Roman-canon full proof standard. Even if he fully trusted the incriminating assertions of two legally incompetent witnesses, he was not supposed to find their testimony sufficient to support the blood punishment sentence.[15] Rules on testimonial disqualification underwent here the metamorphosis to which we have repeatedly alluded: they functioned like cryptic rules of weight, asking the judge to attribute no value to the testimony of legally incompetent persons, even if he found it fully convincing. Like other negative proof rules, those generated by testimonial disqualifications were obviously frustrating to judges eager to impose sanguinary punishments on defendants whom they believed to be guilty. One wonders whether the demand to attribute no value applied also to believable *exculpating* information supplied by incompetent witnesses. No answer to this question was found in the treatises and *consilia* consulted for the purposes of this book. Perhaps the authority of Baldus could have been invoked for the proposition that exculpating assertions are admissible "if the truth could otherwise not be established" (*si aliter veritas haberi non potest*).[16] The argument for admissibility of exculpating information could also have been bolstered by referring to various other asymmetries in treating incriminating and exculpating evidence, springing from the notion that it is better to acquit the guilty than to convict the innocent – the notion to which we alluded in discussing the epistemic assumptions of the Roman-canon fact-finding scheme.[17] At the very least, judges could have used exculpating information to establish weaknesses or possible falsity in incriminating assertions of legally competent witnesses. All told, it seems likely that the fact-finding freedom of judges in the Roman-

---

[13] See Clarus, *Opera Omnia, siue Practica Civilis et Criminalis*, Liber V, para. fin., qu. 24, no. 19; Carpzov, *Practica nova imperialis Saxonica rerum criminalium*, III, qu. 114, no. 38. For a contrary view, see Farinacci, *Tractatus integer de testibus; de oppositionibus contra personas testium*, tit. VI, qu, 62, limit 3, no. 50.

[14] See Prospero Farinacci, *Consilia sive Responsa atque Decisiones Causarum Criminalium*, consilium 50, no. 3 (Lyon, 1610).

[15] Even the minority doctrine would probably balk at a different conclusion. A possible exception existed only in prosecuting *crimina atrocissima*, where incompetent but credible persons could simply be converted into competent witnesses.

[16] See Baldus, as quoted by Carpzov, *Practica Nova Imperialis Saxonica Rerum Criminalium*, Pars III, qu. 114, no. 35.

[17] This notion of Roman origin can be found already in thirteenth-century Roman-canon sources. See Albertus Gandinus, Tractatus de Maleficiis, in Hermann Kantorowicz, *Albertus Gandinus und das Strafrecht der Scholastik, Rubrica: De presumptionibus et indiciis indubitatis ex quibus condemnatio potest sequi*, 1, pp. 93–94 (Berlin: J. Guttentag, 1926).

Illegally Obtained Evidence 97

canon fact-finding scheme was more seriously limited in regard to incriminating than exculpating statements of legally incompetent witnesses.

ILLEGALLY OBTAINED EVIDENCE

Contrary to widespread belief, the inquisitorial criminal process was not so thoroughly obsessed by crime control as to banish all institutions and arrangements we now associate with defensive safeguards. After all, the exacting Roman-canon full proof standard was adopted as such a safeguard. The idea should also not be overlooked, hovering over the inquisitorial process, that certain rules responsive to defense interests are rooted in natural law and constitute the indispensable elements of the just judicial order. This idea found its way into a fourteenth-century constitution of Pope Clement V,[18] and was gradually accepted by continental legal doctrine. One of the indispensable elements of the just order was the requirement that defendants should be given the opportunity to present their defense. As Carpzov put it, "defense could not be denied to beasts, much less to humans, and not even to the devil himself."[19] Yet the question remained rife with dissensions over what this requirement entailed, particularly in the prosecution of the most serious crimes. The only point that was widely, though not universally, recognized was that defense counsel should be permitted to assist the defendant, although restrictions were placed on their activity.[20] The demand that judicial torture should be ordered only on indubitable indications was also often included in the catalog of indispensable elements of the proper procedural order.

More important to our concerns was another constitution of Pope Clement V titled *Pastoralis cura*.[21] A passage at its end proclaimed that all "acts and evidence" are null and void if obtained in breach of procedural provisions based on natural law. It turns out, *mirabile dictu*, that our current provisions on the rejection of illegally obtained evidence have an unsuspected precursor in late medieval papal legislation. Even more surprising is that the passage in question was interpreted by influential legal authorities to require that the nullity extend from evidence illegally obtained to all acts and evidence derived from it.[22] This seems truly odd, considering that even our

[18] *Saepe contingit*, Clem. 5.11.2. For an insightful analysis of this constitution, see Kenneth Pennington, *The Prince and the Law*, 165–191 (Oakland: University of California Press, 1993).

[19] *"Certius est defensionem esse iuris naturalis, adeo ut ne bestiis quidem nedum humani, imo nec diaboli auferri debeat,"* Carpzov, *Practica nova imperialis Saxonica rerum criminalium*, Pars III, qu. 115, no. 1.

[20] A different understanding of what natural law demands in regard to defense entailments was followed in France. Only the defendant's right to address judges before they passed judgment was declared essential to the just procedural order there. In introducing his repressive seventeenth-century codification of criminal procedure, Louis XIV stated that "it is the sense of our Ordinance that the accused can never be deprived of his natural right to defend himself by his own mouth." See Faustin Hélie, *Traité de l'Instruction Criminelle*, Première Partie, 639 (Paris: H. Plon, 1845). On this understanding of the demands of natural law, defense counsel could be excluded from criminal proceedings.

[21] Clem. 2.12.2.

[22] Invoking *Pastoralis Cura*, Farinacci stated two centuries later that *"omnia gesta post denegatas defensiones sunt ipso facto nulla"* (all acts following denied defenses are by that very fact null). See Prospero Farinacci, *Responsorum Criminalium Liber Secundus*, consilium 161, no. 24 (Rome, 1615).

98   The Rejection of Persuasive Evidence

current doctrine on the rejection of "fruits from the poisonous tree" is far from firmly embedded in many jurisdictions. Given the repressive character of inquisitorial procedure, the suspicion arises again that the exclusion of illegally procured evidence was without influence on court practice – an empty gesture of Roman-canon legal doctrine. The judge's fact-finding freedom would have been restricted, of course, only if he attempted to disregard illegal evidence in those situations where it appeared persuasive to him, and especially when it seemed to him crucial for the accurate disposition of a case. As a prelude to abstract remarks on this theme, and as an illustration of how the issue of illegal evidence was argued in an early modern court, let us take a further detour from the mainstream of the narrative and consider another sixteenth-century Italian murder case.[23] The detour should also make our discussion in Chapter 5 of the evidence needed for ordering torture more concrete.

The prosecution of Guido di San Giorgio

A vagrant from Milan named Biffio was arrested in Turin on suspicion of supporting himself by criminal activity. Under the first stage of light torture, he disclosed that another commoner of bad reputation, Curtes, had asked him to kill a Turin nobleman on behalf of Guido, a nobleman from Milan. Subjected to torture, Curtes confessed to having received money from Guido to arrange for the murder. On the strength of these two confessions, a local judge instituted the *inquisitio specialis* against Guido. He admitted to giving money to Curtes, but insisted that it represented remuneration for past services rather than payment for a contract killing. The judge then repeated the interrogation of Biffio and Curtes in Giorgio's presence, and after the two repeated their confessions he brought the "offensive part" of the special investigation to a close, charging Guido with the capital crime of assassination. In the "defensive part" of the investigation, the issue arose whether enough evidence was assembled to order that Guido be subjected to painful interrogation. In his defense Guido urged that the torture of the two commoners had been ordered without sufficient *indicia*, so that their confessions were illegally obtained and could not support a torture order against him. The *Fiscus*, the official whom we encountered earlier in the amorous rivalry case, disagreed. He conceded that evidence normally required for the torture was missing, but claimed that assembling this evidence was not required in the case of the two commoners. The crime of assassination was atrocious and difficult to prove, so that ordinary proof sufficiency rules for torture did not apply. Moreover, he added, Biffio and Curtes were persons of bad reputation who could be subjected to painful

---

Carpzov claimed that the derivative effect of illegally obtained *indicia* applied even in the prosecution of the most serious offenses. "*Nullitas ex effectu indiciorum promanans,*" he penned, "*omnia post facta pariter inficiat, nullaque reddat, etiamsi de crimine excepto ageretur.*" See Carpzov, *Practica Nova Imperialis Saxonica Rerum Criminalium*, Pars III, qu. 108, no. 45.

[23] The case appears in Farinacci, *Consilia sive Responsa atque Decisiones Causarum Criminalium*, consilium 99 (Lyon, 1610).

Illegally Obtained Evidence 99

interrogations on less than normally required evidence. To cap it all, he noted that the governor of Turin requested that the two commoners be put to torture, and added that the governor, being the highest authority in the city, was not bound by the ordinary rules of evidence and could authorize judges to decide according to conscience (*secundum conscientiam*).

Asked to submit an advisory opinion in the case, Farinacci first addressed the validity of Biffio's confession. The *Fiscus* was mistaken, he began, in claiming that mere suspicion sufficed for ordering torture when atrocious crimes difficult to prove were being processed. Even in these cases, he claimed, indubitable indications were required for torture.[24] Nor could persons of bad reputation and with proclivity to criminal activity be tortured without these indications, except in special situations not present in Guido's case.[25] A propos of the gubernatorial request for torture, Farinacci resorted to the distinction between disregard of ordinary procedural defenses and defenses based on natural law. Sufficiency of proof for torture orders, he submitted, fell into the category of natural law defenses which could not be denied to defendants even by the highest authority.[26] All evidence acquired as a result of the denial of these defenses was for this reason null and void. Having concluded that Biffio's confession was invalid, Farinacci turned to the legality of Curtes's confession. Because it derived from Biffio's invalid one, he argued, it was the product of illegal torture and was also null and void.[27] Out of an abundance of caution he invoked yet another reason for the nullity of Curtes's confession – a reason stemming from the fact that this confession had been obtained on repeated torture. Since the first torture was illegal, he opined, the confession extorted on its repetition was tantamount to a confession procured by illegal threats.[28] This was fatal to its validity, he concluded, because learned jurists agreed that a confession extracted by illegal threats could not harm either the confessor or anybody else, "even if it [was] a thousand times ratified and repeated."[29]

Following these preliminaries, Farinacci turned to the question his *consilium* was supposed to answer: could a legitimate torture order be issued against Guido? Since the confessions of Biffio and Curtes were null and void, he submitted, Guido could

---

[24] Nos. 27 and 31.

[25] Nos. 35 and 37.

[26] Nos. 38, 40, and 41. In another *consilium* Farinacci claimed that even the pope and the emperor were bound to observe procedural defenses grounded in natural law. See Farinacci, *Responsorum Criminalium Liber Secundus*, consilium 85, nos. 19 and 25.

[27] No. 46. "*Dato etiam quod ex depositione Bifij contra Curtem orietur indicium ad torturam: hoc tamen intelligi debet, quando ipse Biffius fuisset legitime et praecedentibus indiciis tortus: sed cum ... appareat non legitime et sine praecedentibus indiciis tortum fuisse, sequitur quod talis confessio, nec sibi nec Curti per ipsum nominato nocere potest.*"

[28] This may seem strange to the reader since defendants had to be threatened with torture before it was actually applied. But these threats were permissible only after the judge assembled enough *indicia* for a legitimate torture order. In Curtes's case, however, this requirement was not met.

[29] No. 56. "*Communiter receptum est a Doctoribus quod confessio metu tormentorum extracta, etiam millis ratificata et geminata, nec confitenti nec aliis nocet.*"

not be subjected to painful interrogation. Curtes's confession could not support the torture order, he added, even if its accuracy had been fully established.[30] This additional argument is especially noteworthy for our purposes, because it indicates that the Roman-canon exclusionary doctrine – at least in the opinion of one of its most famous expositors – was not based on the belief that illegally acquired evidence is unreliable. By urging the court to reject the confession of Curtes, even if truthful, Farinacci adopted a position that evinces awareness of values that run counter to an unbridled quest for the truth, and bespeaks a willingness to sacrifice crime control interests even in an abhorrent murder case.

It is unknown whether Farinacci's arguments were accepted by the court and saved Guido from torture. But even if they were rejected, their inclusion in an expert opinion intended for forensic use is significant. It shows that the arguments were within the bounds of acceptable courtroom discourse in sixteenth-century Italy. As a seasoned litigator, reputed to be "the prince of criminal lawyers" (*criminalistarum princeps*), Farinacci certainly knew what arguments could safely be made in court with at least some chance of success. Yet on the issue of excluding illegally obtained evidence the practice of *ancien régime* courts must have greatly varied over time and space. It must have varied depending on the severity of the crime involved and the social status of the defendant. Exclusion of evidence seems to have been seriously contemplated in some jurisdictions when the crimes involved were not considered particularly heinous or dangerous.[31] When they represented grave threats to the established order, the landscape of the law darkened. Even observance of rules believed to originate in natural law could then become uncertain: rejecting illegally obtained confessions could appear too costly.[32] But if the defendant belonged to the upper echelons of society and the crime involved was not considered egregious, the exclusion of illegally obtained evidence became a realistic possibility. Here judges had reason to worry – at least in some jurisdictions – about possible responsibility "*in syndicatu*" for acting on evidence obtained in breach of defense rules stemming from natural law. Hence it is not unusual that in the prosecution of Guido – a nobleman – expert opinion was sought on the question of sufficiency of evidence for torture, and that the issue was seriously contested. But when people belonging to the lower social strata were prosecuted, the response to illegality changed. Guido's case is again telling in this regard. Biffio, a commoner of ill repute, was tortured on

[30] No. 62. "*Confessio metu tormentorum extorta, nihil operator, confitentique aut tertio non nocet, etiam quod aliumque in totum verificetur per inspectiones oculorum, nedum alia verisimilia seu adminicula.*"

[31] Evidence is available for some jurisdictions that irregular torture orders were actually quashed, some of which were based on legally insufficient evidence. See, e.g., Arnd Koch, *Denunciatio: zur Geschichte eines strafprozessualen Rechtsinstituts*, 125–126 (Frankfurt: Vittorio Klostermann, 2006); Alfred Soman, Criminal Jurisprudence in Ancien Régime France, in Louis A. Knafla (ed.), *Crime and Criminal Justice in Europe and Canada*, 61 (Waterloo: Wilfred Laurier University Press, 1981).

[32] Even so, sporadic doctrinal opinion surfaced, holding that normal proof sufficiency rules must be observed even in regard to *crimina atrocissima*. For the case of Hipppolytus Marsilius, see again Giorgia Alessi Palazzolo, *Prova Legale e Pena*, 76 (Naples: Jovene, 1979). Whether such doctrinal musings – liberal *avant la lettre* – were heeded in practice is subject to doubt.

the mere suspicion that he had committed some undefined offense, and Curtes, another person of ignoble status, was tortured twice without any apparent compunction about sufficient evidentiary support for the repeated use of torments. Even here, as in so many other aspects, the inquisitorial process was suffused with social bias.[33]

Illegal Evidence and Fact-Finding Freedom

Let us return now to the main line of our story. Contrary to widespread belief, it does not seem likely that the doctrine requiring the rejection of illegally obtained evidence was without any practical importance in the inquisitorial process, despite its deep disrepute in Western legal history. But even where it played some role, this does not mean that it always limited the judge's fact-finding freedom. As was noted in regard to testimonial disqualifications, his freedom was affected only when he found the tainted evidence credible. When this was not the case, the rejection of evidence was not only the law's demand but also the judge's autonomous preference. Of importance to our concerns is therefore only the question whether judges were sometimes prepared to follow the view – exemplified by Farinacci's opinion in regard to the confession of Curtes – that confessions obtained in a prohibited way should be rejected even if their accuracy is fully established. It is clear that the disregard of incriminating evidence with a high truth quotient bruised the repressive spirit of the *ancien régime*'s criminal justice and the *furor puniendi* of its judges. But while it is therefore improbable that reliable but illegally obtained items of incriminating evidence were routinely rejected, it cannot be ruled out that judges were sporadically prepared to declare them null and void. And where prohibited evidence was declared invalid, an admissibility rule was transformed into a rule of weight. A negative rule of weight appeared, much as it did in the context of testimony of legally incompetent witnesses.

THE ROMAN-CANON HEARSAY BAN

Chapter 2 revealed that the progenitors of the Roman-canon fact-finding scheme failed to develop a unitary doctrine on the treatment of derivative evidence, covering both its oral and written forms. The reason for this failure was that only provisions on oral hearsay figured in the passages of Justinian's codification, on the basis of which late medieval legal scholars shaped the law of evidence.[34] They did not overlook the

---

[33] Farinacci's statement in Guido's case that ordering torture required "*indicia indubitata*" even in prosecuting low-class defendants should be taken with a grain of salt. In another *consilium*, he argued, for example, that in these prosecutions less evidence could suffice. See Farinacci, *Responsorum Criminalium, Liber Secundus*, consilium 103, nos. 5–8.

[34] On the roots of the Roman-canon hearsay doctrine, see the study of Frank Hermann, The Establishment of a Rule against hearsay in Romano-Canonical Procedure, 31 *Virginia Journal of International Law*, 1–51 (1995).

102 *The Rejection of Persuasive Evidence*

epistemic frailty of written hearsay, however. Their negative attitude toward this type of derivative evidence is only veiled by the important role of official documentation in the Roman-canon judicial apparatus. The repository of evidence in this apparatus – the case file – contained written records of official fact-finding activities, and these records were used for fact-finding purposes at both the original and appellate levels of adjudication. But the reliance on them was unavoidable, although hearsay dangers lurking in these documents were not overlooked by perspicacious premodern jurists. The reliance was unavoidable, since investigative activities were performed over time by several levels of officials, so that the file served as the informational lifeline of the judicial organization. "What is not in the file," was its oft-repeated motto, "is not in the world" (*quod non est in actis non est in mundo*). It is important to realize, however, that the use of official records in the file did not involve all the cognitive disadvantages that are the mainspring of reservations about the use of hearsay. Most records contained the sworn testimony of first-hand witnesses, so that the use of these records resembled the reliance on prior testimony which is on certain conditions admissible even in contemporary procedural systems that recognize the ban on written hearsay.[35]

The Implicit Ban on Written Hearsay

As soon as the institutional pressure to rely on official documentation was relieved, the mistrust of written hearsay as extrajudicial testimony and secondary discourse emerged on the surface of the law. This can best be seen in the example of private writings (*apochae, scripture privatae*). Jurists regularly claimed that such writings were inadmissible as proof in criminal cases.[36] There existed exceptions to this rule, of course, since private writings could be used for different purposes, some involving hearsay dangers, others not.[37] Instances in which some jurists found private writing admissible bespeak their remarkable ability to spot the absence of hearsay dangers. Farinacci was clearly one of these jurists. He reported the case of a priest with gargantuan sexual appetites who became a defendant in quasi-criminal proceedings

---

[35] It is true that official documents other than records of prior procedural activities were also included in the file of the case. But they could be used for fact-finding purposes only when produced by officials acting within the bounds of their competences, and in some jurisdictions only if they contained the officials' own observations. Any hearsay concerns these documents raised were thought to be reduced by the "dignity" of their official drafters, and the solemnities attendant to their production. This is akin again to the treatment of official documents in contemporary justice systems of some countries that prohibit the reliance on written hearsay.

[36] Even the levels of written hearsay were not ignored. Farinacci wrote, for instance, that private writings could not be used not only when a private person wrote down someone else's observation, but also when he put down what he himself had perceived. See Farinacci, *Consilia sive Responsa atque Decisiones Causarum Criminalium*, consilium 25, no. 63.

[37] Some nineteenth-century scholars wrote that the ban on the use of private writings did not apply in French courts. It is more accurate to say that French courts admitted "*écrits*" only in "exceptional situations." See Daniel Jousse, *Traité de la Justice de France*, Tome I, Chapter IV, no. 215, p. 740 (Paris, 1771). These situations might well have been those in which hearsay dangers were absent.

The Roman-Canon Hearsay Ban

for the deprivation of ecclesiastical benefits.[38] One of the disputed items of evidence in the case was a short note written by the priest. It contained a signed statement of his servant in which he declared his consent to be touched by the priest, his master, "from in front and from behind," and promised to continue "pleasing" the priest with his body. In three successive opinions, Farinacci argued that the ban on the use of private writings did not apply to this case. In reducing the servant's statement to writing, and then letting him sign it, he opined, the priest committed the crime of soliciting the promise of illicit sex. Because the crime "inhered" in the note, he said, the note was admissible.[39] That writings embodying a crime constituted valid proof was widely accepted in the case of heretical tracts, usurious contracts, defamatory letters, and forged documents.[40]

Oral Hearsay

Chapter 2 also revealed that the Roman-canon fact-finding system required that witnesses convey what they personally observed about the facts to be proven, rather than reproduce what they had heard another person say about these facts.[41] But the resulting ban on hearsay was hedged around by a congeries of exceptions whose mastery required navigating the swirling vortices of "expansions," "limitations," and "sublimitations" established by legal doctrine. Of importance to our purposes is mainly an exception that paralleled the exception we encountered in the law of testimonial disqualifications: testimony of hearsay witnesses could be used in prosecuting crimes secretly committed and crimes difficult to prove.[42] While hearsay exceptions were numerous, Roman-canon legal doctrine did not make recourse to them easy. The judge could use hearsay witnesses only if he was unable to reach the out-of-court declarant. And if a hearsay witness was unable to identify the declarant, his testimony was inadmissible. It is also important that the declarant was supposed to be a person of substance (*persona gravis*), and the credibility of the hearsay witness had to be "above all exception."[43]

---

[38] See Farinacci, *Consilia sive Responsa atque Decisiones Causarum Criminalium*, consilium 25.

[39] See Farinacci, *ibid.*, nos. 59 and 65.

[40] Some jurists argued that writings embodying a crime were not evidence in the strict sense of the term, but objects for the judge's own sensing. As noted in Chapter 2, the judge's own sensing was to them a fact-finding mode cognitively superior to the presentation of evidence.

[41] The architects of the system realized, however, that not all witnesses who testify about what they have heard from others raise reliability concerns. Only those were treated as hearsay witnesses (*testes de auditu alieno*) who reported what they had heard for the purpose of proving the truth of what they had heard. A person was not considered a hearsay witness, for example, who testified that a certain rumor circulated in a community, but not that the rumor reflected reality.

[42] See Farinacci, *Tractatus Integer de Testibus; de Oppositionibus contra Personas Testium*, qu. 69, nos. 13 and 51–53.

[43] For a sense of how these conditions were applied, see Farinacci, *Responsorum Criminalium Liber Secundus*, consilium 193, no. 6.

The Impact of the Hearsay Ban on Fact-Finding Freedom

Witnesses were required to reveal the source of their knowledge (*causa scientiae*), and if it turned out that the source was the statement of an out-of-court person they had to be "repelled." To understand the actual effect of "repelling" the witness, one must consider again the role played by the general inquisition. Because at this procedural stage the judge examined persons informally, his questioning generated narrative accounts containing a great deal of hearsay. He also inspected writings *ad informationem curiae,* including those containing out-of-court testimonial statements. In short, he routinely identified hearsay only after being exposed to it. Observe also that the presence of hearsay in the total pool of information gathered in the general inquisition enabled him to gain a sense of its reliability. What occurred if he found hearsay trustworthy? In the variant of the inquisitorial process where he was also the decision-maker, the ban on the use of hearsay could easily generate a discrepancy between verdicts dictated by the law and verdicts the judge found appropriate in light of believable hearsay information. And in the version of the inquisitorial process where factual findings were made by a panel of judges, the discrepancy between the two outcomes could be avoided only if traces of reliable secondary discourse were removed from the dossier on the basis of which the panel made its decision. But the removal was not even contemplated.

The cornucopia of exceptions to the hearsay ban was meant to avoid this discrepancy and enable judges to use reliable hearsay. Where these exceptions were available, the Roman-canon fact-finding scheme did not constrain their fact-finding freedom, of course. But exceptions were not always available, and, as noted above, recourse to them was not easy. Consequently, situations did arise in which judges were obliged to "repel" a hearsay witness or disregard a document containing hearsay, although they found the forbidden derivative evidence trustworthy. And since the law required that they attribute no probative value to it, the ban on hearsay could morph into a rule on the value of evidence – much as in the context of witness disqualification rules and rules on the exclusion of illegally obtained evidence. This does not mean, however, that formally excluded hearsay, if credible, exerted no influence on the court's decision. As in several other situations, judges could use knowledge acquired from forbidden hearsay in formulating questions to be addressed to legally competent witnesses, and evaluate their responses in light of this knowledge. And if forbidden hearsay made them doubt the testimony of these witnesses, especially those relating incriminating information, judges would find them not to be "above all exception." It would be a mistake to think that premodern judges were insensitive like the gods of Epicurus, facing the prospect of causing death or mutilation of an innocent person with nonchalance.

8

Evading the Roman-Canon Full Proof Standard

The preceding chapters demonstrated that the constraining effect of the Roman-canon proof standard required for capital and serious corporal punishments was not nearly as powerful as conventional wisdom assumes. The standard limited judges' fact-finding freedom only in the negative sense of preventing them from imposing these punishments in the absence of legally required proof, even if they were convinced of the defendant's guilt. But even in this sense the effect of the standard was weakened by numerous dispensations from its application. Nor was the aforementioned metamorphosis of admissibility rules into rules determining the value of evidence capable of greatly affecting their fact-finding freedom. Nevertheless, cases did arise in which judges were persuaded that a defendant had committed a serious crime, but the law barred them from sentencing him to sanguinary punishments. And so long as these punishments were considered the quintessential criminal sanction, the resulting inability to administer them appeared to criminal law enforcers tantamount to letting the guilty person remain unpunished.

As balms to the resulting stress and as compensation for the frustration of punitive urges, instruments were designed in the infancy of the inquisitorial process to avoid the effect of demanding Roman-canon legal proof. The minority legal doctrine discussed in Chapter 6 could be considered an instrument of this kind, but it seems more appropriate to treat it as an alternative to the full proof requirement, rather than as an instrument to circumvent it. A real dodge intended to avoid Roman-canon full proof was the doctrine of notorious crime developed by the lawyers of the Church of Rome. If a crime was well known to the judge and to the relevant community, no witnesses were required for conviction and the imposition of capital and other sanguinary punishments.[1] The doctrine of notorious crime was relatively short-lived and

---

[1] See Albertus Gandinus, Tractatus de Maleficiis, Rubrica: Quomodo de Maleficio Cognoscitur Quando Crimen est Notorius, 9, 15, and Rubrica: De Rumore Manifesto et Occulto, no. 9, 15, in Hermann Kantorowicz, *Albertus Gandinus und das Strafrecht der Scholastik*, vol. 2, p. 103 (Berlin: J. Guttentag, 1926).

106   *Evading the Roman-Canon Full Proof Standard*

will not be discussed here.[2] We will only consider instruments designed to ensure that those who escaped blood punishment would receive at least some penalty, and to keep criminal proceedings suspended in the hope that full legal proof might became available in the future. These two devices to bypass the exacting demands of Roman-canon evidence law were among the salient features of the inquisitorial fact-finding style from its birth to its last gasp.

EXTRAORDINARY PUNISHMENT

When compelling incriminating evidence short of full proof was gathered against defendants accused of serious crimes, the so-called extraordinary punishment (*poena extraordinaria*) was available to prevent their impunity. The punishment was introduced into Church proceedings in the early thirteenth century by Pope Innocent IV, at roughly the same time he allowed the use of torture in special papal courts charged with prosecuting heresy. In the later part of that century, the milder punishment was adopted by secular courts of northern Italy. Gandinus reports a case from Parma in which the defendant accused of homicide could not be sentenced to death because of missing full proof, but was fined upon the advice of learned lawyers "so that crime does not remain unpunished."[3] This milder criminal sanction soon spread to southern France and beyond. It consisted of banishment, fines and corporal punishments other than those causing the spilling of blood. In early modern times various forms of penal servitude, such as the galley sentence, were added to the catalog of sentencing possibilities. The selection of punishments from the catalog was left to the judge's discretion.

What evidence justified the imposition of these milder punishments? Some jurisdictions required the testimony of a single unimpeachable eyewitness, or half proof (*probatio semiplena*). As mentioned above, this evidentiary standard was criticized – especially in the Enlightenment era – on the ground that its progenitors equated half proof with half truth.[4] Now, while it is true that terms like half truth were used in some *ancien régime* jurisdictions – France being an example – the criticism is not justified if intended to apply to the Roman-canon legal doctrine generally. As noted in Chapter 2, its founders believed not that truth could be split,

---

[2]   For a detailed discussion of its fortunes, see Richard Fraher, Conviction According to Conscience: the Medieval Jurists' Debate Concerning Judicial Discretion and the Law of Proof, 7 *Law and History Review*, 23, *passim* (1989).

[3]   See Gandinus, *Tractatus de Maleficiis,, Rubrica: de Homicidiariis et Eorum Poena*, no. 11, p. 288.

[4]   Half truth of guilt does not exist, critics pointed out, and the defendant is either guilty or innocent. An early critic of milder punishments on this ground was Francisco Sarmiento de Mendoza. See Mendoza, *Selectum Interpretationem Libri Tres*, Lib. 1, cap. 1, no. 6 (Rome, 1571). See also Antonius Matthaus, *De Criminibus*, Lib. 48, tit. 16, cap. III, no. 22 (Utrecht, 1644). But the best-known Enlightenment critic using this argument against milder punishments was Beccaria. See Cesare Beccaria, *Dei Delitti e delle Pene*, para 31 (Turin: Einaudi, 1994). This particular critique was resurrected in the last century by Foucault. See Michel Foucault, *Surveiller et Punir*, 46 (Paris: Flammarion, 1975).

Extraordinary Punishment

but that degrees of probability could be distinguished. Half proof meant to them only that nonsanguinary punishment could be imposed on a less demanding standard than the blood sanction. Another proof sufficiency standard for the use of milder punishments was that the judge had to assemble indubitable indications (*indicia indubitata*). We have already encountered this concept in talking about evidence needed for torture orders.[5] In fact, evidence required for torture and extraordinary punishment was in most jurisdictions identical: the judge who gathered *indicia indubitata* could use them either for torture orders or for the imposition of extraordinary punishment.[6] As in regard to torture, so in regard to extraordinary punishment, the prevailing understanding of indubitable indications was that they ought to persuade the judge that the defendant was guilty.[7] Where half proof was required, the actual standard was not much different. Remember that an eyewitness was above all exception (*omni exceptione maior*) only when the judge found no reasons to disbelieve his or her testimony. In other words, the testimony of a single eyewitness had to be convincing to the judge in order to constitute half proof.

According to legal doctrine, then, the basis for imposing milder punishments was the judge's belief that the defendant was guilty. It seems unlikely, however, that this requirement was strictly observed.[8] To believe otherwise is to underestimate the repressive character of inquisitorial procedure. Then as now, judges were exposed to situations in which evidence they marshaled made a defendant's criminal responsibility only very likely. The idea that uncertainty about guilt ought to preclude the imposition of *any* punishment – although already present in medieval moral theology – became firmly established in criminal procedure only as part of modern liberal thought about the relationship between the individual and the state. In the absence of this ideological bedrock, it was not alien to premodern judges to impose nonsanguinary punishments on mere

---

[5] Some authorities referred to the required evidence for extraordinary punishments as "most violent presumptions" (*prasumptiones violentissimae*). Farinacci used the terms "indubitable indications" and "most violent presumptions" indiscriminately. See Prospero Farinacci, *Praxis et Theoreticae Criminalis*, Pars III, qu. 86, nos. 5, 91, 93 (Lyon, 1635). For the terminology used earlier by medieval authorities, see Woldemar Engelmann, *Irrtum und Schuld nach der italienischen Lehre und Praxis des Mittelalters*, 93 (Hamburg: G. Stilke, 1922).

[6] Using *indicia indubitata* to order torture in the hope of obtaining a confession was in some countries risky, since the defendant who withstood painful interrogation had to be acquitted. Where this was the case, it was safer to use them for the imposition of extraordinary punishment. An additional use of indubitable indications in some courts was to require the defendant to take a purgatory oath. This was also hazardous, because the defendant who swore that he was innocent had to be acquitted.

[7] Carpzov wrote, for example, that *indicia indubitata* must be so "clear and certain" as to be capable of completely persuading, albeit not of fully proving (*apta ad plene persuadendum, licet non plene probandum*). See Benedict Carpzov, *Practica Nova Imperiali Saxonica Rerum Criminalium*, Pars III, qu. 120, no. 13. For a similar formulation of indubitable indications, see Prospero Farinacci, *Responsorum Criminalium Liber Secundus, consilium* 108, no. 89 (Rome, 1615). ("*Verissima est ergo mea conclusio, quod indicia indubitata sint illa quae trahunt iudicem ad firmiter credendum delictum.*")

[8] For a contrary opinion, see Walter Sax, Zur Anwendbarkeit des Satzes "in dubio pro reo," in *Studien zur Strafrechtswissenschaft: Festschrift für Ulrich Stock*, 153 (Würzburg: Holzner, 1966).

108   *Evading the Roman-Canon Full Proof Standard*

suspicion of guilt.[9] They were also faced with cases revealing that the defendant presented a danger to the community, although the crime he was charged with could not be proven. In cases of this kind extraordinary punishments were sometimes imposed as security measures *avant la lettre*.[10] The imposition appeared acceptable especially in prosecutions of suspicious idlers and low-class persons of ill repute. The notion of life-style or status crimes was not perceived as reprehensible.[11]

The proof sufficiency standard for extraordinary punishments is now criticized on the ground that the demand for evidence was changed in response to the magnitude of punishment. The proof sufficiency standard must be constant, the prevailing legal doctrine now insists, no matter what punishment is threatened for a crime. But it is less than clear that our current demands for proof sufficiency are constant as a matter of decision-making practice. It may well be that the doubts and certainties our fact-finders experience in arriving at a verdict are not fixed entities, but vary depending on a host of factors, including the magnitude of the punishment. Is it not as natural as the winds that the regret of erroneously imposing capital punishment exceeds the regret of erroneously imposing a short prison term or a fine? And if these regrets are indeed different, then our fact-finders are likely to experience different degrees of certainty as tolerable in reaching the verdict. Even now, could the imposition of the death penalty require, albeit *sub rosa*, more compelling evidence than the imposition of a milder punishment?[12] Observe the subtle irony here. While Roman-canon evidentiary barriers to conviction were lowered for milder punishments, they were lowered to the level of "indubitable indications," corresponding roughly to our reasonable doubt standard for the imposition of *any* punishments. And since the Roman-canon system required two eyewitnesses or an in-court confession for its harshest punishments, it was in this regard more demanding than we are

---

[9]   Some believe that punishments on mere suspicion of criminality emerged only in the seventeenth century. See Georgia Alessi Palazzolo, *Prova Legale e Pena*, 40, note 6 (Naples: Jovene, 1979). But as prosecutions of heretics demonstrate, milder punishments based on suspicion of guilt were already imposed in late medieval times. See Mathias Schmoeckel, *Humanität und Staatsraison*, 300–334 (Vienna: Böhlau, 2000).

[10] Although the distinction between punishment and security measures was developed only in late eighteenth century, already medieval lawyers were using a form of extraordinary punishment – banishment – to get rid of dangerous folks whose guilt of specific crimes could not be proven. It is hard to read Gandinus, for example, without gaining this impression.

[11] A low-class suspicious idler ("*nebulo*") of this kind was Biffio, from whom a confession was extorted without legally required evidence in the case of the nobleman Guido.

[12] For an argument along these lines, see Mirjan Damaška, Evidentiary Barriers to Conviction and Two Models of Criminal Procedure, 121 *University of Pennsylvania Law Review*, 506, 542–543 (1978). Contemporary decision-making theory seems to lend some support to this intuitively plausible insight. See Eric Lillquist, Recasting Reasonable Doubt, 36 *U. C. Davies Law Review*, 85, 91 (2002). For empirical research on this subject, see Rita Simon and Linda Mahan, Quantifying Burdens of Proof, 5 *Law & Society Review*, 319, 325, 329 (1971). On variable regrets for error in decision-making, see Richard Lempert, Modeling Relevance, 73 *Michigan Law Review*, 1021, 1032 (1977).

today.[13] All in all, the relaxation of the strict Roman-canon full proof standard for the imposition of punishments milder than death or mutilation does not deserve to be ridiculed as wrongheaded. The relaxation is offensive to our values only because the doctrinal standard requiring "indubitable indications" was often disregarded in the inquisitorial process, and the milder punishments became the penal reaction to mere suspicion of criminality or to perceptions of a person's dangerous life-style.[14] In the liberal political environment of the nineteenth century, extraordinary punishments were rightly rejected precisely on these grounds.

How did the lower proof standard for *poena extraordinaria* affect judges' fact-finding freedom? Since the punishment could be predicated on circumstantial evidence, and since its probative potential resisted determination by abstract *ex ante* rules, an argument could be made that the lower standard liberated judges from legal shackles in fact-finding. Several decades ago John Langbein propounded a theory predicated on this insight. As outlined in Chapter 4, he argued that extraordinary punishment was seldom used until the sixteenth and seventeenth centuries, because prior to that time death and mutilations were regarded as the only proper punishments for serious crime. Free evaluation of evidence, inherent in the use of extraordinary punishments, was for this reason barely visible in, and failed to have a noticeable impact on, the administration of justice. But in early modern times, as *poenae extraordinariae* became acceptable as the response even to the most serious misdeeds, their spreading deprived the Roman-canon full proof standard of its reason for existence. Evidence law was liberated from dependence on eyewitnesses and confessions as a precondition for proper punishment, and free evaluation of evidence became the norm.[15]

Available sources contradict this theory. In countries that retained the Roman-canon fact-finding scheme, the belief persisted as late as the nineteenth century that some crimes are so serious that the only condign punishment for their perpetration was the death sentence. As a result, judicial efforts to obtain the Roman-canon full proof continued unabated, albeit in a much more limited area.[16] More important, while the lower evidentiary standard for extraordinary punishments freed the judges

---

[13] The problem with the higher Roman-canon standard was, of course, that it was unrealistic in its demand for two unimpeachable eyewitnesses.

[14] Extraordinary punishment is also repulsive to us because it could be imposed for *fully proven* behavior not defined by law as crimes. See, e.g., Carpzov, *Practica Nova Imperiali Saxonica Rerum Criminalium*, Pars III, qu. 116, no. 103, and Pars III, qu. 142, no. 51. Discussion of this use belongs to the history of the legality principle, however, rather than to the history of evidence. And while it was for good reasons offensive to nineteenth-century reformers of *ancien régime* criminal justice, it is not relevant to this study.

[15] See John Langbein, John Langbein, *Torture and the Law of Proof*, 12, 59 (Chicago and London : University of Chicago Press, 1977). More recently, and following Langbein, also Jean-Marie Carbasse, *Introduction historique au droit pénal*, 105, 182, 321 (Paris: Presses Universitaires de France, 1990).

[16] Sporadically, even long prison terms could not be imposed on circumstantial evidence. See Arnd Koch, *Denunciatio*, 206–207 (Frankfurt: Vittorio Klostermann, 2006). On nineteenth-century

Evading the Roman-Canon Full Proof Standard

from dependence on the most exacting Roman-canon proof standard, it did not liberate them from other Roman-canon legal proof rules capable of limiting their fact-finding freedom. Some courts continued to require an eyewitness for the imposition of milder punishments, for example, and some provisions on circumstantial evidence required for these punishments were specifically designed to act as constraints on the decision-maker's freedom.[17]

Langbein's theory is right, however, in pointing out that most evidence rules required for milder punishments left ample room for the subjective assessment of probative value – not only in determining the existence of indirectly relevant facts, but also in drawing inferences from them. Even if a single indirectly relevant item of evidence was as compelling as Thoreau's trout found in milk, other items of circumstantial evidence could have removed or reduced its impact. The Italian murder case related in Chapter 5 illustrated the elasticity of decision-making on circumstantial evidence. Is it then not appropriate to designate the evidentiary standard for the imposition of milder punishments as one of free evaluation of evidence? The full answer to this question must again be postponed until the modern concept of free proof is elucidated in Chapter 10. What can be said in anticipation is that the disregard of proof sufficiency rules for *poena extraordinaria*, no matter how pliable they may have been, was subject to rebuke on appeal, and to challenge in professional responsibility proceedings. Sporadically, appellate review of decisions made on circumstantial evidence was even mandatory. This is significant because the review of factual findings required a normative foothold for its exercise. If constraints on the judge's evaluation of evidence did not exist, meaningful supervision of his findings would have been impossible. What conclusion follows? If free proof is understood to imply the absence of normative constraint on the judge's assessment of evidence, then the era of free proof was not ushered in by the spreading of extraordinary punishments. They served only to reduce the frustration of judges whom Roman-canon full proof prevented from administering sanguinary punishments. If, on the other hand, free evaluation of evidence is understood not to exclude normative constraints on decision-making, then the

---

legislation in German political units reflecting the continuing need for in-court confessions, see Mirjan Damaška, The Death of Legal Torture, 87 *Yale Law Journal*, 860, 871 (1978). The Austrian Penal Code of 1803 went so far in its effort to facilitate obtaining confessions and obtaining the required legal proof that it abolished the defendant's right to assistance of counsel in first-instance proceedings. Isolating the defendant and holding him incommunicado to obtain a self-incriminating statement was the main reasons for this early nineteenth-century regression.

[17] On the persistence of other rules limiting fact-finding freedom, see Brigitte Thäle, *Die Verdachtsstrafe in der kriminalwissenschaftlichen Literatur des 18 and 19 Jahrhunderts*, 34, 38 (Bern: Peter Lang, 1993). Further indicative of the continued downgrading of circumstantial evidence were provisions of some early nineteenth-century codifications requiring automatic review of all decisions based on *indicia*. On their automatic review under the Austrian Penal Code of 1803, see J. Kropatscheck (ed.), 17 *Sammlung der Gesetze* (Vienna, 1803). Part I, para 435(a) for felonies, and Part II, para 400 for minor offenses.

Intermediate Judgments 111

evidentiary standards for the imposition of milder punishment could be seen as introducing a variant of now-prevailing fact-finding systems.

INTERMEDIATE JUDGMENTS

The other instrument capable of alleviating the discontent caused to judges by the demanding Roman-canon evidentiary standard consisted of intermediate judgments tucked in between acquittal and conviction. Several kinds of these judgments existed, but the only ones relevant to this study are those available in situations when the assembled evidence satisfied the *indicia indubitata* standard both for imposing extraordinary punishments and for ordering torture. Observe that ordering torture was risky in jurisdictions where incriminating evidence was invalidated ("purged") if the defendant withstood the painful examination without confessing. An outright acquittal would then result, despite powerful incriminating material gathered in the course of the investigation.[18] Imposing extraordinary punishment, on the other hand, could in some circumstances be viewed by judges as being too mild a response to serious crime. Pronouncing intermediate judgments could in this situation appear preferable both to ordering torture and to imposing extraordinary punishments. The judgments did not produce the *res iudicata* effect, leaving the issue of the defendant's criminal responsibility undecided, so that proceeding against him could be continued and blood punishments imposed if and when full proof became available. In the interim, the defendant could be placed under surveillance, and various restrictions could be imposed on his activities. An intermediate judgment of this kind, called *absolutio ab instantia*, appeared in the practice of late medieval courts. Italian jurists elaborated its features, and as of the fourteenth century the judgment spread across the continent.[19]

In a purely epistemic sense, the idea of inserting judgments between conviction and acquittal is not objectionable. To realize this, consider possible attitudes the fact-finders may adopt toward the defendant's criminal responsibility at the close of evidence. Not only can they feel persuaded that he is guilty or innocent, they can also remain uncertain whether factual predicates exist for finding him guilty. Between the two mental states of certainty a range of beliefs can persist expressing the fact-finder's probability estimates – some gravitating toward a belief in guilt and others toward a belief in innocence. From the epistemic standpoint, then, judgments designed to capture these intermediate states of mind make sense. An argument can even be mounted in their favor. Observe that when acquittal is

---

[18] See Carpzov, *Practica Nova Imperiali Saxonica Rerum Criminalium*, Pars III, qu. 125, nos. 3, 5, 6, 9–15. See also supra, n.6

[19] For a study of the origin and dissemination of this judgment, see Mathias Schmoeckel, *Humanität und Staatsraison*, 367–383. French courts developed several types of intermediate judgments to express varying degrees of evidentiary support for them and to attach different sanctions to them "*pro modo probationum.*" On the details of this complex French system, see also Schmoeckel, *ibid.*, at 384–403.

Evading the Roman-Canon Full Proof Standard

the only alternative to conviction, the innocent defendant is placed in the same category as defendants burdened with serious incriminating evidence, and deprived of procedural mechanisms to fully clear himself from the stigma of crime.[20] Hence if intermediate judgments expressed only the fact that a crime has not been proven, they would not belong to the odious features of *ancien régime* criminal justice. What makes them repulsive to our values is that they did not become *res iudicata*, and kept the possibility of the death penalty looming over the heads of defendants like the sword of Damocles. They also caused deleterious consequences – such as travel restrictions – to persons who were merely suspected of crime. If stripped of these two objectionable attributes, however, intermediate judgments are not abhorrent. It is therefore not strange that they outlived the inquisitorial process of the *ancien régime* and have still not completely disappeared.[21] If they remain problematic even in this innocuous form, it is because they cannot be reconciled with the presumption of innocence properly understood. Absent legal legerdemain, the presumption demands that the defendant be acquitted whenever his or her guilt has not been proven. If innocence is presumed, it must be treated as such until rebutted.

After extraordinary punishments were rejected at the beginning of the nineteenth century, intermediate judgments were not only retained in German political units, but were pronounced by courts with increasing frequency.[22] This is understandable because they were the only legal instrument left to reduce the annoyance of judges when the surviving Roman-canon full proof prevented them from imposing the harshest punishments on defendants whom they considered guilty. It was only in the middle of the nineteenth century that *absolutio ab instantia* was finally abolished.[23] By then, the difficulty of reconciling intermediate judgments with values protected by the presumption of innocence and the requirement of proof beyond a reasonable doubt was no longer veiled by the invocation of crime control arguments.

---

[20] The European Court of Human Rights has recently rebuked a German judge for hinting in reasons for his judgment of acquittal that the defendant might nevertheless be guilty. See *Cleve* v. *Germany*, ECHR, 5th Section (January 15, 2015).

[21] Enlightenment luminaries did not advocate the rejection of intermediate judgments. They were satisfied instead with introducing temporal limits on the postponement of *res iudicata* effects radiating from them. See Cesare Beccaria, *Dei Delitti e delle Pene*, para. 19, at 45 (Turin: Einaudi, 1994). In Italy, a type of judgment other than that of conviction and acquittal – the judgment *per insufficienza delle prove* – survived until the last decades of the twentieth century. And the Scottish "not proven" verdict is another example of the longevity of the notion that intermediate judgments are appropriate.

[22] In France, intermediate judgments were abolished in the last decade of the eighteenth century, but not as result of the aversion toward them. Their disappearance was the side effect of the wholesale rejection of the inquisitorial process during the French Revolution.

[23] See Peter Holtappels, *Die Entwicklungsgeschichte des Grundsatzes in "dubio pro reo,"* 84–86 (Hamburg: Cram, de Gruyter & Co, 1965).

9

Recapitulation

It is time to gather together the threads of our survey of the Roman-canon fact-finding scheme for the criminal process. As noted in Chapter 3, the purpose of the survey was to establish the extent to which Roman-canon legal proof limited the judge's freedom to assess the probative value of evidence. In so doing, we have focused on the discord that could arise between factual outcomes resulting from the mechanical application of legal proof rules and outcomes resulting from the judge's personal assessment of evidence in particular cases. The reason for this cynosure was that the judge felt constrained in his decision-making freedom only when factual findings he believed were accurate differed from those required by fidelity to legal rules. Two possible constraining effects of these rules were distinguished, one "positive," the other "negative." First examined was the question whether legal proof produced the positive effect by forcing the judge to impose punishment on defendants he believed were innocent. This proved not to be the case. As applied in the criminal process, Roman-canon proof sufficiency rules did not force the judge to impose capital and mutilating punishments on defendants he believed were innocent. The sworn testimony of two eyewitnesses obligated him to convict and impose blood punishment only if he found them credible and their testimony concordant and persuasive.[1] In the course of the judicial investigation, and especially at its informal initial stage, he had not only the opportunity but also the duty to assess the probative value of testimony. In other words, the imposition of punishment required both objective legal proof and the judge's belief in its probative value. The same was true of the defendant's courtroom confession: whether spontaneous or coerced, the judge was supposed to accept it only if he found it trustworthy.[2]

In contrast to its absence of positive potential, Roman-canon legal proof was capable of exercising a negative impact, preventing the judge from imposing capital or mutilating punishment in the absence of legally prescribed evidence, even if other evidence in the case persuaded him of the defendant's criminal responsibility.

---

[1] For a similar conclusion, see Matthias Schmoeckel, *Humanität und Staatsraison*, 193–194 (Vienna: Böhlau, 2000).

[2] Cf. again Schmoeckel, *ibid.*, 204.

It is true that a minority doctrine allowed the use of blood punishment on circumstantial evidence whose evaluation required the exercise of personal judgment, so that the divorce between legally mandated outcomes and outcomes the judge believed to be correct could be forestalled, or at least the discrepancy between them could be reduced. Yet the view prevailed in legal doctrine that the imposition of capital and mutilating punishments requires direct evidence – two eyewitnesses or a defendant's in-court confession. Although exceptions provided by the doctrine weakened the rigidity of this position, it was still capable of preventing judges in some jurisdictions from imposing sanguinary punishments on defendants of whose guilt they were convinced on legally insufficient evidence. Thus, while in regard to its positive impact, legal proof was dispositive only if accompanied by the judge's belief in its actual probative value, in regard to its negative impact, legal proof alone could be decisive and the judge's personal assessment of evidence irrelevant. Only in this negative sense, then, did Roman-canon legal proof generate discords between factual findings mandated by the law and factual findings the judge believed to be correct. And although these discords were experienced as a lesser problem than they would have been if the law had compelled the judge to impose sanguinary punishment on persons he considered innocent, the discrepancy was still a serious problem in the criminal process of the *ancien régime*: it impeded the satisfaction of strong punitive urges of law enforcers, and it complicated the realization of the then-prevailing criminal policy. But the divorce between legally mandated and substantively correct outcomes could also be caused by rules on testimonial disqualifications, illegally obtained evidence, and exclusion of hearsay evidence. Although these rules were meant to decide what evidence should be admitted, rather than what value to attribute to it, we have seen that the institutional setting of the judicial apparatus often converted them into rules barring the judge from deciding the case on evidence he found persuasive. He could be thwarted again from imposing sanguinary punishment in situations in which he thought it was called for. The gap could arise once more between decisions he believed were accurate and decisions mandated by law.

Where negative legal proof impeded the realization of criminal policy, instruments were designed to circumvent the law, or to alleviate the undesirable consequences of its implementation. The most important instrument was the imposition of punishments milder than death or mutilation, on less demanding evidence than the normally required evidentiary standard. Proof required for the use of these punishments consisted mainly of circumstantial evidence whose assessment accorded judges considerable fact-finding freedom: they could combine *indicia* in complementary ways to arrive at factual findings corresponding to their beliefs. But not all rules on circumstantial evidence had the required valences to be braided in such flexible fashion. If all of them had been equally flexible, the fact-finding freedom of the judges would have been unfettered, and no meaningful review of

Recapitulation

their findings would have been possible. But the review of decisions based on circumstantial evidence existed, and could even be made mandatory.

Although the terrain we traversed in canvassing the Roman-canon fact-finding scheme revealed many legal constraints on the freedom of judges to evaluate evidence, it also revealed how untenable is the trope that the scheme turned them into puppets on the strings of evidence law. Almost everywhere the rigidity of legal proof was cushioned by what we now call judicial discretion. This enabled judges to escape the obligation of imposing blood punishments on evidence they believed was weak, and, although to a much lesser degree, of acquitting defendants whose guilt was obvious on legally insufficient evidence. The exercise of personal judgment inherent in this discretion avoided the objections raised by Christian moral theology, as discussed in Chapter 1. For when judges disbelieved the veracity of an eyewitness incriminating a defendant, or the truthfulness of his confession, their disbelief prevented rather than caused the spilling of blood, so that theology had no reason to oppose the personal involvement of judges in determining the actual value of legal proof in particular cases.[3] Nor was the negative effect of legal proof rules disturbing to theologians: it too prevented rather than required the imposition of sanguinary punishment. And since crime appeared through theological lenses as a sin, theologians could find solace in the thought that criminals who avoided the terrestrial punishment they deserved would not escape it in the hereafter.

In referring to the room for maneuver possessed by the judge in applying legal proof, Roman-canon sources did not use the Latin equivalent of the word "freedom" (*libertas*). Instead they used terms such as deciding according to "conscience" (*conscientia*), "religion" (*religio*), or "the impulse of the soul" (*motus animi*). Most frequently used, however, was the term *arbitrium*, devoid at the time of pejorative connotations and corresponding roughly to our concept of discretion. But, as we have repeatedly emphasized, the judge's latitude in applying legal proof rules – no matter how labelled – did not imply the absence of normative constraints. The dose of subjectivity allowed him in assessing the value of evidence was held in check: the reasons for departing from legal proof, or relaxing its rigidity, were supposed to be based on verifiable grounds. Disregarding the testimony of a legally competent eyewitness required that the reasons therefor be noted by the judge or a notary in the case file and preserved for possible review.[4]

One way in which jurists described the limits of discretion was to invoke reason and virtue as models for the judge's behavior. A medieval example of this hortatory

---

[3] On the contrary, the theological "safer path" doctrine required that the judge should acquit the defendant if unsure of his guilt. Announced at the birth of the inquisitorial process by Pope Innocent III, the doctrine could have led in some circumstances to verdicts required by our proof standard of reasonable doubt. One of the reasons why this doctrine could not lead to outright acquittals was the insertion of intermediate judgments between conviction and acquittal pure and simple.

[4] The companion requirement that the judge explain his final decision was introduced into Church proceedings as early as the thirteenth century. See the decretal *Sicut Nobis* (X, XXVII) of Pope Innocent III.

116   *Recapitulation*

approach can be found in Gandinus. Writing about the judge's discretion (*arbitrium*) in assessing the sufficiency of evidence for torture, he remarked that nothing else could be said on the subject other than that the judge "should proceed with good conscience, according to what his conscience dictates."[5] Conscience was not associated with inscrutable inner motives, however, or with other matters pertaining to the chemistry of the unknown. According to Baldus, it was a mental state involving not only "cognizance of one's own heart" but also "the commands of reason," whose observance could be checked by supervising authority.[6] The most common way of describing the limits on the judge's fact-finding freedom, especially in early modern times, was to say that judicial discretion was "regulated". The source of this regulation and what it entailed led to obscure formulations. "The judge with power to act according to discretion," Damhouder opined, "should not follow his own judgment, or his own discretion and conscience, but public ones, regulated and shaped according to law and the canons."[7] What the enigmatic concepts of "public" conscience and "public discretion" demanded, Damhouder failed to specify. One question that remained conspicuously unsettled was whether constraints on the exercise of discretion emanated only from civil and canon law, or also from normative sources transcending the positive legal order. Menochio, who wrote extensively on the subject, claimed that the limits of discretion could spring from domains that need not belong to positive law. According to him, judicial discretion was of two kinds. One was "full discretion," allowing the judge to make decisions according to his own desire (*proprio ductus appetitu*). Another kind applicable to criminal cases (*arbitrium regulatum*) was discretion regulated not only by civil and canon law, but also by reason and equitable considerations approximating natural law.[8]

Although resistant to transparent summation, the judge's limited or regulated discretion emerges as of the greatest importance to the proper understanding of the Roman-canon fact-finding scheme for criminal cases: it mediated tensions inherent

---

[5] *"Videtur, quod sic, qui dare arbitrium potestati nihil aliud dicere, nisi ut cum bona conscientia procedat, secundum quod eius conscientia dictaverit."* See Albertus Gandinus, Tractatus de Maleficiis, Rubrica de Questionibus et Tormentis, 38, 24, in Herman Kantorowicz, *Albertus Gandinus und das Strafrecht der Scholastik*, vol. 2, p. 175 (Berlin: J. Guttentag, 1926). According to Bartolus, the judge had to exercise discretion following the paradigm of a good person (*vir bonus*) or a wise man in the Aristotelian tradition. For an analysis of his views, see Susanne Lepsius, *Von Zweifeln bis Überzeugung*, 165, 318 (Frankfurt: Vittorio Klostermann, 2003).

[6] *"Conscientia autem dicitur a conscio conscis, id est cognitio sui ipsius cordis, et est conscientia dictamen rationis, et si recta non est ratio esse non potest."* Baldus, *In Sextum Codicis Librum Commentaria*, qu. De Schismaticis, in nomine Patris et Filii et Spiritus Sancti, no. 10 (Venice, 1599).

[7] *"Qui habet potestatem disponendi secundum arbitrium, discretionem, ac conscientiam, nequoquam debet segui proprium abitrium vel propriam conscientiam, sed publicam, quae est regulata et reformata secundum leges et canones."* See Josse de Damhouder, *Praxis Rerum Criminalium*, Caput 36, no. 3 (Antwerp, 1601).

[8] *"Qualia sit huius judicii potestas in causis criminalibus,"* he asked. His answer was: *"non liberum et absolutum arbitrium, sed de jure et ratione regulatum et ob id ius et equitatem juri naturae proximam servare debet."* See Jacobus Menochius, *De arbitrariis iudicum questionibus et causis centuriae sex*, Lib. 1, centuria 77, casus 90 (Geneva, 1671).

in the scheme from its inception to its final days. While the demanding proof sufficiency standards required relaxation in order not to impede the realization of criminal policy, the judge's unconstrained fact-finding freedom was anathema in a judicial apparatus dedicated to uniform and supervised decision-making. Limited discretion provided a solution to the resulting predicament. It permitted charting the course for navigation between the Scylla of rigid normativity and the Charybdis of uncontrollable decision-making freedom. And while it required the relaxation of the *rigor canonum*, it promised that the relaxation would occur in a regular and orderly fashion.

How does the *arbitrium regulatum* of the Roman-canon judge relate to the understanding of the judge's fact-finding freedom in contemporary systems of criminal justice? We saw that a few legal historians believe that our understanding of free evaluation of evidence was adopted in late medieval times by both Roman-canon jurists and court practice. Others take the view that fact-finding freedom in our sense became established only in early modern times as a by-product of the decline of blood punishments. Still others think that the modern understanding is the fruit of modern views on the relationship between legal norms and forensic fact-finding activity, views without precedent in premodern times. As we have noted repeatedly, evaluation of evidence free from normative constraints is differently understood in contemporary systems of criminal justice. These differences must be elucidated before the relationship between premodern and modern approaches to fact-finding freedom can meaningfully be addressed. The time has come to do so: the differences must be identified and their relationship explored. But because prevailing views on the subject are not equal in continental and common law jurisdictions, their relation to the Roman-canon fact-finding scheme must be examined separately.

10

Continental Successors to Roman-Canon Legal Proof

Modern continental systems of criminal justice profess allegiance to the so-called principle of free evaluation of evidence, but the principle is understood in two different ways. The difference between them will now be determined and their relationship to the Roman-canon legal proof explored. Of interest for our purposes will be only those relations between modern and premodern fact-finding arrangements that have a bearing on the latitude accorded judges in assessing the value of evidence. Accordingly, our analysis will be untethered by the momentous contrasts between the social, political and cultural milieux in which criminal justice systems embracing Roman-canon legal proof functioned, and the milieux in which systems professing allegiance to free evaluation of evidence now operate.

INTIMATE CONVICTION AND ROMAN-CANON LEGAL PROOF

Modern continental attitudes toward legal constraints on the evaluation of evidence emerged in the French revolutionary regime of the late eighteenth century, whose legislators decided to copy the English machinery of justice and introduce the jury trial. The main reason for their rejection of Roman-canon legal proof was their belief that rules on the value of evidence and its sufficiency for findings of fact were too complicated for lay use, and therefore incompatible with a justice system in which cases were decided by lay persons enlisted in the criminal justice apparatus *ad hoc*. To the extent that admissibility rules and judicial instructions to the jury were caught in the beam of the revolutionary legislators' lamp, they too appeared unacceptable. For they implied that judges – politically suspect in revolutionary France – would control the flow of information to the jurors, imagined at the time as avatars of the sovereign French people. What was then to guide the jurors in arriving at conclusions of fact? Revolutionary legislators adopted a standard propagated by Beccaria, among others. In his view, decision-making in the factual domain depended on inner experiences – including murmurings of intuition – generated by the totality of presented evidence. The certainty required for establishing the defendant's guilt, he wrote, "can more readily be felt than be accurately

Intimate Conviction and Roman-Canon Legal Proof

determined."[1] Following this understanding of mental processes involved in arriving at conclusions of fact, a French revolutionary statute required each juror to take the following oath: "I swear that I will decide according to evidence presented by the prosecution and the defense according to my conscience and my inner conviction, impartially and with fairness befitting a free man."[2] Sufficiency of evidence required for verdicts – implicit in this oath – became a legally untouchable matter of inner psychological acceptance and personal intuition, resistant to transparent summation. The resulting decision-making standard came to be called "intimate conviction" (*conviction intime*).

Although somewhat obscured, yet another reason existed for discarding legal proof. If a legal scheme for measuring probative value superior to that of Roman-canon law were available to revolutionary legislators, they would have been tempted to retain a few legal proof rules as guidance to the jury. This seems likely, since the potential for abuse of normatively unconstrained evaluation of evidence was not ignored by the French Revolutionary Assembly during the heated debates that culminated in the rejection of Roman-canon rules of proof.[3] But in tune with the views that gained ground in Western philosophical and scientific discourse from the seventeenth century, the opinion prevailed that the value of evidence depended so much on the circumstances of particular cases that it was impossible to make satisfactory rules on the subject. It should not be overlooked, however, that not only rules of weight, but also intrinsic admissibility rules – like the hearsay ban – were suspect on this epistemic ground, because they also rested on categorical depreciation of certain types of evidence. These rules too became vulnerable to the objection that in the infinitely varied circumstances of particular cases ingested in the justice system, abstract rules on the subject would often be either over- or under-inclusive.

How does free evaluation of evidence as *conviction intime* relate to Roman-canon proof sufficiency rules? In regard to the Roman-canon evidentiary standard for the imposition of sanguinary punishment, conventional wisdom locates an antipodal contrast to free evaluation: *conviction intime* is purely subjective, while Roman-canon full proof appears to be purely objective. But as Chapters 4 and 5 have shown, as far as the *positive* aspect of the Roman-canon full proof is concerned, this understanding of the relationship is overstated. We saw that the objective component of Roman-canon full proof was insufficient for the imposition of sanguinary punishments: the judge had to be convinced that the two eyewitnesses or the defendant's

---

[1] See Cesare Beccaria, *Dei Delitti e delle Pene*, paragraph 14, p. 35 (Turin: Einaudi, 1994).

[2] The Law of 16–29 September 1791, art. 24, title 6.

[3] See Antonio Padoa Schioppa, La Giuria all'Assemblea Costituente Francese, in A. P. Schioppa (ed.), *The Trial Jury in England, and Germany*, 118 (Berlin: Duncker & Humblot, 1987). Even prior to the Revolution some Enlightenment luminaries worried that miscarriages of justice might occur if only conscience and commonsense remained as guides to forensic decision-making. See, e.g., Voltaire, Prix de la Justice et de l'Humanité, 80B *Oeuvres Complètes*, para. XXII, p. 170 (Oxford: Voltaire Foundation, 2009).

confession are reliable. A less dramatic difference between the two standards is obvious, however: in contrast to the Roman-canon standard, *conviction intime* needs no objective substratum, no specified quantity and quality of evidence. An antipodal contrast between the two standards comes into view only when the *negative* effect of the Roman-canon full proof becomes the object of comparison. For while *conviction intime* makes the fact-finders' decision dependent on purely subjective factors, some of which may be rooted in the subsoil of consciousness, the mainstream Roman-canon doctrine made the judge's belief in the defendant's guilt irrelevant in the absence of two eyewitnesses, or a defendant's confession to back up his belief. So while *conviction intime* is an eminently subjective evidentiary standard, the Roman-canon standard was in its negative aspects eminently objective.

What about the opinion of some legal historians that the Roman-canon full proof was so elastic that free evaluation of evidence was already the tenet of medieval jurists? If free evaluation of evidence is understood as *conviction intime*, this opinion is mistaken. The Roman-canon judge was not allowed to make factual findings on inscrutable personal grounds. Our reconnaissance of the Roman-canon legal terrain revealed that he was not permitted to depart from legal proof without outwardly discernible reasons.[4] His discretion was bounded and his findings were amenable to review by superiors. Most important, his belief in the defendant's guilt obtained on the basis of legally insufficient evidence was completely beside the point in the absence of legal proof required for the imposition of sanguinary punishments. In a word, the subjective yardstick of *conviction intime* was completely alien to the Roman-canon evidentiary standard needed for the imposition of capital and mutilating punishments.

Could the Roman-canon standard of evidence needed for the use of milder punishments (*poenae extraordinariae*) be equated with free evaluation of evidence understood in the sense of *conviction intime*? The answer is again negative. It is clearly mistaken to identify *conviction intime* with the way in which circumstantial evidence was treated in the Roman-canon fact-finding scheme. Although Roman-canon provisions on circumstantial evidence were flexible, we have seen that they were nonetheless capable of constraining judges' fact-finding freedom. Judgments based on circumstantial evidence could also be subjected to appellate review. On the other hand, factual findings made under the regime of *conviction intime* are supposed to reflect the inner acceptance of factual hypotheses, and should for this reason be impervious to external scrutiny of their rectitude.

All things considered, then, if free evaluation of evidence is understood in its pristine French sense, it turns out that free evaluation was neither professed nor practiced in criminal procedures using Roman-canon fact-finding evidence law. Whether the theory equating the treatment of evidence for milder punishments with

---

[4] See *supra* Chapter 4, text above note 23.

Reasoned Conviction and Roman-Canon Legal Proof

free evaluation of evidence differently understood is sustainable, is a question that will emerge gradually as our inquiry continues.

REASONED CONVICTION AND ROMAN-CANON LEGAL PROOF

The continental revolutionary enthusiasm for untutored lay people as triers of fact did not last long. Given the hierarchical and bureaucratic attitudes of the judicial apparatus which survived revolutionary upheavals, unreviewable jury verdicts were soon criticized as arbitrary and erratic. As a result, the jury as a body of lay persons who sit alone and independently return verdicts was replaced in most continental lands by tribunals in which amateurs decide factual and legal issues jointly with professional judges. Even in France, the original jury was transformed into such a body.[5] But while contemporary French legislation still proclaims loyalty to *conviction intime*,[6] the majority of continental countries have adopted a different understanding of free evaluation of evidence for both mixed tribunals and purely professional courts. According to this understanding, the fact-finders' freedom in attributing value to evidence includes only freedom from *legal* rules determining the quantity and quality of evidence required for the verdict. The freedom does not include dispensation from rules of rational inference, or license to disregard the maxims of experience. And since rules regulating fact-finding activity exist, albeit not legal in nature, the propriety of factual findings can be subjected to superior review. To facilitate the review, trial courts must supply written reasons for their findings.[7] This more recent understanding of free evaluation, which now prevails in continental criminal procedure, is often referred to as "reasoned conviction" (*conviction raisonnée*).[8]

---

[5] Despite disenchantments with its performance, the transformation of the jury came late to France, because of sentimental attachment to this child of the grand Revolution. The transformation occurred only in Vichy France during World War II. After the war, all the legislation enacted by the quisling government was abrogated, save the statute which transformed the jury into a mixed tribunal. See Gaston Stefani and George Levasseur, *Procédure Pénale*, 331 (10th ed.) (Paris: Sirey, 1977). This sole exemption from abrogation speaks volumes about how important the transformation of the jury into a mixed tribunal must have appeared to the cognoscenti.

[6] See the Code de Procédure Pénale, arts. 304, 352, and 427. Even the romantic notion that the adjudicator's decision in criminal cases originates from his or her deepest self ("*au plus profund de soi*") has still not disappeared. See, e.g., Jean-Denis Bredin, Le Doute et l'Intime Conviction, 23 *Droits* (1996), p. 21; Etienne Vergès et al., *Droit de la Preuve*, 434, 436–438 (Paris: Presses Universitaires de France, 2015).

[7] This requirement can apply even to a few untransformed continental juries that are composed solely of lay people. A noteworthy example is the Spanish jury, required to give reasons for its special verdicts. If the "supervising judge" finds these reasons inadequate, jury verdicts can be returned to jurors for correction, or be reversed by higher courts. See Ley Organica del Tribunal del Jurado, art. 63 (1) and art. 65 (1995).

[8] See Massimo Nobili, *Il Principio del Libero Convincimento del Giudice*, 8 (Milan: Giuffrè, 1974); Günter Deppenkemper, *Beweiswürdigung als Mittel prozessualer Wahrheitserkenntnis*, 208 (Göttingen: V&R Unipress, 2004).

Observe, however, that where superior review of factual findings exists, be it in direct or indirect form, the claim that the evaluation of evidence is free from legal rules trembles in the gusts of invading realism.[9] The claim can be sustained only by the unrealistic – albeit still widely accepted – legal doctrine that court decisions are not a source of law. It is true that appellate court decisions dealing with factual issues are often deeply contextual, so that no sharp-edged rules can be abstracted from them. Yet, rules capable of constraining fact-finding freedom emerge over time in all jurisdictions. In most countries, they are collected and published. If a judge is ignorant of these rules, or purposely disregards them, it is strained to say that he or she has run afoul of extralegal precepts of logic or experience, rather than that he or she was insufficiently aware or respectful of the law. Take the example of a witness who asserts in his testimony that video footage contains decisive incriminating evidence, while the defendant refuses to consent to the playing of the recording. If an appellate court rules that defendants have the right to do so, and that no incriminating inference should be drawn from their refusal, a rule has emerged capable of constraining the decision-maker's fact-finding freedom. And if a trial judge in a subsequent case justifies the judgment of conviction by the defendant's refusal to consent, it is only legal legerdemain to blame him or her for failing to observe extralegal considerations, rather than for failing to follow the law. Nor is it unprecedented for some continental appellate courts openly to interfere with judges' freedom to determine the probative value of evidence. For instance, a high court may deny trial judges the power to substitute their own opinions for the differing opinions of experts. They are then left with the option of either accepting the original expert's opinion, or appointing another expert in the hope of obtaining an opinion corresponding to their own.[10] Either way, their fact-finding freedom is circumscribed.

Constraints on the fact-finding freedom of continental judges do not emanate solely from within the judicial apparatus, however. An increasing number of provisions can now be found in continental legislation whose avowed purpose – or indirect effect – is to tell judges whether they can legitimately use specified items of information in their decision-making. An example of legislation *directly* affecting judicial freedom is provisions exclusively enumerating the means of proof, or ways

---

[9] The review is direct in those continental jurisdictions where appellate courts are authorized to reverse, and sometimes even to alter, factual findings of trial courts. The review is indirect in jurisdictions like Germany, where the legacy of jury trials caused the law to permit challenges to judgments only in regard to *legal* error. Here appellate courts cannot reverse findings they find faulty by invoking disregard of maxims of experience or canons of proper reasoning, since they are not considered legal in nature. What, then, do these courts do when they are disinclined to let a factual mistake stand? They hold that the trial court has breached a *legal* provision whose purpose is to assure accurate fact-finding. Rather than holding that a trial court's inference is unreasonable, for example, they rule that the trial court has breached a statutory provision on proper ways in which reasons for the judgment ought to be written.

[10] See the judgment of the German Supreme Court of general jurisdiction (BGH) as published in *Neue Juristische Wochenschrift*, 2061 (Munich: C.H. Beck, 1961).

in which evidence must be presented in court. If persuasive information emerges at the trial from means of proof the law does not recognize, or from evidence presented in an inappropriate manner, judges are not allowed to use it, no matter how important it may appear to them for ferreting out the truth. Another example is legislative provisions in some continental jurisdictions making expert testimony mandatory for the determination of specified facts, irrespective of whether judges are persuaded of the truth of these facts by other testimony. Legislative provisions can also be found prohibiting the drawing of negative inferences from the defendant's invocation of his right to silence, even if persuasive inferences from his selective taciturnity can sometimes be drawn.

Equally important are *indirect* constraints on judges' fact-finding freedom emanating from legislative provisions. Constraints of this nature mushroomed across continental Europe in the aftermath of traumatic experiences with twentieth-century totalitarian regimes. These experiences induced legislators to accept the idea that evidence, no matter how cognitively precious, should not be used against the defendant if obtained in violation of human rights. The result was the adoption of a vast array of exclusionary rules in statutory and sometimes even constitutional form. The importance attached to the defendant's right to confront witnesses against him also led many continental countries to reintroduce the ban on the use of oral hearsay, rejected in the aftermath of the French Revolution as one of the "legal chains" limiting jurors' fact-finding freedom.[11] Consider that continental judges sit in unicameral courts and decide on both the admissibility and the value of evidence. They can therefore easily become exposed to prohibited evidence and be required to disregard it even if they find it persuasive.[12] What then happens parallels what we observed happening in the Roman-canon procedural context: rules aimed at keeping information out of the pool of usable evidence undergo transformation into rules requiring judges to attribute no probative value to evidence no matter how impressed by it they might be.

Can judges remove knowledge that has been lodged in their minds? This question has already been addressed in reviewing the Roman-canon fact-finding scheme, but it deserves to be amplified at this point. The answer depends on how humans process information. If they are capable of reasoning about facts by attaching separate value to items of information, and then coming to a conclusion by aggregating or

---

[11] Following the Roman-canon precedent, however, the continental hearsay concept is still limited to its oral form. Sporadic court decisions can even be found prohibiting conviction based solely on hearsay. On the current hearsay ban in Italy, Portugal and Spain, see Elisabetta Grande, Legal Transplants and the Inoculation Effect: How American Criminal Procedure has Affected Continental Europe, 64 *American Journal of Comparative Law*, 583, 607 (2016).

[12] It is true that comprehensive pre-trial stages of continental criminal procedure – ending with the full discovery of the prosecution's case – enable identification of inadmissible evidence prior to trial. Tainted evidence can then be excluded from the file of the case transmitted to trial judges, so that they remain ignorant of what they are not supposed to consider. But the forbidden character of some evidentiary items can still emerge only at the trial.

disaggregating these values, then they can follow the law's mandate and attribute no probative value to prohibited evidence.[13] Empirical research suggests, however, that faced with the reconstruction of complex events, humans experience difficulty disentangling the value of discrete information from global judgments and process information in a compartmentalized or monadic fashion.[14] If conclusions drawn from this research are correct, what can judges do if they want to follow the dictate of the law to disregard evidence they have found persuasive? If the untainted evidence is clearly insufficient for conviction, the answer is easy: they ought to acquit the defendant. Where this is not the case, and incriminating evidence is strong, they can only engage in a thought experiment, trying to switch to the viewpoint of a person uncontaminated by forbidden information, and imagine what verdict that person might reach. But if they engage in such counterfactual hypothesizing, they end up deciding cases on considerations extraneous to their actual beliefs. This presents a problem if their thought experiment results in the conclusion that the defendant committed the crime, because the conclusion compromises the requirement that judges convict a defendant only when personally convinced of his or her guilt. And since the requirement of personal conviction persists in continental evidence law like aged redwoods in a forest, the standard of reasoned *conviction* can be observed only by transferring the case to judges ignorant of prohibited evidence. But since this is a costly proposition, the most common solution to the problem is for judges to refrain from referring to prohibited evidence in compiling written reasons for the verdict, even when this evidence has actually influenced their decision.

Let us now examine how constraints on the judge's fact-finding freedom inherent in the *conviction raisonnée* systems compare to those embedded in the Roman-canon fact-finding scheme.[15] Conventional wisdom discovers here another radical opposition. We are told that while the Roman-canon scheme deprived the judge of freedom by legal rules determining the value of evidence, reasoned conviction rejects all *legal* rules on the subject. It only requires judges to obey extralegal considerations – logic and experience – in arriving at their conclusions. Actually,

---

[13] In the early nineteenth century this approach was designated as "analytic" and contrasted with the "synthetic" one. See Giovanni Carmigiani, *Teoria delle Leggi della Sicurezza Sociale*, vol. 1, p. 308, vol. 4, p. 31 (Pisa: Fratelli Nistri, 1832). Contemporary scholarship usually refers to this approach as "atomistic" and juxtaposes it with the "holistic" antipode. Cf. Mirjan Damaška, *Evidence Law Adrift*, 35–36 (New Haven: Yale University Press, 1997). Logical, psychological, and commonsense dimensions of processing evidence are now studied by the so-called new evidence scholarship. See William Twining, *Rethinking Evidence*, 349–353 (Evanston: Northwestern University Press, 1994).

[14] See Jeffrey Rachlinski et al., Can Judges Ignore Inadmissible Information?, 153 *University of Pennsylvania Law Review*, 1251 (2005); David Sklansky, Evidentiary Instructions and the Jury as Other, 65 *Stanford Law Review*, 407, 414–440 (2013).

[15] At this point, the caveat mentioned at the outset of this chapter is worth repeating. Of interest for the purpose of this study are only differences in the *degree* of these constraints. Differences in the *reasons* for establishing these constraints are vast, not only because of differences in the enveloping political, social and cultural context, but also because of specific procedural reasons, such as paucity of physical evidence in the formative period of Roman-canon evidence.

Reasoned Conviction and Roman-Canon Legal Proof 125

the contrast between these two fact-finding arrangements is again far less dramatic. This is most readily apparent when Roman-canon evidence necessary for administering nonsanguinary punishments (*poenae extraordinariae*) is compared to evidence satisfying the standard of reasoned conviction. We noticed that Roman-canon rules on circumstantial evidence required for the imposition of *poenae extraordinariae*, although numerous, seldom prevented the judge from arriving at factual conclusions corresponding to his actual beliefs. He was capable most of the time of arriving at these conclusions by applying then-prevailing common sense and logic. The case of amorous rivalry was recounted in Chapter 5 for the specific purpose of illustrating the flexible approaches to *indicia*, presumptions and various other kinds of circumstantial evidence invoked by lawyers in the inquisitorial process.[16] But while the judge was not tightly bound by rules, his fact-finding freedom was not unlimited. As Chapter 8 has shown, some legal rules on circumstantial evidence possessed a freedom-limiting potential.[17] More important, the judge's findings of fact were subject to review and reversal if found faulty. They were found faulty, among other reasons, when his inferences from indirect proof made no sense to the reviewers. Compare the limited freedom of the Roman-canon judge to the freedom of judges acting under the regime of *conviction raisonnée*. When the actual impact of continental appellate court decisions and legislative provisions on the processing of evidence is included in the comparison, it transpires that they generate a degree of constraint on judges that is similar to that produced by Roman-canon rules. Logic and experience constrained the Roman-canon judge in ways not greatly dissimilar to the ways in which they constrain our judges. Legal rules limiting fact-finding freedom exist on both sides of the comparison, and so does appellate review of factual findings, which is incompatible with the absence of normative constraints on decision-making. Remember the theory that the use of nonsanguinary punishment introduced free evaluation of evidence into the Roman-canon system? We found that this theory does not stand up to criticism if free evaluation is understood as *conviction intime*.[18] But if free evaluation is understood as "reasoned conviction," then the theory points to a similarity between premodern and modern approaches to circumstantial evidence and the judge's bounded discretion in assessing its probative force.

What about the relationship of *conviction raisonnée* to the Roman-canon full proof standard required for the imposition of sanguinary punishments? Even in this context the contrast between the two fact-finding schemes is not as stark as is often assumed. The contrast does not turn on the need for the judge's belief in the defendant's guilt on one side, and the irrelevance of this belief on the other. We demonstrated that the Roman-canon judge was not compelled to impose blood punishments on legally prescribed evidence if it failed to convince him that

[16] See *supra*, Chapter 5, note 25.
[17] See *supra*, Chapter 8, note 17.
[18] See *supra*, Chapter 8, note 15.

the defendant committed the crime. What this means is that the adjudicator's belief in the defendant's guilt – the *sine qua non* for conviction in modern continental criminal procedure – was also the precondition for conviction in the Roman-canon scheme. The difference between the two systems lies elsewhere. While the mainstream Roman-canon doctrine demanded that the judge's belief in guilt be supported by a legally prescribed quantity and quality of evidence, the *conviction raisonnée* fact-finding system rejected rules requiring legally postulated evidence as an objective basis for the judge's conviction. It is satisfied instead if the judge's belief in guilt is based on legally unspecified evidence, provided that it is capable of generating a high degree of intersubjective probability that his or her factual findings are correct. This difference in framing principles is greatly reduced, however, when one looks at the details of the two fact-finding schemes. As Chapter 7 has shown, the mainstream Roman-canon doctrine subjected the need for the prescribed quantity and quality of evidence to important exceptions. Of greatest practical importance was the provision that in regard to crimes difficult to prove, strong circumstantial evidence (*indicia indubitata*) suffices for conviction.[19] This provision alone lessens the distance between the two fact-finding systems considerably. But the distance is further reduced if we observe that while modern continental evidence does not prescribe what quantity and quality of evidence is needed for conviction, it contains more or less visible rules of what we have called negative legal proof.[20] That these rules are capable of reducing the decision-maker's freedom in arriving at factual determinations is crystal clear, and denying them legal character means closing one's eyes to reality.

How is one to think, then, about the relationship between the standard of *conviction raisonnée* and the Roman-canon standard of proof sufficiency? While the needs of the hierarchical Roman-canon court organization induced the architects of the Roman-canon scheme to start from an abstract preference for rule-bound evaluation of evidence, the attachment of the progenitors of the modern continental scheme to jury trials led them to start from an abstract preference for rule-free evaluation of evidence. But while the need for accurate outcomes and the imperatives of effective criminal policy made Roman-canon jurists reduce the rigidity of legal proof, the need of modern continental lawmakers for uniformity and avoidance of arbitrariness induced them to reintroduce rules constraining the judge's fact-finding freedom. And as Roman-canon law enforcement authorities used the judge's limited discretion (*arbitrium regulatum*) to adapt legal proof rules to the needs of substantively correct outcomes in particular cases, they created a space for judicial maneuver that is similar in its degree to the latitude modern continental judges enjoy in meeting the evidentiary standard of *conviction raisonnée*. In one seldom-noted respect, Roman-canon judges possessed even greater latitude for expressing

---

[19] See supra, Chapter 6, notes 3 and 5.

[20] Think of corroboration rules like those on mandatory expertise, or of admissibility rules that can turn into rules of weight if the judge becomes exposed to inadmissible evidence and finds it credible.

their assessment of evidence than their modern successors. Recall our discussion of intermediate judgments between convictions and outright acquittals.[21] They clash with our liberal sentiments for reasons that need not be rehearsed. But while offensive to our values, they enabled Roman-canon judges to express their beliefs on the state of evidence with greater discrimination than is possible for the modern judge, limited as he or she is to the dichotomous choice between acquittals and convictions. Evidence presented in the case not only could have persuaded Roman-canon judges of a defendant's guilt or innocence, but could have left them uncertain about his criminal responsibility. Intermediate judgments did not compel them, as modern fact-finding arrangements compel our judges, to treat a defendant whom they strongly suspected of guilt as if they had established that he or she was innocent. In the end, both schemes produced fact-finding arrangements in which the evaluation of evidence is neither entirely bound by rules nor entirely free from them. The expectation to find a radical difference between the two fact-finding schemes in terms of the judge's degree of freedom in attributing value to evidence evaporates on closer inspection like mist on summer mornings.

[21] See *supra*, Chapter 8, note 19.

11

Roman-Canon Legal Proof and Common Law Evidence

The common law fact-finding scheme is much more difficult to relate to the Roman-canon scheme than are modern continental fact-finding arrangements. This is mainly due to institutional differences between the two schemes that have no real counterpart on the continent of Europe. The modern judicial apparatus of continental countries inherited quite a few attitudes, values and features from its Roman-canon predecessor, despite the French Revolutionary love affair with the jury. The new grew out of the old. So while the comparison of Roman-canon to modern continental evidence involves the exploration of variety within institutional similarity, the comparison of Roman-canon to modern common law fact-finding arrangements involves the exploration of much less commensurable disparities. Of central importance among them is the fact that while continental courts of the *ancien régime* were unitary, staffed with professional judges, and their decisions subject to review, the archetypical common law trial courts are bifurcated, with judges interacting with the lay jury whose verdicts are difficult and sometimes even impossible to reverse. In these two widely different settings even the question whose fact-finding freedom the law is supposed to constrain is not identical. While on the Roman-canon side of the comparison the target of legal constraints on fact-finding was always the judge, on the common law side their primary target was the jury.[1] Nor can the orientation of the jury toward the object of proof easily be equated with that of the Roman-canon judge. Differences on this point date back to medieval times and still survive, although they are now as barely visible as a Gothic smile. But in some regards they are of interest to the theme of this book and must be accounted for. In order to obtain the proper perspective on these and some other contrasts between a living and a defunct procedural system, a quick reconnaissance over the past cannot be avoided. Skimming rather than plunging into common law history,

---

[1] As a late sixteenth-century Englishman wrote in trying to explain the English mode of trial to the French, "judex is with us called the judge, but our fashion is so diverse that those who either condemned or acquite the man for guiltie or not guiltie are not called judges but twelve men." See Thomas Smith, *De Republica Anglorum*, Lib. II, cap. 8, p. 66 (Alston ed.)(Cambridge: Cambridge University Press, 1960).

The Changing Role of the Jury 129

the varying degrees of the jury's freedom from judicial control must be outlined and the residue of ancient attitudes toward the object of proof identified. However, the strong trial-avoidance tendency of common law criminal justice reflected in contemporary guilty plea arrangements is beyond our ken, as evaluation of evidence in this context falls outside the scope of this study.

THE CHANGING ROLE OF THE JURY

As was pointed out in talking about the origin of the Roman-canon fact-finding scheme, the thirteenth-century papal prohibition of clerical participation in trials by ordeal caused the emergence of two divergent paths leading from the shared background of earlier medieval forms of justice. The path followed by England consisted in the adaptation of the medieval practice of communal participation in the administration of justice. At trials before an itinerant royal judge no evidence was taken: lay jurors would come to court to announce the verdict based on knowledge they acquired on their own, out of court. Some may have been witnesses to the incriminating event, others may have been recipients of rumors circulating about the event in the community, and still others may have conducted their own informal inquiries about what had happened. The royal judge would ratify the jurors' verdict, and where appropriate impose the sentence – capital punishment in the case of all serious crimes. In trials so organized, testimonial and adjudicative functions were merged and verdicts rested on extrajudicial knowledge of jurors, a feature that was anathema in the continental administration of justice.[2] Why did English kings fail to follow the continental model and prohibit the use of adjudicators' private knowledge, especially in cases leading to the imposition of capital punishment? After all, theologically inspired dangers to the souls of judges who caused the spilling of blood were known to Christian elites throughout Europe. In explanation, the theory has been propounded that English kings shifted the moral hazard of imposing blood sanctions from their judges to jurors.[3] But it seems more likely that the unanimous expression of local community belief – or the public knowledge of incriminating facts – dispelled spiritual misgivings about sanguinary decisions based on this belief or this knowledge. This possibility is suggested by a summary procedure invented by Church lawyers for processing notorious crimes, defined as misdeeds whose commission is so well known to the local populace that the perpetrator's guilt cannot be

---

[2] English lawyers claimed well into early modern times that this fusion of functions was superior for truth-discovery purposes to the continental model of witnesses presenting evidence to the judge with no extrajudicial knowledge of the facts. For a fifteenth-century example, see John Fortescue, *De Laudibus Legum Angliae*, Cap. 26, 62 (Chrimes ed.) (Cambridge: Cambridge University Press, 1942).

[3] See James Whitman, *The Origin of Reasonable Doubt*, 127–129, 150–157 (New Haven: Yale University Press, 2008). On his theory, jurors could be spared the moral hazards of general verdicts by acquitting the defendant, or returning special verdicts. Observe, however, that if they returned special verdicts, their decision would cause the *renvoi* of moral hazard back to the judge.

130 *Roman-Canon Legal Proof and Common Law Evidence*

"concealed by any tergiversation." In proceedings involving these crimes, the defendant appeared before the judge only to hear the sentence pronounced against him.[4]

For our purposes it is important to note that medieval English jurors did not pursue exactly the same objective as the Roman-canon judge. As mentioned in Chapter 1, the inquisitorial procedure was animated by the concern of the late medieval papacy with control over its vast judicial organization, whose task was to protect values uniting the community of the faithful (*populus christianus*). This concern required sustained efforts to establish whether specific *acts* dangerous to the Church were committed, with the view to applying appropriate criminal sanctions. The response to crime required the abandonment of the medieval conceit that the administration of justice was primarily a peace-upholding mission, in the execution of which "*concordia*," or the settlement of the rift produced in a community by wrongdoing, constituted the paramount objective. In light of the papal criminal policy it became irrelevant whether a local community was prepared to grant dispensation to the wrongdoer for his misdeed by virtue of the global assessment of his personality and the situation surrounding the misdeed. Settlements between miscreants and victims, popular in many parts of Europe, became suspect or even turned into crimes. While this change took place on the continent, the medieval English jury continued to respond to crime in ways that were congenial to ordeals, concerned not only with the specific *act* but also with judgments about the *person* suspected of having committed the act. The primary objective of self-informing jurors was to achieve a loosely defined right result in which fact and law had been fused. It was therefore not alien to them to return the not guilty verdict in the case of a person who appeared virtuous and morally upright, although he may have committed the prohibited act. In other words, jurors were prepared to acquit a person for reasons we would now find relevant for pardoning the guilty rather than for finding him innocent.[5] An acquittal on this ground would have made the Roman-canon judge vulnerable to sanctions in tribunals of professional responsibility.

Room for the development of evidence law appeared in England only sometime in the fifteenth century, when testimonial evidence to the jury ceased to be sporadic and became essential to criminal trials. As the royal judge came to be exposed to the testimony of witnesses, he could begin to comment on its probative value, creating the source of influence on the jury. A peculiar and insufficiently understood feature of early presentation of evidence was its asymmetrical character: only witnesses for the prosecution were permitted to testify under oath. Whatever the reason for this asymmetry, it was not a glaring problem so long as jurors could also be witnesses, and so long as the social elite had little reason to fear

---

[4] See *supra*, Chapter 8, note 1.

[5] A historian has rightly remarked that trials by ordeal went into decline when their objective came to be seen as that of revealing the truth of particular acts. See Karl B. Shoemaker, Criminal Procedure in Medieval European Law, 116 *Zeitschrift der Savigny Stiftung für Rechtsgeschichte*, 174, 184, 193, 202 (1999).

criminal prosecutions.[6] As this fear became acute in popish trials of the late seventeenth century, this asymmetrical procedural arrangement was abolished, and defense witnesses were allowed to testify under oath. The new fact-finding regime turned into a fertile breeding ground for evidence law, owing to the concern that the upgrading of the defendant's evidence to sworn status might damage the effective repression of crime. Worries about how jurors would assess clashing testimony of equal formal character were greater in eighteenth-century England than they had been in the continental procedural setting five centuries earlier. In England, the resolution of testimonial conflict was in the hands of amateurs whose verdict had to be unanimous, while on the continent it was in the hands of case-hardened professionals, who decided by majority vote when sitting in panels. And while jurors were expected to return the verdict after brief day-in-court trials, providing little opportunity for considering the trustworthiness of witnesses, especially when their testimony was clashing, Roman-canon judges rendered their decisions after methodical investigations, following repeated interrogations, even confrontations, of disagreeing witnesses.

What tools were available to the common law judge to influence the jury and alleviate concerns about the rectitude of their verdict? One such tool consisted of instructions to the jury at the close of the evidence. Many bore such resemblance to rules developed five centuries earlier by Roman-canon jurists that it is hard to exclude continental influences on their articulation.[7] But more effective in exercising control over the jury's treatment of evidence were informal instruments the common law judge had in his tool kit. Although, as of the later part of the seventeenth century, he could no longer fine or jail jurors for returning verdicts contrary to his views, he could forcefully intrude on their evaluation of evidence by informally communicating his own opinions while the presentation of evidence was still in progress. He could also withdraw the case from the jury if he suspected that its verdict would depart from his preferred outcome. He could even reject a proffered jury verdict with which he disagreed: he could argue with the jury about the proper decision, give additional instructions to it, require repeated deliberations, and even order a new trial, since double jeopardy then attached only at the end of the trial.[8]

---

[6] One of the reasons may have been the survival of the medieval notion of compurgation by oath-helpers. The concern may have existed that the populace would interpret the defendant's use of sworn witnesses as his "purgation."

[7] An example was the instruction that affirmative evidence (most likely to come from prosecution witnesses) is of greater probative force than the negative one. The admonition *"falsus in uno falsus in omnibus"* reproduced the much older Roman-canon rule almost verbatim. See Prospero Farinacci, *Tractatus Integer de Testibus*, Tit. VII, qu. 65, pars 3, no. 200 (Osnabrück, 1678). The instruction that jurors should give more credit to the side that produced the greater number of witnesses also resembled a rule of Roman-canon jurists, although, as noted in Chapter 1, the Roman-canon version of the rule did not evince a numerical approach to evidence. Roman-canon jurists insisted that greater weight ought to be attributed to the "dignity" of witnesses and the persuasive force of their testimony than to their number.

[8] See John Langbein, The Criminal Trial before the Lawyers, 45 *University of Chicago Law Review* 263, 284–300 (1978).

132   *Roman-Canon Legal Proof and Common Law Evidence*

Common law's fact-finding scheme began to acquire its recognizable present-day form, and the jury its present-day fact-finding freedom, only from the middle of the eighteenth and across the nineteenth century. Informal exchanges between judge and jury on the weight of evidence disappeared, and the possibility of judicial interference with proffered verdicts was greatly reduced after double jeopardy started to attach at the beginning of the trial. The resulting relaxation of judicial control over the jury's decision-making fitted well the nineteenth century's liberal image of the criminal trial as a dispute between the state and the defendant in front of jurors as independent representatives of civil society. A more tangible explanation of these changes was offered by John Langbein, who attributed them to the capture of criminal trials by the lawyers.[9] Lawyers were permitted to act as counsel in felony cases only sometime in the first part of the eighteenth century. Prior to that time, English criminal justice, in contrast to its continental counterpart, was largely a laymen's enterprise. Once admitted, lawyers took charge of an increased chunk of trial activity, dwarfing the role of the judge in the presentation of evidence. They, rather than the judge, were familiar with the evidentiary material, and their examination of witnesses came to be regarded as the best vehicle for spying out testimonial falsehood. Witness disqualification rules,[10] based on the idea that useful categorical rules could be devised for the prophylactic exclusion of spurious testimony, lost their reason for existence and began to disappear. And with the increasing passivity of the judge and the decline of informal communications between him and the jury, his formal evidentiary instructions to jurors became and remain the main vehicle for influencing the jury.

JUXTAPOSITION WITH ROMAN-CANON LEGAL PROOF

Viewed through conventional lenses, the Roman-canon and common law fact-finding schemes seem to be polar opposites in terms of fact-finders' freedom from legal constraints. While the common law jury appears as the avatar of decision-making freedom, Roman-canon judges seem to have been slaves shackled by rules on the value of evidence. We know by now that the actual contrast is not so pronounced, if only because Roman-canon judges were accorded wide discretion in the processing of evidence. But while the difference between the two schemes in terms of fact-finders' freedom is not as great as may superficially appear, the lineaments of the difference elude confident diagnosis. A major stumbling block in trying to get a clear idea of the actual differences is that the institutional frameworks in

---

[9]   See his path-breaking study Historical Foundations of the Law of Evidence: A View from the Ryder Sources, 98 *Columbia Law Review* 1168, 1170–1171 (1996).

[10] They resembled the Roman-canon "oppositions to the person of witnesses," several centuries older, so closely that it is again unlikely that the similarity was fortuitous. One possible channel for their import from across the Channel could have been Farinacci's *Tractatus Integer de Testibus*, to which frequent references have been made in our survey of the Roman-canon fact-finding system. The book was widely held by Oxford college libraries, and was cited in 1682 as an example of admirable evidence scholarship by the editor of a popular English trial handbook (*Trials per Pais*).

which evidence is evaluated in continental and common law courts are hardly commensurable. Luckily, the difficulty can be reduced by separately examining the aspirations of the two fact-finding systems and their success in realizing them. In the paradigmatic common law court, divided into professional and lay parts, aspirations regarding the question of how evidence should be processed are formed by the judges, while the degree of their realization depends on the jury. In the Roman-canon system, on the other hand, aspirations were embodied in rules made by the system's scholarly progenitors, while the degree of their realization depended on the structured discretion of judges in applying these rules. Since the relation between evidentiary doctrine and court practice in the inquisitorial process has already been noted in our tour of the Roman-canon scheme, what needs to be examined here are only aspirations and their realization in the criminal procedure of countries following the common law tradition.

Aspirations

Starting off with aspirations, an unsuspected similarity of the two systems comes into view. Both exhibit no principled opposition to providing legal scripts for the processing of evidence. In fact, both reveal an inclination to legalize fact-finding by rules capable of uniform application. They have in common the belief that useful rules can be crafted on the question what evidence should be admitted, and even on some aspects of the question how admitted evidence should be processed. The common law's aspiration to provide a legal script for treating evidence is easy to understand. In its pristine fact-finding arrangement, verdicts were returned by normatively unconstrained lay decision-makers. The starting point of the scheme was rule-free fact-finding. This preference could not be sustained beyond medieval times, and evidence law gradually emerged from judicial efforts to influence laypersons selected *ad hoc* to administer criminal justice. The resulting inclination to legalize fact-finding was manifested first and foremost in rules regulating the question what evidence should be presented to the jury. Some of them strikingly resemble admissibility rules found in Roman-canon evidence law. Conspicuous among them is the ban on the use of hearsay. As noted in Chapter 2, even reasons advanced for the ban are similar in Roman-canon and common law.[11] The main weakness of hearsay is attributed in both systems to the unavailability of the original declarant for interrogation. His absence, both systems recognize, makes his sworn testimony unavailable and prevents the judge from observing possible bodily indications of his insincerity.[12] The main difference

---

[11] See supra, Chapter 2, note 23 and surrounding text.

[12] The belief in what is most pernicious about the unavailability of original declarants was not identical, however. While modern common lawyers consider most pernicious the absence of the declarant's cross-examination by the party opponent, Roman-canon jurists stressed the impossibility of the declarant's examination by the awe-inspiring judge (*in terrorem iudicis*). See Mirjan Damaška, Hearsay in Cinquecento Italy, *Studi in Onore di Vittorio Denti*, vol. 2, 65 (Padua: Cedam, 1994).

between hearsay and other admissibility rules in Roman-canon and common law procedure stems from the surrounding institutional setting. While the bifurcation of the paradigmatic common law court enables the judge to resolve many admissibility questions without jurors being exposed to the evidence involved, in the unitary court of the Roman-canon type, where the same judges not only decided admissibility issues but also ultimately disposed of the case, this separation was impossible. So while in the classic common law courts admissibility rules can retain their pristine character – even if inadmissible evidence is highly persuasive – in the Roman-canon procedural environment inadmissible but convincing evidence underwent the now familiar transformation into rules of weight, requiring the judge exposed to inadmissible information to attribute no probative value to it. This difference disappears, of course, in juryless common law trials where the judge sits alone: the law's demand that he exclude an inadmissible but convincing item of evidence places him in the same position in which the Roman-canon judge often found himself. Here the similarity between the two fact-finding systems is at its apogee.

It is true that in contrast to Roman-canon law, common law systems contain no rules on the quantity and quality of evidence needed for conviction.[13] But their inclination to legalize the processing of evidence is manifested in other ways. It is reflected in evidentiary instructions aimed at telling jurors how to evaluate and reason from evidence. Consider evidentiary instructions given to the jury in those situations in which jurors become exposed to inadmissible evidence, despite the opportunities to avoid contamination by tainted evidence presented by the bifurcated trial court. The usual concern is that jurors could evaluate some information improperly, or that some information could unfairly predispose them to decide the case in a particular way. So the judge asks them to disregard the forbidden information. But if jurors find it convincing, instructions of this kind function like Roman-canon negative legal proof in that they aspire to influence the fact-finders' commonsense reasoning, and prevent them from arriving at factual findings by following their autonomous reasoning processes. This aspiration also inheres in instructions regarding the few surviving common law rules requiring corroboration of incriminating evidence – such as the testimony of accomplices, children, or rape victims. For they aspire to induce jurors not to take some factual propositions as true without additional evidence – irrespective of whether they formed their belief in the truth of these propositions without any additional information.[14] Nor should instructions be neglected capable of influencing the processing of evidence by the jury, although this may not be their primary purpose. Instructions asking jurors to use an item of evidence only for some inferences but not for others fall into this category. Although their primarily aspiration is to serve other purposes, they are clearly capable of inducing jurors to abandon ordinary practical reasoning and try to dissect

---

[13] A negligible exception in some jurisdictions is the requirement of two witnesses for treason cases.

[14] They resemble Roman-canon *adminicula*, requiring the judge to bolster the probative value of weak *indicia* by additional information.

Juxtaposition with Roman-Canon Legal Proof

evidence in legally postulated ways. Or take the case of information elicited at the trial by an improper question, or other improper behavior of trial participants. Judges will direct the jury to disregard this information. And although the primary purpose of these instructions is again not to influence the processing of evidence, they can still interfere with the jurors' natural reasoning.

It will be objected that instructions of this kind tend to be merely ceremonial, delivered by the judge in ways signaling to the jury that they are not meant to be taken seriously. But while this may be true of instructions felt by judges to be senseless or incoherent, the objection is misplaced as a general proposition. Many instructions to disregard evidence, or to process it in a particular way, are given by judges in earnest, in the hope of influencing the jurors.[15] It may also be objected that these instructions are mere practical guidelines, or flexible standards, rather than mandatory precepts. But their flexibility stems not from the absence of the aspiration to legalize fact-finding, but from the circumstance that the realization of the aspiration is not in the hands of the judge. And as our survey of the Roman-canon fact-finding scheme revealed, many Roman-canon legal proof rules, properly understood, were also in the nature of flexible guidelines for the exercise of judicial discretion.

The Realization of Aspirations

While both Roman-canon and common law fact-finding schemes share legalistic aspirations, great differences between them surface when the realization of these aspirations comes into view. Although the rigidity of Roman-canon admissibility rules and rules on the value of evidence was greatly relaxed by judicial discretion, we saw that the factual findings of the judge were subjected to supervision by hierarchical superiors, or by judges of special courts adjudicating cases of professional responsibility. The judge's proof-taking activity had to be recorded in the file of the case, and his reasons for refusing to find legally prescribed evidence credible had to be transparent. Unexplained or unjustified departures from rules were threatened with punishments, especially in sensitive matters such as the sufficiency of evidence for torture. Modern Anglo-American jurors, by contrast, can disobey instructions transmitting evidence law to them without untoward consequences. The appearance of regular appellate remedies – a comparatively late event in common law history[16] – failed to restrain the modern jury's capacity to arrive at a verdict largely free from effective legal control.

---

[15] For a thoughtful discussion of this issue, see David A. Sklansky, Evidentiary Instructions and the Jury as Other, 65 *Stanford Law Review*, 407, 419, 447 (2013).

[16] While a regular and comprehensive system of appellate review appeared on the continent in the twelfth century, a much less comprehensive system appeared in England only in the last years of the nineteenth century as a product of Victorian reforms. In America, appellate courts were established after the Revolution, and are very old by common law standards.

136   *Roman-Canon Legal Proof and Common Law Evidence*

This freedom of the jury is due to the legacy of the single level of decision-making that characterized English judicial organization for the largest part of its history. From the standpoint of the single plane of authority characterizing this organization, trial court judgments were final, so that their review constituted an independent new proceeding rather than the continuation of the original one. In criminal cases, this view of the matter raised the specter of double jeopardy, and made the jury's not guilty verdicts resistant to appellate attack.[17] As a result, the jury has the power to acquit defendants even for legally irrelevant reasons, such as pity, even though it has established that they committed the crime with which they were charged. In this *de facto* pardoning power of the jury one can recognize, preserved and only partly transformed, the medieval conceit mentioned in our historical sketch that the jury sits in judgment not only over the criminal acts of defendants but also over their personal character and life experiences. The original single level of adjudication is also responsible for the fact that not so long ago even appeals from conviction required the waiver of double jeopardy protection as a precondition for their lodging. Although guilty verdicts can now be reviewed without this precondition, the review of the accuracy of the factual foundation on which they rest is seriously limited: it focuses only on the reconstruction of possible lines of reasoning which could have led jurors to their factual findings. As a result, jury verdicts are reversed only when appellate judges cannot identify any plausible reasoning paths to findings on which the guilty verdict is based.[18] The main reason for this torso of full superior review is that common law jurors decide alone, in secrecy, and return unexplained general verdicts.

We observed that the absence of the bicameral court in juryless trials placed both Roman-canon and common law judges in a similar position when the law required them to abstain from using evidence they found persuasive. Even so, common law judges are freer to disobey this requirement than was the Roman-canon *iudex*. Responsible for their greater freedom is the limited scope of appellate review of their decisions – another legacy of attitudes that prevailed for centuries in the single-level English judicial apparatus. In accord with the remnants of these attitudes, appellate courts grant wide deference to trial judges, setting their factual findings aside only when they find them clearly erroneous. The hierarchical setting of the Roman-canon judicial organization, on the other hand, attributed much less respect to factual findings made by judges on lower echelons of authority.

---

[17] It is only of late that England and Wales enable prosecutors to retry defendants who have been acquitted if compelling new evidence appears in the case. Observe, however, that this does not involve the reconsideration of evidentiary material presented at the trial, but only the appearance of previously unconsidered evidence.

[18] *Wright* v. *West*, 505 U.S. 277, 296 (1992) and *Lavender* v. *Kurn*, 327 U.S. 645, 653 (1946), illustrate American case-law on the subject.

Conclusion

While the ambition to legalize fact-finding permeates the common law fact-finding scheme as it did the Roman-canon one, the realization of this aspiration differs greatly in the two institutional environments. Even when the large dose of discretion granted to the Roman-canon judge in the inquisitorial process is taken into consideration, his fact-finding freedom pales in comparison with that of the paradigmatic Anglo-American decision-maker – the jury. After the common law judge finds that the evidence in the case is sufficient to go to trial, the question whether rules of evidence laid out in his or her instructions are observed depends almost entirely on the jury. The Roman-canon judge was unable to turn into such an autonomous decision-maker, since he acted within a hierarchical judicial organization and was subjected to the supervision of professional responsibility courts. Another contrast related to institutional differences is deserving of notice at this point. Although it was mentioned earlier for another purpose, the contrast deserves reiteration, because it affects the importance of personal belief as the basis of factual findings. Our survey of the Roman-canon fact-finding scheme for criminal cases revealed that it attributed great importance to the judge's belief in the probative value of evidence. His personal assessment of evidence become immaterial only when he was convinced that the defendant was guilty, but the legally prescribed evidence was missing. In other words, his belief was immaterial only when defensive safeguards were involved. In the common law procedure, on the other hand, where the typical decision-maker is a small group of *ad hoc* lay adjudicators, interpersonal considerations can become dominant and overshadow personal belief. This is especially likely in common law jurisdictions where the original unanimity rule is still maintained.[19] In some procedural situations, such as a deadlock in jury deliberations, it is not inappropriate for the judge to urge recalcitrant jurors to abandon their beliefs formed on the basis of presented evidence.[20] Intersubjectively acceptable positions rather than personal beliefs can prevail: only *reasonable* doubts as to the evidentiary material are relevant, not just *personal* doubts.

---

[19] European common law countries – England, Wales and Ireland – departed from long tradition and now permit jury verdicts by majority vote.

[20] This is reflected in the still-surviving American "supplemental" jury instruction. See *Allen v. United States*, 164 U.S. 492 (1896).

Epilogue

Although the major part of this book has been concerned with fact-finding in the vanished world of premodern criminal procedure, the preceding pages had a larger purpose than burrowing through the past. Rather than providing lavender for the closet of superannuated evidentiary arrangements, the book's concern with the past was meant to prepare the ground for exploring the issue of the law's interference with the freedom of judges to evaluate and reason from evidence. Is their freedom from legal constraints in determining the value of evidence the final and irreversible stage in the evolution of forensic fact-finding? Do attempts to introduce legal rules in this domain invite the danger of regression to an inferior stage in the historical development of forensic fact-finding? In a word, is the apotheosis of the free evaluation of evidence warranted? The issue is usually debated against the background of the contrast between the processing of evidence in the criminal process of the *ancien régime* and in contemporary systems of criminal justice. Our extended tour of the Roman-canon fact-finding scheme and its comparison with modern ones has shown that no sharp-edged contrast between them exists in regard to the degree of the adjudicators' freedom from normative interference. On a continuum from an ideal type of factual inquiry governed by legal rules to an ideal of factual inquiry without them, both premodern and modern fact-finding arrangements arrived at positions not far from the middle. No gaping divide yawns between them, although, as we have noted, the progenitors of the Roman-canon system started from a preference for evaluation of evidence bound by legal rules, while the architects of modern systems started from a preference for the evaluation of evidence free from legal rules. These initial preferences are largely responsible for exaggerations of the divide, because ideologues of the two systems tend, or tended, to highlight only those aspects of their respective fact-finding arrangements that can be reconciled with initial preferences.

What caused the movement of premodern and modern fact-finding systems toward the middle of the continuum between rule-bound and rule-free evaluation of evidence? Roman-canon jurists discovered that the probative effect of evidence is so deeply contextual that legal rules predicated on *ex ante* judgments of its value easily turn into overgeneralization capable of impeding fact-finding accuracy and the realization of criminal policy. By a sort of bricolage, they were driven to make legal rules on this subject malleable, so that judges retained considerable fact-finding freedom. Modern lawmakers, on the other hand, came to realize that some legal restraints on the adjudicators' freedom to evaluate evidence are useful not only for cognitive reasons, but also as safeguards against arbitrariness and as guarantors of procedural fairness. Thus, even as allegiance to free evaluation of evidence continued to be professed, rules appeared in modern evidence law restricting the exercise of the adjudicators' innate cognitive processes. Only the common law jury appeared to be gravitating toward the rule-free terminus of the continuum. But even the jurors' fact-finding freedom emerged as incomplete. Limits on their freedom stem from judicial efforts to induce them to process evidence in specified ways, but especially from the subjection of the factual substratum of guilty verdicts to a degree of appellate supervision.

Premodern and modern fact-finding systems have something else in common. Our inquiry revealed that both display a different attitude toward what this book has called positive and negative legal proof. Conspicuous by their rarity in, or total absence from, both systems are positive legal proof rules, obligating judges to convict a defendant on specified evidence irrespective of their belief in his innocence.[1] Contrary to conventional accounts, Chapters 4 and 5 have shown that Roman-canon legal proof never produced this effect: legally required evidence obligated the judge to convict a defendant only if he found this evidence persuasive. We also saw that Roman-canon jurists resisted the teachings of medieval theologians that the judge ought to convict a person on the incriminating testimony of two legally qualified eyewitnesses, even though he was persuaded of his innocence by privately rather than officially acquired knowledge. Roman-canon authorities recognized the moral anguish that would afflict judges if the law compelled them to impose capital or mutilating punishment on a defendant they thought was innocent.

SURVIVAL OF NEGATIVE LEGAL PROOF

A different conclusion is warranted in regard to rules preventing judges from convicting a defendant in the absence of specified evidence, and also in regard to rules prohibiting them from using specified evidence in support of conviction. Both types of rules are capable of limiting the deliberative freedom of judges and belong in the classificatory niche of what we have called negative legal proof. Our tour of Roman-canon evidence law revealed an abundance of these rules in various contexts, including the law on the use of *poena extraordinaria*. Most prominent among them was the rule requiring two eyewitnesses or the defendant's confession for the imposition of capital and mutilating punishments. No matter how persuaded judges may have been of a defendant's criminal responsibility by other evidence in the case,

---

[1] Some positive rules of this kind will be mentioned in talking about the foreseeable future.

the law prohibited them from imposing blood punishments on him in the absence of this legally specified proof. Although the inability to impose proper punishment on the guilty was easier to accept than the obligation would have been to send an innocent person to the executioner, and although this proof sufficiency standard was riddled with exceptions, the scarcity of two eyewitnesses impeded the realization of crime control interests to such an extent that the standard turned out to be the neuralgic spot of the entire Roman-canon fact-finding scheme. Law enforcers sought to circumvent it in various ways, or to satisfy it by brutal means.[2] The most ignominious consequence of high barriers to conviction created by the standard was that they facilitated the introduction of judicial torture into the inquisitorial criminal process. But this gruesome consequence of the Roman-canon full proof standard does not mean, of course, that all negative legal proof rules deserve opprobrium. Although they may lead to the acquittal of the guilty, when properly selected they may also be precious safeguards to the innocent, offering him protection from easy or arbitrary convictions. And when they assume the form obligating judges to disregard evidence irrespective of how persuasive it seems to them, they can also be useful in protecting values independent from the factual accuracy of verdicts. The ban on the use of convincing but illicitly procured evidence is only the most prominent example of these rules.

It is therefore easy to understand why negative proof rules survived the demise of the *ancien régime*. Chapter 10 has traced them in modern continental procedures, seeking to show how unrealistic it is to deny them legal character and treat them as mere rules of logic and experience guiding judges in the analysis of evidence. But whatever their nature may be, they restrict the modern judge's fact-finding freedom to a degree that is not significantly different from the degree to which they limited the freedom of the judge in the Roman-canon fact-finding scheme. It is true, however, that a difference exists between premodern and modern negative proof rules. Those requiring confirmation of reputedly weak evidence – that is, corroboration rules – while abundant in the Roman-canon fact-finding scheme, are now few and far between and viewed with disfavor. Favorably regarded, meanwhile, are some rules which mandate that specified items of evidence be disregarded even if they are highly persuasive. Although they can lead to the acquittal of the guilty – the exclusion of illegally obtained evidence comes again to mind – the inaccurate outcomes they may cause are treated as an acceptable price for ensuring the fairness of criminal prosecutions. Chapter 11 has shown that the state of the law on the subject is not much different in countries following the common law tradition. Negative proof rules of both kinds exist there as well. While corroboration rules are also in decline, exhorting jurors to disregard specified items of evidence is routine in judicial instructions. Whether these exhortations are recognized as legal precedents

---

[2] One is left to wonder what evasive tactic contemporary law enforcers would adopt if confronted with equally high barriers to conviction.

Epilogue

and are obeyed by the jurors is another matter, of course. As in regard to many other aspects of common law fact-finding arrangements, this depends on the multifaceted interaction of judicial aspirations with the actual power of the jury.

THE STATUS OF CORROBORATION RULES

Why is it that negative proof rules are now viewed with disfavor when they assume the form requiring confirmation of presumptively weak incriminating evidence? Two main reasons exist for their lowly status, although they are in the nature of defensive safeguards. One is that negative proof rules intrude on the venerated free proof principle; the other, more important, one is the belief that the danger of wrongful convictions can better be averted by other means. Corroboration rules, like all rules based on abstract *ex ante* determination of probative value, can be over-inclusive and erect obstacles to the accuracy of verdicts in particular cases. Presumptively weak evidence does not always need confirmation, and corroboration evidence is not always available. Consequently, so goes the argument, the danger of wrongful convictions can better be averted by flexible procedural instruments that take account of the individual circumstances of particular cases. Two such instruments are believed to make corroboration rules unnecessary. One is the requirement that trial judges provide written reasons for their factual findings, and the other is the contemporary proof sufficiency standard requiring that evidence supporting convictions should leave no doubt in the adjudicator's mind. These two instruments are supposed to complement each other naturally, like a wink and a smile. Used in tandem, they are believed to provide sufficient guarantees against miscarriages of justice.

Safeguards against Weak Evidence

But do they really offer sufficient protection against erroneous verdicts that could emanate from shaky evidence? Let us first examine the requirement that judges provide written reasons for their factual findings.[3] In order to pass the threshold of being meaningful, these reasons must include not only the statement of relevant facts the court has found, but also statements of the evidence used in arriving at

---

[3] The requirement is attributed great importance in continental legal systems, independently of its capacity to offer protection from hasty or arbitrary convictions. Unexplained verdicts are considered offensive there on the ground that decisions made by governmental power-holders must be transparent, irrespective of whether these power-holders are governmental officials or ordinary citizens enlisted in the governmental apparatus. The European Court of Human Rights has recently read the right to reasoned judgment into article 6(1) of the European Human Rights Convention. In its 2010 *Taxquet v. Belgium* case, the Grand Chamber of the Court made a valiant effort to reconcile unexplained verdicts of the English jury with this requirement. For a discussion of the difficulties involved in this reconciliation, see Karoly Bard, Can the Jury Survive after the Judgment of the European Court of Human Rights?, in Bruce Ackerman, Kai Ambos and Hrvoje Sikirić (eds.), *Visions of Justice*, 77–93 (Berlin: Duncker & Humblot, 2016).

142   *Epilogue*

them, as well as the grounds for rejecting conflicting evidence. But even if written reasons contain all these statements, it is unlikely that they will replicate the mental processes of adjudicators in arriving at their conclusions. Beneath reasons advanced by them there may be others, some even outside the realm of conscious thought. To paraphrase a poet, beneath the surface-stream of what judges say motivated them, there flows "the current obscure and deep of what has motivated them indeed."[4] The difficulty of replicating actual decision-making processes is increased in collective courts, whose members seldom travel identical paths in assessing the probative force of evidence. In mixed continental tribunals the outvoted professional judge may even be required to explain the decision's origin in terms that are alien to him or her. A more realistic reason for insisting on written reasons is that they provide rational support for verdicts in terms of acceptable legal conventions. But while reasoned judgments so understood do provide some insurance against arbitrary evaluation of evidence, a rosy veil should not be thrown over reality and the effectiveness of reasons overstated. In many jurisdictions, the *stylus curiae* abounds in conclusory statements and circular arguments from which it is difficult to draw confident conclusions about the factual rectitude of verdicts. Seasoned judges also acquire the skill of using legal conventions to explain their findings in ways that may satisfy the reviewing higher court even when they rest on problematic evidence. In a word, when convictions are based on presumptively weak evidence, the limited effectiveness of reasons could become a cause for concern.

The second instrument is referred to by continental lawyers as the absence of doubt (*in dubio pro reo*) standard, while their common law brethren add the requirement of reasonableness and speak of the absence of "reasonable" doubt. While the continental formulation preserves the emphasis on the subjective belief of a single Roman-canon judge (*iudex singulus*), the common law's stress on reasonableness reflects the already mentioned need for intersubjective yardsticks in a small group of lay adjudicators expected to come to a unanimous decision. In assessing the potential of this instrument to reduce the danger of wrongful convictions on presumptively weak evidence, our earlier remarks should be recalled that the absence of doubt does not always imply the same level of certainty. It fluctuates in response to the magnitude of punishment and the relative difficulty of proving physical facts and mental states, as well as a host of other variables. Whether the propriety of the judges' reaction to these variables can effectively be supervised is not obvious. The potential of the standard as defensive safeguard also varies depending on whether each fact from which inferences are made must be proven beyond doubt, or whether doubt relates to the global impression obtained from the totality of marshaled evidence – not all of which needs to be proven beyond doubt. The former approach can be found in instructions given to Anglo-American juries, while the latter is said to be used by continental judges. Here the totality of evidence can satisfy

---

[4]   Matthew Arnold, *St. Paul and Protestantism*, 3rd edn. (London: Smith, Elder & Co, 1875)

the standard even if no fact of consequence taken separately has been proven beyond doubt. But it is most important to note that the absence-of-doubt formula viewed as defensive safeguard has little independent purchase apart from the requirement that judges provide reasons for their factual findings. For whether the absence of doubt is appropriate can be established mainly by examining the reasons they give for their findings. If these reasons fail to establish a high degree of probability that the defendant has committed the crime, the verdict is unjustified.

THE PREDICAMENT OF CORROBORATION RULES

In light of what has just been said, would it not make sense to look more favorably upon some negative proof rules even when they assume the corroboration form? Would it not be prudent to welcome rules prohibiting conviction on evidence considered weak or easily misleading without some legally specified confirmation, even if judges find that the proof sufficiency standard has been satisfied without it? The answer depends on whether some species of admissible evidence are indeed so shaky that their reinforcement could reduce the danger of wrongful convictions. The decline of corroboration rules in modern criminal justice systems attests to the fact that the danger is currently not taken seriously enough to outweigh the possible increase in unjustified acquittals which could result from the absence of legally required corroboration. But is it not possible that the danger of miscarriages of justice caused by reliance on shaky evidence is underestimated? That this possibility should not be rejected out of hand is indicated by the number of persons recently exonerated by DNA tests after they had been convicted on the basis of false police confessions, erroneous eyewitness identification, evidence supplied by jailhouse informants, and shoddy forensic evidence.[5] And if it turned out that the danger of erroneous convictions is presently underestimated, then the adoption of some well-chosen corroboration rules might be warranted.[6] Inroads their adoption would cause on the free evaluation of evidence should not justify keeping them in darkly lit corners of evidence law. Rather than letting them linger in the limbo between legal and extralegal constraints on the judges' fact-finding freedom, it would be more appropriate to accord them a legitimate place in contemporary evidence law.

[5] For American jurisdictions, see Samuel R. Gross, Exonerations in the United States 1989 through 2003, in 95 *Journal of Criminal Law & Criminology*, 523, 551 (2005). Significant numbers of erroneous convictions were also reported elsewhere. An old German empirical study suggested, for instance, that there were between 150 and 350 erroneous convictions in Germany each year. See Karl Peters, *Fehlerquellen im Strafprozess*, 9 (Munich: Müller, 1970). On similar studies in other countries, see Stephen C. Thaman, Reanchoring Evidence Law to Formal Rules, in Bruce Ackerman, Kai Ambos, and Hrboje Sikirić (eds.), *Visions of Justice*, 384–385 (2016).

[6] For a recent suggestion that mandatory corroboration rules should be adopted as safeguards against false convictions, see Stephen Thaman, *ibid.*, 398–406.

144 *Epilogue*

THE FUTURE OF NEGATIVE LEGAL PROOF

But let us suppose that *rebus sic stantibus* corroboration rules are an unnecessary encumbrance. What about their future? Our antennae for future events will have no difficulty in picking up signals that the improvement of their status is in the cards, along with the improvement of the status of negative legal proof generally. The improvement is likely to occur in the wake of rapid advances of science and its technological implementation, which may already have begun to weaken the allure of fact-finders' legally unconstrained freedom to assess the value of evidence. Symptomatic in this regard is that the testimony of fact witnesses on which judges in the Roman-canon process depended almost completely – and on which our judges still greatly depend – is increasingly confronting a competitor in the silent testimony of sophisticated technical devices, capable of establishing facts not within reach of manifest human perception. The silent testimony of these devices is translated to judges by expert witnesses, whose importance is likely to grow as a result of the dissemination of these devices and the likely invention of new ones.

We noticed that it is already not unprecedented in some jurisdictions to prohibit judges to replace expert testimony with their own lay opinion: they can only seek to find other experts who share their point of view.[7] Facts are also increasingly becoming the subject of formal expert testimony, which until recently were not subject to proof at all, but belonged to the basket of background information used by fact-finders to evaluate evidence formally presented in court. For the proof of these facts, common sense and ordinary experience may not be sufficient much longer: rules are likely to appear requiring expert testimony about some of these facts in addition to, or even in lieu of, lay testimonial accounts. Gradual changes can even be imagined in the vitally important matter of assessing witness credibility. The observation of witnesses' demeanor may not be regarded much longer as the most reliable way of establishing veracity. The testimony of stress-detecting experts could emerge as a superior source of information on the subject. At present these experts pose no threat to the adjudicators' dominance in making credibility determinations. For even if all presently existing obstacles to the admission of polygraph evidence were removed, for example, judges would still remain in charge of evaluating the credibility of polygraph experts. But advances in the precision of stress testing, or the appearance of instruments invented by cognitive scientists for stress-detecting purposes, could precipitate a change, especially if accompanied by empirical studies casting doubts on the capacity of ordinary people to detect falsity in the demeanor of witnesses. One can easily envisage the emergence of rules requiring that the testimony of ordinary witnesses, especially those offered by the prosecution, be corroborated by the testimony of experts.

Many thoughtful observers believe that science and technology are not Trojan horses in the citadel of free evaluation of evidence. Forensic fact-finding will, in

---

[7] See *supra*, Chapter 10, note 10.

Epilogue 145

their opinion, not be handed over to men and women in white coats. Scientific consensus is rare, they argue, and the attitude of ordinary people to science and technology is ambivalent, so that courts composed of ordinary people will not unreflectively defer to experts.[8] It is also possible that ordinary people will not unreflectively defer to experts because they will acquire knowledge needed to draw inferences from scientific evidence, perhaps even in domains where these inferences could be counterintuitive.[9] On a more general plane, it can also plausibly be argued that ordinary cognition is the ethical and political predicate of our administration of justice, so that abandoning ordinary reasoning in adjudicative fact-finding would undermine the legitimacy of judgments as presently conceived.[10]

For the foreseeable future it is indeed hard to imagine that science and technology will crowd out ordinary processes of cognition from the courtroom. It seems unlikely that the near future will see acceptance of legal rules disregarding these processes, and mandating that the results of scientific tests constitute conclusive evidence in criminal cases, irrespective of whether adjudicators are persuaded by them or not. In other words, *positive* legal proof rules based on scientific insights are unlikely to proliferate anytime soon – at least not in a form that totally excludes ordinary reasoning.[11] Their acceptance would indeed require major social, cultural and political transformations whose precise character is impossible to foresee. To realize how difficult it would be for positive legal proof rules to spread in present circumstances, it is enough to note the preference of judges for case-specific or anecdotal testimony, and their reluctance to convict a person on statistical evidence, no matter how powerful it might be. They find it hard to abandon beliefs generated by credible case-specific testimony on the ground that what it asserts is statistically rare or even extremely rare. Their reluctance is easy to comprehend. Anecdotal and statistical evidence addresses different dimensions of reality: while the former invites causal explanations, the latter expresses quantified regularities.

But *negative* legal proof in both its forms can much more easily be integrated into current fact-finding schemes, and is likely to face a bright future. Consider the prospect of rules requiring scientific corroboration of evidence. To imagine their increased acceptance, one need not envision a state of affairs in which fact-finding is handed over to experts entirely. It is enough to conjure the emergence of a climate of

---

[8] See the thoughtful reflections on this theme by Paul Roberts, Faces of Justice Adrift?, in John Jackson, Maximo Langer and Peter Tillers (eds.), *Crime, Procedure and Evidence in a Comparative and International Context*, 295, 324 (Oxford: Hart Publishing, 2008).

[9] See, Richard Friedman, Anchors and Flotsam; Is Evidence Law "Adrift"?, 107 *Yale Law Journal* 1965 (1998).

[10] See, e.g., Jonathan Cohen, Freedom of Proof, in William Twining (ed.), *Facts and Law*, 16 *Archives for Philosophy of Law and Social Philosophy*, 1–6 (1983).

[11] It is true that conclusive weight is already attributed in some jurisdictions to evidence produced by technical instruments. Think of the rule that driving incapacity can conclusively be established by finding a specified amount of alcohol in a person's blood. But rules of this kind seldom require judges to decide contrary to their personal beliefs. The mantle of science, coupled with the absence of alternative credible information, tends to make properly performed tests persuasive to them.

146 *Epilogue*

opinion in which establishing a growing number of facts in the absence of scientific support appears as dilettantish dabbling. Given the increasing reliance on the fruits of scientific and technological progress in many aspects of social life, this climate of opinion may already be nascent. Consider only the emerging challenges to the rulings of referees in some sports by recourse to instruments capable of determining certain facts more accurately than the sensorium of the referees. If justice were to shut the door to newly emerging methods and instruments likely to mushroom in this century, forensic fact-finding would soon become vulnerable to charges of exhibiting quasi-Luddite attitudes and being obscurantist. And when the mind-set favoring the use of science and technology establishes itself in the administration of justice, an increasing number of rules are likely to appear requiring expert corroboration of ordinary witness testimony, despite the likely encroachments of these rules on the adjudicators' legally unconstrained evaluation of evidence. In other words, the number of cases is likely to decrease in which judges will be able to find facts solely on their subjective or untutored assessment of evidence.

THE IDEAL OF NORMATIVE CONSTRAINT

As has repeatedly been intimated, the opinion is widespread that evaluation of evidence free from legal intrusion is the ideal fact-finding scheme and the cornerstone of enlightened justice.[12] According to this opinion, the increase of negative legal proof rules appears as a departure from optimal evidentiary arrangements. But is this negative view of possible future developments justified? Does the free evaluation of evidence deserve to be so highly appreciated as to be considered ideal? What should give us pause is that the ideal implies the undesirability of injecting law into one of the most important activities in the administration of justice. To devotees of the rule of law, this must seem wrong. An ideal fact-finding system for them would be one in which legal rules determine the weight of evidence *ex ante* and lay down what proof is needed for factual determinations. Like the rule of law in general, these rules would function as safeguards against arbitrariness and prejudice, guaranteeing uniformity and facilitating predictability. An added benefit of their existence would be the protection against common charges of partiality in decision-making. Why should such a legally regulated system not be put on the pedestal, rather than legally unregulated evaluation of evidence?[13] The main reason is that the probative effect of evidence depends so much on the context and particularity of experience that adopting a system of rules on such an unstable subject would be like attempting to

---

[12] For an elegant exposition of this view, see Massimo Nobili, *Il Principio del Libero Convincimento del Giudice*, 5–6 (Milan: Giuffrè, 1974).

[13] As late as the last decade of the seventeenth century, Leibnitz argued that all problems of inference could be mechanically calculated, and that evidence should be entrusted to judicial discretion as little as possible. See Gottfried Wilhelm Leibnitz, Study of Universal Characteristics, in C. Gerhardt (ed.), *Philosophische Schriften*, vol. 7, 201 (Hildesheim: Olims, 1978).

Epilogue   147

legislate against a chameleon by reference to its color. Remember the primary impulse of the progenitors of the Roman-canon fact-finding system? Their ideal was to saturate the evaluation of evidence with rules affixing the value of evidence in advance. But they realized their inability to extricate the real value of evidence from the contingencies of particular cases, and to ensure that rules on the subject would produce accurate factual findings. So they softened the rules by allowing departures from them, and moved quite a distance toward rule-free evaluation of evidence. Nor did the architects of modern fact-finding schemes choose free evaluation of evidence because they believed that rule-free fact-finding was an epistemically ideal arrangement. Continental reformers adopted the system because they thought that legal proof rules were unfit for the jury system, but also because they believed that rules cannot capture the actual decision-making processes of the fact-finders. The freedom of common law juries to process evidence was also not the result of purposeful choice of the epistemic ideal. Their freedom developed from the peculiar institutional features of the English machinery of justice.

It thus seems more appropriate to treat the free evaluation of evidence as only the second best solution – a *faute de mieux* – rather than the ideal of forensic fact-finding. Even the most widely known enemy of the legal regulation of evidence, Jeremy Bentham, acknowledged that the presence of rules in the fact-finding area would be preferable to their absence. He only argued that no satisfactory system of rules on the value of evidence had been developed so far, and that the task of formulating the system should be reserved, as he said, "for the improvement powers of some more mature age."[14] What follows from this insight is that if useful legal rules on the processing of evidence can be drafted, they should not be treated as a departure from but rather as movements toward an ideal. And while the freedom of judges to *acquit* a defendant whom they find innocent on their personal assessment of evidence should for the foreseeable future be respected, interference with their freedom to *convict* a defendant on this evidence should remain a possibility. In other words, negative legal proof rules based on scientific insight, if properly chosen, should not be regarded with suspicion as relics of the *ancien régime*'s criminal justice.

The Prologue alluded to the opinion that the evaluation of evidence free from legal rules is the final and irreversible stage in the evolution of forensic fact-finding. This opinion is even more problematic than the apotheosis of the free evaluation of evidence. Even in this century, the miracles of science could produce knowledge and technologies capable of extending evidence law into areas presently monopolized by the fact-finders' legally unconstrained cognition. And in the distant future, fact-finding systems may emerge which are so deeply dominated by scientifically based evidence rules that they dwarf the significance of ordinary cognition in the

---

[14]   See Jeremy Bentham, *Rationale of Judicial Evidence*, vol. 5, 216 (Edinburgh: William Tait, 1843).

148   *Epilogue*

evaluation of evidence to a degree that is now hard to imagine.[15] But we need not worry about such remote threats to the presently cherished principle of free evaluation of evidence. As far as we can see, we should only expect a significant increase in the number of legal rules that require scientific support of factual findings made by judges. Disapproval of well-chosen rules of this kind on the ground that they reduce the space for the adjudicator's fact-finding freedom will become increasingly misplaced. Instead of being looked at with disfavor, these rules should be treated as small steps in the direction of the true, though probably unattainable, ideal of the rule of law in the sphere of forensic fact-finding.

---

[15] A German legal philosopher speculated in the middle of the last century that Western procedural systems were moving in the direction of what he called "scientific proof." See Gustav Radbruch, *Einführung in die Rechtswissenschaft*, 147, 329 (Leipzig: Quelle & Meyer, 1929).

Index

absolutio ab instantia, 111, 112
accusatorial procedure, 7, 23
admissible evidence *See* evidence
amorous rivalry, case of, 74, 75, 88, 95, 98, 125
ancien régime, 1, 2, 6, 33, 40, 43, 47, 57, 67, 71, 85, 88, 92, 100, 101, 106, 109, 112, 114, 128, 138, 140, 147
Anselm *See* St. Anselm
appeal, right to, 20, 65, 110
Aquinas, Thomas, 28, 54
arbitrium See judicial discretion
arbitrium regulatum, 4, 116, 117, 126
articuli inquisitionales, 60
Augustine of Hippo, 13

Baldus de Ubaldis, 8, 29, 30, 31, 32, 34, 36, 37, 61, 62, 63, 64, 70, 71, 73, 78, 83, 84, 86, 87, 88, 94, 95, 96, 116
Bartolus de Saxoferrato, 8, 20, 24, 25, 28, 29, 31, 33, 34, 37, 51, 56, 64, 65, 74, 116
Beccaria, Cesare, 8, 38, 119
Bentham, Jeremy, 1, 10, 30, 49, 147
Bernardo Cenci, case of, 78
blood punishment, 3, 4, 22, 23, 24, 25, 43, 50, 51, 52, 53, 54, 57, 59, 68, 69, 70, 71, 80, 81, 82, 84, 85, 86, 87, 89, 90, 92, 95, 96, 106, 113, 114, *See* poena sanguinis
blood sanction, 48, 82, 107
Bodin, Jean, 29, 49, 89
Butrio, 53

canon law, 18, 38, 47, 49, 58, 65, 78, 81, 116, 119, 126, 134
capital punishment, 14, 21, 67, 83, 87, 89, 108, 129
Carpzov, Benedict, 8, 20, 26, 31, 35, 38, 41, 42, 44, 45, 47, 48, 60, 63, 69, 71, 72, 73, 76, 77, 78, 79, 83, 84, 95, 96, 97, 98, 107, 109, 111
case file, 19, 66, 80, 92, 95, 102, 115

Church, 2, 6, 7, 13, 14, 16, 17, 19, 20, 22, 23, 24, 25, 29, 32, 55, 60, 94, 105, 106, 115, 129, 130
Clarus, Julius, 42, 48, 87, 89, 95, 96
competent witnesses, 10, 11, 15, 57, 63, 64, 93, 95, 96, 104
confession
  coerced confession, 3, 44, 78, 80
  Confessionem necessario sequitur condemnatio, 79
  courtroom confession, 37, 41, 57, 69, 80, 81, 85, 89, 113
  verification, 38, 45, 78, 79
conjecture, 76, 91
conscience, 20, 21, 53, 55, 56, 62, 66, 84, 99, 115, 116, 119
Constitutio Criminalis Carolina, 35, 62, 65, 72, 82
conviction intime, 5, 119, 120, 121, 125
conviction raisonnée, 5, 121, 124, 125, 126
corroboration rules, 126, 140, 143, 144
court
  ecclesiastical courts, 13, 19, 60, 94
credulitas, 33
crimes
  crimen laesae Maiestatis, 84
  crimen magiae, 45, 48
  crimes difficult to prove, 83
  crimina atrocissima, 83, 84, 85, 96, 100
  crimina infanda, 41, 77, 83
  crimina nocturna, 83
  crimina occulta, 23
criminal policy, 2, 19, 22, 23, 24, 25, 90, 114, 117, 126, 130, 139

Damhouder, Josse de, 8, 40, 41, 59, 69, 84, 85, 116
defendant's guilt, 3, 41, 50, 54, 58, 68, 80, 81, 82, 88, 89, 105, 118, 120, 125, 127
defense counsel, 49, 97
Digest *See* Justinian's Digest
dignity, 41, 44, 61, 102, 131

149

150 *Index*

direct proof, 35, 83
discovery, 7, 44, 45, 52, 73, 123, 129

England, 1, 16, 32, 39, 60, 94, 129, 130, 135, 136, 137
epistemology, 29, 30
evidence *See* probatio
  admissible evidence, 69, 92, 93, 96, 102, 143
  circumstantial evidence, 3, 8, 22, 24, 31, 35, 36,
    37, 40, 42, 44, 46, 48, 69, 71, 72, 74, 81, 82, 87,
    88, 90, 91, 109, 110, 114, 120, 125, 126
  common law evidence, 8
  conflicting evidence, 62, 142
  illegally obtained evidence, 97
  inadmissible evidence, 92, 93, 102, 103, 123, 124,
    126, 134
  legal proof, 51
  probative value, 4, 10, 12, 24, 27, 34, 37, 42, 43, 44,
    46, 57, 61, 62, 65, 66, 69, 81, 87, 94, 104, 110, 113,
    114, 119, 122, 123, 124, 130, 134, 137, 141
  weak evidence, 140, 141, 142
evidence law
  Roman-canon evidence law, 6, 7, 8, 15, 17, 20, 49,
    50, 67, 81, 94, 106, 133, 139
expert opinion, 61, 100
extorted confession *See* confession
eyewitness *See* testimony, single eyewitness, two-
  eyewitnesses rule

fact
  factum a quo, 35
  factum ad quem, 35
  factum probandum, 36
  factum probans, 36
fact-finding
  Roman-canon fact-finding, 2, 4, 9, 10, 17, 18, 20, 22,
    35, 44, 50, 59, 92, 96, 117, 124, 135, 137, 138, 140
Farinacci, Prospero, 8, 31, 32, 36, 62, 70, 73, 74, 75,
  76, 77, 78, 79, 82, 83, 86, 88, 89, 91, 95, 96, 97,
  98, 99, 100, 101, 102, 103, 107, 131, 132
file of the case *See* case file
France, 17, 33, 43, 49, 55, 78, 82, 89, 97, 100, 102,
  106, 112, 118, 121
French Revolution, 112, 119, 123, 128
full proof, 3, 4, 7, 16, 23, 25, 34, 36, 40, 48, 50, 51, 55,
  59, 62, 63, 64, 65, 66, 67, 68, 69, 71, 82, 83, 84,
  85, 86, 87, 88, 89, 90, 95, 96, 97, 105, 106, 109,
  110, 111, 112, 119, 120, 125, 140
fundamenta inquisitionis See investigation

Gandinus, Albertus, 8, 18, 42, 52, 54, 63, 74, 82, 96,
  105, 106, 108, 116
general inquisition, 59, 60, 65, 66, 95, 104, *See*
  investigation
God, 1, 11, 13, 14, 15, 16, 18, 23, 44

Guido di San Giorgio, case of, 98
guilty plea, 39, 129

half proof *See* probatio semiplena
hearsay, 32, 33, 46, 92, 101, 102, 103, 104, 114, 119,
  123, 133
heresy, 41, 45, 48, 79, 84, 89, 106
heretics, 23, 93, 108

inadmissible evidence *See* evidence
indication *See* circumstantial evidence
  indicia, 28, 35, 36, 48, 69, 70, 71, 72, 73, 74, 75,
    76, 77, 78, 82, 83, 86, 87, 88, 89, 95, 98, 99, 101,
    107, 110, 111, 114, 125, 126, 134
  indicia dubitata, 87
  indicia indubitata, 71, 73, 82, 86, 87, 88, 89, 96,
    107, 111, 126
  indicia proxima, 87
  indicia remota, 87
  indicium, 34, 35, 36, 37, 72, 75, 87, 88, 99, *See*
    indication
  indicium indubitatum, 88, 91
  indicium plenum, 34
  indicium semiplenum, 34
indubitable, 71, 73, 79, 89, 97, 99, 107, 108
innocent, 3, 17, 27, 44, 50, 53, 54, 70, 76, 79, 82, 90,
  96, 104, 106, 107, 111, 113, 114, 127, 130, 139,
  140, 147
inquisitorial procedure, 3, 4, 7, 9, 20, 29, 47, 52, 53,
  54, 57, 60, 61, 63, 68, 70, 79, 80, 83, 92, 101, 105,
  109, 112, 130, *See* investigation
  circumstantial evidence, 125
  evidence law, 4
  fact-finding, 10, 24, 27, 51, 68, 81, 106
  full proof, 16, 59, 65, 67
  history, 22, 23, 42, 55, 90, 94
  illegally obtained evidence, 97, 98, 101
  judicial discretion, 137
  repressive character, 78, 82, 107
  testimonial disqualifications, 93, 94
  truth-finding, 3
inquisitorial process, 6, 7, 15, 20, 24, 48, 56, 60, 79,
  112, 115, *See* inquisitorial procedure
inspectio ocularis, 31
investigating judge, 13, 65, 66, 79
investigation, 6, 38, 42, 43, 48, 54, 59, 69, 70, 73, 74,
  84, 95, 98, 111, 113
  fundamenta inquisitionis, 60
  inquisitio generalis, 59, 94
Italy, 7, 8, 17, 19, 20, 100, 106, 112, 123, 133
iudex ad maleficia, 20
iudex iudicat secundum allegata et probata, 56
iudex singulus, 142
ius commune, 6, 18

Index

151

Jousse, Daniel, 9, 55, 82, 83, 102
judicial discretion, 21, 25, 74, 76, 106, 115, 116, 135, 146
judicial organization, 19, 20
jury, 5, 14, 80, 92, 118, 119, 121, 122, 124, 126, 128, 130, 131, 132, 133, 134, 135, 136, 137, 139, 141, 147
Justinian's Digest, 6, 33, 56, 62, 63, 64, 65, 71, 86

Langbein, John, 16, 49, 50, 68, 78, 109, 110, 132
law of evidence, 47, 68, 101, *See* evidence law
legal proof, 1, 4, 5, 8, 9, 21, 23, 24, 25, 28, 40, 47, 49, 50, 53, 54, 57, 61, 62, 65, 66, 80, 81, 82, 85, 88, 90, 105, 110, 113, 114, 115, 118, 119, 120, 126, 134, 135, 146, 147
  negative, 50, 51, 58, 114, 139, 140, 144, 145
  positive, 3, 50, 57, 67, 81, 85, 113, 114, 116, 119, 139, 145
legislation, 11, 66, 76, 97, 110, 121, 122
Leibnitz, Gottfried Wilhelm, 146
liberal ideology, 38, 39, 100, 107, 109, 127, 132
Lombard, Peter, 13

miscarriage of justice, 51, 54
Mittermaier, Carl, 8, 62, 67, 68

notoria, 30, 34

oath, 10, 11, 12, 13, 14, 15, 16, 32, 43, 60, 119, 130
  oath-helpers, 13, 131
  purgatory oath, 13, 43, 107
ordeal, 11, 14, 16, 17, 129, 130
ordines iudiciarii, 20

pactum vincit legem et amor judicium, 22
papal decree, 11, 12, 16, 24, 129
perjury, 14, 43, 51
podestà, 20
poena extraordinaria, 4, 106, 109, 110, 120, 125, 139
poena inobedienciae, 38
poena ordinaria See poena sanguinis
poena sanguinis, 2, 21, 22, 34, 40, 47, 49, 52, 54, 57, 68, 81, 85, 88, 89, 96, 105, 110, 114, 119, 120, 125
pope *See* papal decree
  Pope Clement V, 97
  Pope Gregory VII, 19
  Pope Innocent III, 16, 23, 52, 115
  Pope Innocent IV, 84, 86, 106
presumption, 34, 35, 36, 71, 72, 75, 76, 86, 87, 89, 107, 125
private knowledge of the judge, 54, 56
probatio, 33, 71, 106
  probatio plena, 25, 34, 59, 71
  probatio semiplena, 35, 71, 106, 107

processus per accusationem See accusatorial proceeding
processus per inqusitionem See inquisitorial proceedure
proof *See* evidence
  burden of proof, 57
  proof rules, 1, 5, 8, 21, 24, 49, 50, 80, 96, 110, 113, 115, 119, 126, 135, 139, 140, 141, 143, 145, 146, 147, *See* evidence law
prosecutor, 6, 25, 39, 57, 75
punishment
  blood punishment *See* poena sanguinis
  divine punishment, 13, 23, 43
  mutilating punishment, 21, 41, 113, 139
  sanguinary punishment *See* poena sanguinis

quod non est in actis non est in mundo, 102

rational judgment, 17
retribution, 13, 43
right to silence, 39, 123
rules of torture, 70, *See* torture

self-incrimination, 39, 40, 44, 46
  self-incriminating statements, 38, 44, 70, 77, 79
single eyewitness, 48, 81, 107
special inquisition, 60, 61, 63, 66
species probationum, 31
St. Anselm, 18
suggestive questions, 77

testes de credulitate See oath
testes de scientia See witnesses with actual knowledge of relevant facts
testimony *See* witness
  concordant testimony, 15, 62
  eyewitness testimony, 63, 64, 66, 67
  false testimony *See* perjury
  testimonial disqualification, 15, 93, 94, 95, 96
  testimony of a single eyewitness, 35
  truthful testimony, 14
theology, 2, 13, 18, 19, 21, 22, 52, 55, 107, 115
torture, 18, 20, 38, 39, 41, 42, 43, 44, 46, 47, 48, 63, 69, 70, 71, 72, 73, 74, 75, 76, 77, 78, 79, 84, 85, 87, 89, 90, 95, 97, 98, 99, 100, 101, 106, 107, 111, 116, 135, 140
  exemptions from torture, 41
  law of torture, 44, 45, 46, 70, 79
  mental torture, 43
  tortura ad eruendam veritatem, 42
  water-boarding, 43
treason, 48, 84, 89, 134
trial judge, 122, 123, 136, 141

Index

truth
- God's truth, 11, 14
- truth of testimony, 12, 13

two-eyewitnesses rule, 3, 4, 15, 16, 22, 23, 24, 37, 38, 40, 48, 51, 59, 66, 67, 68, 73, 80, 85, 86, 87, 88, 89, 90, 108, 113, 114, 119, 139

vera scientia, 28

verisimilitude, 11

victim, 22, 23, 30, 62, 72, 75, 81, 86, 88

victimless crime, 23

Vouglans, Muyart de, 8, 9

vox Dei, 16

vox populi, 16

Whitman, James, 21, 52, 55, 129

Wigmore, John, 10, 11, 30, 49

witchcraft *See* crimen magiae

witness *See* eyewitness, testimony
- personal status, 61
- qualified witnesses, 52, 60, 61, 65, 66
- sensory perception, 27, 29, 30, 31, 32, 46
- *testes habiles*, 95
- *testes inhabiles*, 94, 95
- testimonial disqualifications, 12, 15, 93, 96, 101, 103, 114
- witnesses with actual knowledge of relevant facts, 13, 14

wrongful conviction, 54, 141, 142, 143